Kodak and

the Lens of

Nostalgia

Cultural Frames, Framing Culture

ROBERT NEWMAN, *Editor*

Kodak
and the
Lens of Nostalgia

Nancy Martha West

UNIVERSITY PRESS OF VIRGINIA

◇ *Charlottesville and London*

The University Press of Virginia
© 2000 by the Rector and Visitors of the University of Virginia
All rights reserved
Printed in the United States of America
First published in 2000

Library of Congress Cataloging-in-Publication Data
West, Nancy Martha, 1963–
   Kodak and the lens of nostalgia / Nancy Martha West.
     p. cm. — (Cultural frames, framing culture)
   Includes bibliographical references and index.
   ISBN 0-8139-1958-4 (cloth : alk. paper) — ISBN 0-8139-1959-2 (pbk. : alk. paper)
   1. Advertising—Photographic equipment—Psychological aspects—History.
  2. Nostalgia. 3. Eastman Kodak Company. I. Title. II. Series.

HF6161.P36 W47 2000
659.1′977131—dc21   99-055371

This book is dedicated to my mother,

with love, always

After all, there is only one perfect memory

. . . the Kodak's.

Contents

Color plates follow page 108

Preface

I WAS INSPIRED to write this book after seeing a set of Kodak advertisements in a local antique store. Saved from the Dumpster by the grace of a collector, these ads had become commodified objects of the past, tagged at $20 to $30 each for their sentimental value. I balked at the prices and then wound up buying the entire collection, so charmed was I by the images I saw, the slogans I read, the products I had never heard of before. In a 1901 advertisement for the Folding Pocket Kodak, a beautiful young woman holds a parasol in one hand and a Kodak camera in the other, both objects represented as fashionable accouterment (plate 1). Framed now on the wall of my office, that advertisement hangs beside another one from the 1920s featuring a man carrying a picnic basket and Kodak camera (figure 1). Shot in close-up, the camera seems to glide along of its own accord, inviting us to open and use it, its shiny leather case as enticing as the basket of food. And in my favorite ad purchased that day, dated 1910, a couple wave good-bye from a train. The woman snaps a photo of someone occupying the spectator's viewpoint, which creates an odd sense of familiarity between subject and viewer and thus personalizes the image through simulated intimacy (plate 2).

No set of images had ever attracted me as these did. Like many other antiques, these ads represented experiences that seemed impossibly distant in time yet somehow intimate. It almost felt like falling in love, compelling me to do what made absolutely no sense at the time: three weeks after I discovered these ads, I was on my way to Rochester, New York, home of the Eastman Kodak Company, to look at others.

I rummaged through Kodak's archives for six days on that trip, examining box after box of hundreds of ads. At five o'clock I would make my way back to the inn where I was staying and start pressing the owner, a retired Kodak employee, for information about the company

Have your Kodak handy

Autographic Kodaks, $5 up

Eastman Kodak Company, Rochester, N. Y., *The Kodak City*

Figure 1. Advertisement for the Autographic Kodak camera, early 1920s.
(Reprinted courtesy of Eastman Kodak Company)

and its founder, George Eastman. Back in the archives the next morning, I gasped with delight when I spotted especially interesting ads, much to the wonder—and probable annoyance—of other researchers. Two of them eventually came over to my table. "Charming," one woman said. "You should write a book about them." With the same combination of certainty and illogic that sent me on a plane to Rochester, I decided at that moment to take a stranger's advice.

Since the first day I saw them, I have often asked myself why these advertisements so appeal to me, and more generally why another exploration of advertising should be written when advertising histories fill nearly three rows of shelves, totaling over 2,000 books, in my home institution's library. The answers are closely connected, but since it is easier for me to explain why I am intellectually drawn to this subject, I will begin there. Advertising studies number among the thousands because ads reveal the fantasies and ambitions of modern culture, their ubiquity having granted them an unrivaled iconic significance. Coupled with words, pictures in advertising tell stories that, in the words of the historian Jackson Lears, "are both fabulous and didactic," that "evoke fantasies and point morals" (2).

Until that day in the antique store, however, I had never paid much attention to advertisements, soured by the traditional readings of them as agents of crass materialism and promoters of sexist, racist, and classist stereotypes. But these ads differed in at least one sense, for what was being sold here was not lipstick but photography, as potent a force in American culture as advertising itself. Perhaps more than ever before, we depend on photography not only to enrich but to "certify" our experiences, according to Susan Sontag, who cavalierly argues "it hardly matters what activities are photographed so long as photographs get taken and are cherished" (8). Sontag would have been amused by the actions of my old boyfriend's sister, Candice: after discovering that the photographer had accidentally destroyed the film of her wedding pictures, she demanded that he fly out the entire wedding party (months later and at his expense) for a retake. Tuxedoed men and taffeted women posed in a church without guests and danced in a ballroom without music, pretending to be living moments that were already long gone.

Candice ("Re-Bride," we called her) assumed complete control over the representation, overriding the photographer with her command of specific shots and poses. Although her behavior struck me as

xii
◇ absurd at the time, and still does to some extent, Re-Bride's unabashed insistence on staging those phony photos also makes sense in a way. It admits that memory is predicated on an intractable forgetting, and that no simple line should be drawn between what Scott McQuire calls the "psychic interiority of living memory and the exteriority of artificial or technological memory" (165). It urges us to get over our anxieties about photography's "threat" to memory by admitting that everything—even the unforgettable—is liable to be forgotten. Candace was wise enough to accept this idea, and to look on photos not so much as substitutes for memory—she knew that viewing the photos of this mock wedding would probably accentuate the loss not only of the original images but of her memories as well—but as objects we must have in order to possess pictorial control over our past.

One premise of this book is that Kodak has done more than any other single enterprise or individual to determine the uses and expectations for snapshot photography, thereby also reshaping perceptions of such abstract concepts as memory and evidence. Despite the popularity of photography in the United States before the Kodak camera was invented, it seems unlikely that even the most exacting of clients would have demanded a posthumous shoot of a wedding to furnish "proof" of its occurrence. The other premise is that, through such advertisements as those described earlier, Kodak has sanctioned a poetics of domestic life celebrating what Don Slater calls "the modern family at play" ("Consuming Kodak" 58). In investigating the first forty-four years of Kodak history, I soon realized that most of the personal and domestic associations that come to mind with Kodak's name—from June weddings to children seated underneath the Christmas tree—were vigorously promoted even then. Then, as now, Kodak ads minimized technical content while creating a world many viewers would love to step into, the way Mia Farrow's character enters the screen in *The Purple Rose of Cairo* and tastes champagne for the first time in her life.

It is this celebration of leisure, family, and home, coupled with Kodak's indelible association of photography with one's ability to remember as well as one's responsibility to preserve memories through photos, that has made snapshot photography and the institution of Kodak such an integral part of American life. Another important component of Kodak's influence in modern culture is the company's continuing effort to cultivate an image of itself as a benevolent, even pa-

ternalistic institution through ads and promotional literature that repeatedly employed such words as "home" and "family" to refer to the
company and its employees.[1]

Ironically, this legacy of paternalism, originating in Eastman's own
image as the company's "Yellow Father," many critics now identify as
the source of Kodak's current fiscal troubles.[2] Citing such employee
benefits as huge bonuses and leisurely work hours, Alecia Swasy
blandly notes that "there wasn't much that Kodak didn't provide for
its employees" (19). Such extravagance, exacerbated by what Swasy
identifies as "decades of complacency," has resulted in the company's
current beleaguered position. In the twenty-first century Kodak's status as world leader in film manufacturing seems highly precarious,
threatened most notably by Fuji. A book on what may be described as
Kodak's golden years is thus timely and desirable, given the very real
possibility that in the future we may no longer be looking to Kodak to
shape our perceptions of photography. In this sense, the company that
taught us to view photography through the lens of nostalgia may find
itself an object of nostalgia.

Throughout the years I have worked on this project, I have tried to
write a critical history that also recognizes the undeniable attraction
of Kodak's advertisements and other marketing strategies. The seductiveness of advertising, it seems to me, has for too long been matched
by the tight-laced rhetoric of its intelligentsia. As Lears notes, until recently most efforts to interpret advertising's cultural significance have
been embedded in a tradition that includes the writings of Thorstein
Veblen and John Kenneth Galbraith, who wrote their critiques out of
vaguely masked "Protestant commitments to plain speech and plain
living, as well as from republican fears of conspiracy against the independence of the individual self" (Lears 3). Taking a different approach, though producing similar arguments, are those histories that
emerge from a more liberal tradition, such as the feminist movement,
which attack advertising for promoting hopelessly stereotyped images.
Within these bodies of criticism, advertising has been repeatedly
rewritten—almost beyond cliché—as corrupt and all-powerful, the
consumer as passive and hapless, consumer culture as wasteful and
doomed.

While I recognize the value of such critiques, I also contend
that they have drained advertising of its undeniable attraction. Gilles
Lipovetsky makes a similar argument regarding the field of fashion.

xiv
◇

"Fashion," he writes, "has become a problem devoid of passion, lacking in theoretical stakes, a pseudo-problem whose answers and explanations are known in advance. The capricious realm of fantasy has managed only to impoverish the concept and reduce it to monotony" (4). Like fashion, advertising caters to fantasy. And like criticism on fashion, advertising studies have tended until recently to define fantasy as delusion rather than as the boon it can also be: the liberation of someone viewing advertisements from a world of poverty and sadness.

I am one such viewer. Unlike most Americans, I grew up without photography. Patricia Holland notes that the most avid snapshooters are parents of young children, but neither my mother nor my father took many photographs of me as a child. My mother never owned a camera. My father did, but he left my mother and me when I was two, making only an occasional appearance and never thinking to bring a camera when he did. It is this lack of a pictured past, I suppose, that has inspired my attraction to all photographs, even the impossibly idealized ones represented by Kodak, or perhaps especially those.

Of the few photos I possess of my childhood, the one I love most is of my mother holding me as a baby (figure 2). My arm extends in front of me, as if I am reaching for the photographer, who happens, in this only instance I know of, to be my father. Shot in 1964, it contains all the elements of a typical Kodak advertisement: young mother, happy child, sunny day, father recording it all. It is thus easy to forget when I look at this photo that my parents separated two months later, and that the setting it depicts is actually the devastated city of Newark, New Jersey. Like millions of other consumers, I owe this temporary ability to escape painful memories to Kodak, which allowed my parents for one day to create the family scenario I have always desired and that perhaps they desired as well. And yet, even as I look upon this snapshot as an object of tender regard, I note that my father stands outside the frame, his invisibility in the photo signifying what would soon become his invisibility in my life. I remind myself that photos record only one (constructed) moment, that they exclude as well as include, that what isn't represented in the photo often possesses more meaning than what is.

And, finally, I observe that this photograph, like most of my snapshots, has imprinted on its back the name "Kodak," in letters so faded

Figure 2. Snapshot of author and her mother, 1964

that I can barely read them. But I know they exist, stamped not once but eight times, cut from adhesive I imagine to be infinite in length (Stieglitz's famous comment that Kodak ushered in an era of "photography by the yard" possessed more literal meaning than he supposed).[3] I pause to contemplate what I generally overlook—that the corporation writes its name on my experience, authorizing its moment in history. This tension between the intimacy of the snapshot and the impersonality of the corporation grounds every page of this book, just as the tension between my first nostalgic response to these advertisements and the commodifying space of the antique store in which I discovered them informed my original interest in this project.

Nostalgia thus provides both the critical subject of this book and the point of view from which I write, my love of photographs and the advertising images presented here always having to confront the haunting probability that a corporation has taught modern American culture how to see, to remember, and even to love.

Acknowledgments

I F NOSTALGIA filters memory so as to render the past warmly remembered, then I have succumbed to its influence. I barely recall the arduous revisions, the research leads that led nowhere, the individual sentences I sometimes wrangled with for hours. The memories I have now revolve mainly around the generosity of many friends and colleagues—the very thing I lost sight of, as writers too often do, when in the throes of their work.

I thank my home institution, the University of Missouri–Columbia, for a semester's leave, travel grants, and a generous subsidy to help finance reproduction costs for the illustrations, despite the fact that I submitted an application for that subsidy at zero hour. My department couldn't have been more supportive, especially my chairman, Howard Hinkel, who sailed me through various obstacles with characteristic good humor. The people at Academic Support, especially the photographers Paul Szopa and Linda Owen-Pedroley, put up with all my last-minute requests and produced high-quality work throughout. I thank especially my students at Missouri, who have expressed such interest in this project that I never once thought of my research as separate from my teaching. I must single out my indefatigable research assistants, Steven R. Bender and Laura Rotunno, as well as Madalyn Painter, Mary Davis, John Tait, Kel Munger, Sandy Camargo, Eric Leuschner, Amanda Davis, Kim McCaffrey, Kristen Harmon, Dorthy Eberhardt, Scott Eidson, Michele Hornisch, Jackie Chambers, and Cindy and Matt Durham.

Several of my colleagues at the University of Missouri and elsewhere read parts of this book, and I owe them immense thanks for making my arguments so much smarter. Lynne McMahon, Mike Bernard-Donals, Bill Kerwin, Carsten Strathausen, and Karen Piper all devoted hours of their time to critiquing various chapters. My special thanks go to Elaine Lawless, Pat Okker, Trish Roberts-Miller, and

Trudy Lewis, with whom I formed a writing group during my first year xvii
at Columbia. To Elaine, my good friend and continual inspiration, I ◇
owe the decision to do this project. To Pat, I owe the huge gift of figur-
ing out how to organize chapters and a first-hand perspective on the
value of baby photos. I thank Trudy for her discerning questions and
Trish for all those obscure references no one else in the world could
possibly have come up with.

I also have fond memories of my research trips to the Kodak
archives, the George Eastman House, and Duke University's Hartman
Center for Sales, Advertising, and Marketing History. Andrea Imbur-
gia, Linda Bouchard, and Kim Hoffend at Kodak were especially help-
ful. Kathy Connor, Todd Gustavson, Joseph R. Struble, and Janice
Madhu at the George Eastman House all deserve my thanks, especially Todd, who answered at least a hundred questions about Kodak
cameras patiently and efficiently. The gracious owners of Rochester's
Dartmouth House, Ellie and Bill Klein, put me up in grand style while
I was there and even lent me their car so I could see Niagara Falls.

The people at the Hartman Center, especially the director, Ellen
Gartrell, have handled all my requests with amazing efficiency. I also
thank Janie Morris, who probably has no idea who I am because we
met so briefly. But in a two-minute exchange at the Hartman Center
one day, she told me about Kodak's "Death Campaign" quite accidentally—and gave me a delightfully eerie ending for this book.

I also thank the Eastman Kodak Company for granting me permission to reproduce all of the Kodak advertisements featured here;
Leeds University for reproduction of the fairy photograph featured in
chapter 3; and the George Eastman House for reproduction of the
Kodak Salesman cartoon in chapter 1, the William Shewell Ellis photograph in chapter 4, and the postmortem daguerreotype in chapter 5.

Everyone at the University Press of Virginia has been incredibly
enthusiastic and supportive. Thanks to Ellen Satrom, the managing
editor, for seeing that my manuscript sailed through all the production
stages as smoothly as possible, and to Barbara Salazar for her out-
standing editing of the manuscript. I am also grateful to Robert
Newman, the editor of the Cultural Studies series, for his intelligent
suggestions and criticisms. My warmest thanks go to Cathie Brett-
schneider, acquisitions editor at the Press, who remembered me after
nine years and believed in this project from the first.

My love and thanks go to those friends who lent personal support,

xviii including Denise Davis, Mary Lago, Tim Logue, Karen Holmberg,
◊ Brad Tucker, Chris Semansky, Beverly Taylor, Greg Hyder, Jan and Al
Kluever, Derrick Martin, Rod Santos, Helen Osana, Steve and Diana
Hammond, and Penelope Pelizzon, who writes about photography with
a poet's poignancy and can turn any situation into a party. No one
helped out more with this book than my dear friend Ronald Schleifer,
whose extraordinary generosity inspires me daily. I am also grateful to
him for granting me permission to reproduce parts of my essay "Her
Finger on the Button: Kodak and the Age of UnRipening," *Genre* 29,
nos. 1–2 (Spring/Summer 1996), in chapters 2 and 4.

I also thank Craig Kluever for his unwavering support and un-
conditional love, and for driving two and a half hours to make me soup
one night after one of my writing crises. I look forward to all the
occasions for snapshots we'll have in the future, starting with our
wedding.

Most of all, I thank my mother, whom I have never seen take a
single photograph, and for whom I feel more love and gratitude than
I can ever express. During crunch times, she cooked meals for me,
walked my dog, tended my garden, and never asked for a single thing
in return. To her I dedicate this book.

*Kodak and
the Lens of
Nostalgia*

Introduction

The Picture

This is a book about how Kodak marketing—its packaging, its promotional literature, and especially its advertisements—created a new kind of desire for photography in the late nineteenth and early twentieth centuries. More specifically, it is about how Kodak transformed American consumers' perception of how they could organize, present, and even remember their lives through snapshots. I begin with 1888 because that was the year George Eastman patented the Kodak name and issued his revolutionary hand camera (originally called the Kodak No. 1) and roll film. Although Eastman had advertised his dry plates in photographic journals as early as 1881, it was not until the invention of the Kodak No. 1 camera and roll film that he took the first major step toward creating a mass market for photography. The year 1888 thus witnessed Kodak's birth and became a major milestone in the history of photography. As the year when Eastman took his life, 1932 closes an era in which the image of the company was inextricably bound with that of its father.

The central argument of this book is that Kodak taught amateur photographers to apprehend their experiences and memories as objects of nostalgia, for the easy availability of snapshots allowed people for the first time in history to arrange their lives in such a way that painful or unpleasant aspects were systematically erased. Before the Kodak burst upon the scene, Americans were much more willing to allow sorrow into the space of the domestic photograph; as we shall see, postmortem photographs were very popular in the United States between the 1840s and 1880s. Kodak's advertising purged domestic photography of all traces of sorrow and death and in the process taught amateur photographers that in a consumer society, to make the real consumable is to affirm it. Kodak affected such conditioning by

2
◇ exploiting five motifs in its marketing: leisure, childhood (and specifically toys), fashion, antiques, and narrative, each of which forms the
basis of a chapter in this book.

With the exception of narrative, whose atemporal and eschatolog-
ical associations I deploy in bringing this investigation to a close, I
treat the topics addressed in each chapter more as cultural formations
than as themes; that is, I look at the ways in which each of these subjects flourished as industry and idea during the late nineteenth and
early twentieth centuries. In writing this book, I wanted to hear Kodak
as one voice in what I imagined as an ongoing series of cultural conversations about such topics as travel, automobility, childhood, toys,
feminine beauty, family, memory, and even World War I.[1] I wanted to
hypothesize about how Kodak collaborated with other industries in
molding the aspirations and concepts of identities of people living in
the United States. I approach Kodak, then, not as a point of origin but
as a point on a continuum, while at the same time arguing for the
company's profound influence over our perceptions of snapshot photography and the personal experiences we use it to record or forget.

I chose these five particular motifs because they played such a recurring role in the formation of Kodak marketing and because each
participates, like snapshots themselves, in the aestheticizing of experience. Susan Sontag argues that all photographs aestheticize reality
because the photographer selects what seems worthy of special and
lingering attention to capture on film. In other words, the poignancy
that resides in arresting time and movement lends even the ugliest or
most disturbing of subjects a certain beauty.[2] Before Kodak, however,
no system existed to condition such a purely aesthetic and emotional
response to photographs. Just as important, no corporation produced
photographs with the kind of material abundance—what Jackson
Lears has called a "lyrics of plenty"—offered by Kodak.[3] The Kodak
No. 1 camera came equipped in 1888 with 100 exposures, probably over
ten times as many photographs as the average middle-class American
family owned at the time.[4] Simply by "pressing a button," ads assured
the American public, amateur photographers could realize what had
been a dominant hope of American culture since the early nineteenth
century: the hope of effortless abundance.

Sontag claims that one of the defining characteristics of modern
culture has been its systematic drive to stockpile photographs of every
imaginable subject, photographs thus providing a means of collecting

the world. No force has so conditioned this modern drive toward collection of photographs as Kodak, whose name has appeared not only ◇
on our snapshots but on our slides, home movies, and videos, transforming us into what Sontag calls "image junkies" (24). Collection implies an attempt at completion, a desire for narrative wholeness.

This observation applies most poignantly to the collection of photographs. Modern culture has come to regard the isolated moments
represented by photographs as producing collective truth when in fact
they represent at best only relative truths and their sheer proliferation
negates meaning rather than helps construct it: "The presence and
proliferation of all photographs contribute to the erosion of the very
notion of meaning, to that parceling out of truth into relative truths
which is taken for granted by the modern liberal consciousness," argues Sontag (106). In other words, we have learned to accept the par-
tial truths offered by photographs as standing in for an understanding
of the world itself (or on a smaller scale, for an understanding of our
own individual lives and histories).

We might oppose meaning or understanding here to erotics, to the
pleasure of staying on the surface of things that abundance inevitably
generates—what Sontag defines as an opposition between "understanding" and the "amorous relation," the difference between knowing
how something functions and knowing how it looks (23). "Poignant
longings for beauty, for an end to probing below the surface, for a re-
demption and celebration of the body of the world—all these elements of erotic feeling are affirmed in the pleasure we take in photographs," claims Sontag (24). Leisure, childhood and toys, fashion,
antiques, and even narrative all provide a means of staying on the
surface. So do photographs. And so does nostalgia, which is always
caught up in erotics—in the desire for a surface appreciation of the
"beauty" of the past and a narrative of wholeness even as it isolates
particular objects for contemplation.

This desire for staying on the surface we might see as a direct result of the advent of commodity culture in the mid- to late nineteenth
century, a culture Kodak helped shape with its transformation of
memory and experience into an infinite supply of objects that could be
bought and sold.[5] *Random House Webster's College Dictionary* defines
a commodity as "anything produced for use or sale, an article of commerce, an object of trade." It possesses, argues Marx, both a use value
and an exchange value, the latter defined as the ability to participate

4
◇

in a network of social relations. Commodities, Marx wrote, are "social things whose qualities are at the same time perceptible and imperceptible by the senses" (72). Thomas Richards observes that in the short space between the mid—nineteenth century and World War I, the commodity "became and has remained the one subject of mass culture, the centerpiece of everyday life, the focal point of all representation, the dead center of the modern world" (1). Before the formation of a new commodity culture in the 1850s, the getting of things had become a "bland business conducted by the middle class," argues Richards; commodities were simply there, piled one on top of the other, ready and waiting to enter a process of circulation.

But beginning at mid-century, as dramatically exemplified by the Great Exhibition of 1851 in England and the proliferation of "world's fairs" in the United States near the turn of the century, the commodity literally came alive and began to "teem with signification" (Richards 2). Objects assumed an increasingly symbolic value, emerging as signs for or symbols of a seemingly endless variety of social meanings. Such a transformation occurred because formations such as advertising emerged during this period to represent commodities as spectacles, as objects that possessed unprecedented special meanings. As Richards explains, "By the time Marx wrote his famous analysis of the fetish character of commodities in *Capital* in the 1860's the situation had changed dramatically from Adam Smith's time. In a variety of striking and subtle ways, Marx's text registers a new spectacular mode for the representation of things" (68). And by the time of the second Industrial Revolution in the 1880s and 1890s, an economy of need was supplemented by an economy of desire, best exemplified in the transformation of classical economics into marginal economics.[6]

One might see a similar history in photography: the transformation of routine into spectacle and the supplementation of need by desire. By the 1880s, studio photography had already lost much of its novelty; for many middle-class Americans it was, as it largely is for us today, a kind of necessary ritual for the preservation of formal occasions such as weddings and baptisms. Judging by writings in popular magazines as well as letters and diaries, many people complained of the boredom of sitting through relatively long sessions as well as the necessity of adopting formal poses and expressions.[7]

Kodak removed the possibilities for boredom by injecting *play* into the experience of photography, allowing consumers for the first time

to take their own portraits and to adopt informal poses and gestures
in informal settings—beaches, parks, city streets. Moreover, Kodak's
marketing created a coherent representational universe for the commodity of the snapshot (just as the world's fairs did for commodities
in general), controlling the unprecedented abundance of photographs
by supplying a new set of codes and images aimed at celebrating the
nostalgic pursuit of beauty, pleasure, and innocence. And finally, by
embodying nostalgia, the snapshot charged representations with desire. Kodak, in other words, taught us how to see and use photographs
as sites of longing.

Kodak and the four other industries I discuss in this book—
leisure, toys, fashion, and antiques, all of which underwent dramatic
transformations in the late nineteenth century—aim at providing a
special kind of commodity. Each serves to transform a surface attention to the world—the desire for beauty, pleasure, and innocence—
into things or, more precisely in the case of leisure and fashion, into
the semiotics of packaged experiences and appearances. The difference, however, is that while these other industries acknowledge their
participation in the construction of fantasy—in the case of leisure,
a pleasurable antidote to labor or daily routine; in the case of toys,
a nostalgic view of childhood; in the case of fashion, an erotics of novelty; and in the case of antiques, an intimate and innocent past—
Kodak advertising presents its idealizations as real. In other words, it
borrows the fantastic or nostalgic rhetoric of these other industries
while at the same time contextualizing its own promotional strategies
within the framework of the true and authentic.[8]

The photograph also persists in its seeming existence as a unique
"gift," magically outside commerce.[9] As John Frow argues, gifts traffic in "inalienable objects" and establish a "qualitative" relationship
among subjects, whereas commodity exchange traffics in "alienable
objects" and establishes a "quantitative" relationship among objects.
The striking feature of photography—especially the ubiquitous production and dissemination of amateur photography "produced" by the
Kodak corporation—is that it creates the illusion of its existence as a
gift (inalienable, qualitative, the product of a human subject) even
while it is bound, part and parcel, within a system of commodities
(alienable, quantitative), a seemingly freestanding "thing" in a system
in which "persons and things both become thinglike" (141). It should
come as no surprise, then, to learn that Kodak capitalized on holidays

Figure 3. Christmastime advertisement for the Autographic Kodak camera, early 1920s. (Reprinted courtesy of Eastman Kodak Company)

and such events as Christmas and weddings to promote its cameras as "ideal and intimate gifts," as in figure 3, an advertisement from the early 1920s. Framed in close-up, the hands gently placing a camera on the Christmas tree suggest that photography partakes in the personal nature of gift giving—a sentiment accentuated by the card that reads "For Mother." The absence of textual description (a three-word slogan with no accompanying caption or information regarding price, features, etc.) suggests that photography presents itself *naturally* as gift and thus requires no explanation for endorsement.

The snapshot's status as a commodity is also unique in that it maintains an aura of simplicity whose meaning derives in part from the illusion that the snapshot—unlike most other commodities—is made by its users. Of all photographic genres, snapshot photography has stubbornly maintained the illusion of naiveté.[10] Val Williams, for example, argues that "snapshot photography poses as the only photographic genre which could be said to be naive, the result of a simple consciousness or an uncluttered wish to obtain a record and to find proof and evidence of a particular course of events, of certain individuals, or of a pattern of experience" (186). Not only does snapshot photography disregard the importance of technical or artistic expertise; it thrives on codes of "simplicity" as a means of shaping perceptions of experience. In the world of snapshots, the view is almost childlike. All one has to do to appreciate its radical difference from earlier forms of photography is to look at photographic portraits taken from the 1840s through the 1880s, with their formal poses and costuming, the grim faces that peer at us amidst all the heavy props, velvet suits, starched cravats, ruffled collars.

This transformation—what we might see as embodied in the emergence of the smile as the dominant icon of portrait photography—was ushered in with Kodak advertising. Such a "simple" approach to the world is reinforced, moreover, by the fact that for most makers of snapshots, control stops once the exposure has been taken. The developing, cropping, printing, mounting—the technical processes that legitimize all other forms of photography—are here made invisible. Shipped through the mail or handed over a counter (often at such places as Wal-mart, where we can shop as our photos develop), snapshots arrive ready-made for us, as Patricia Holland describes (5). Completed by unseen hands, snapshots foster the illusion that a mere

8
◇

press of the button transforms our private visual images into bordered, radiant pictures.

Kodak—and most notably its advertisements—thus rendered the snapshot a unique commodity, one that not only commodified beauty, pleasure, and innocence but also created the illusion that these fantasies were real because consumers had *made* them. The alienating effect of commodities, as Marx so famously described, is that they allow us to forget the processes of labor that went into them, thereby cutting entities off from their own history. Snapshot photographs clearly participate in commodification's erasure of history by appearing in our mailboxes ready-made, completed for us by the invisible hands at the Kodak factory.

At the same time, Kodak ads have consistently assured us that *we* produce these images: "You Press the Button, We Do the Rest," claims the famous slogan, which had appeared in ads by 1889.[11] By beginning with the word "You," the slogan announces its primary focus: the consumer—the new amateur photographer—now has the capability to create her own photographs. The second half of the slogan reassures us that all the mess and mystery of the darkroom will be handled by the company. Snapshot photographs, unlike most other commodities, thus manage to have it both ways: they veil the history of their production while at the same time maintaining the illusion that they, and the meanings they represent, are produced by us. Thus they represent the ultimate commodity: the embodiment of infinite reproducibility with the aura of the unique.

As Richard Terdiman has argued, the erasure of history and social relations implicit in the processes of commodification, exemplified so strikingly by Kodak, speaks to the larger issue of how memory itself is at stake. Because commodities veil the memory of their production from their consumers, as from the very people who produced them, they create a field of what Theodor Adorno called "hollowed-out" objects, which may be invested with any meaning whatsoever, even though they are intrinsically or naturally connected with none at all. "To understand what we have made," claims Terdiman, "we have to be able to *remember* it" (12). Because commodities suppress the memory of their own process, they subvert or violate this fundamental law. Such an observation is especially disconcerting, argues Terdiman, because objects invite us into an intimate relation with them:

> This subversion of memory is all the more unexpected because
> normally objects have an intimate relation to remembrance.
> Through their associations, they play a familiar triggering or an-
> choring role in the mnemonic process. Indeed, the nineteenth
> century institutionalized and exploited this connection between
> memories and objects in the form of a brisk trade in "keepsakes"
> and "souvenirs." So it is astonishing when somehow the mne-
> monic potential of the objects fundamental to an entire social
> formation turns up radically disrupted or disabled. Then the ob-
> ject—in its "metaphysically" enigmatic commodity form—mu-
> tates into a privileged icon symbolizing the whole crisis of mem-
> ory and the sudden opacity of the past. (13)

Our relationship to commodities, a relationship that began in the
mid–nineteenth century, thus speaks to the larger issue of how modernity witnessed a gradual disintegration of a collective confidence
in the ability to remember. In a world of change, memory cannot sustain an uncomplicated belief in its capabilities. Bombarded by too
much information and too many new commodities, many nineteenth-
century writers expressed their uncertainty over the present's relation
with the past.[12]

The gist of Terdiman's argument is that commodification's suppression of memory stands for the larger "memory crisis" he sees as infecting nineteenth-century culture. Endemic to much of this period
was a sense that "the past had somehow evaded memory, that recollection had ceased to integrate with consciousness" (4). It was an age
of "too little memory and too much" (14). One of the major causes—
and symptoms—of this crisis was the increased abstraction of commodities from the history of their production, an abstraction that
paradoxically heightened the mystique of the commodity while ensuring its banality. A similar point might be made about nineteenth-
century perceptions of memory; the more memory was subjected to
analysis and speculation by such writers as Gustave Flaubert and Sig-
mund Freud, the more it seemed to slip away.

Kodak, of course, commodified memory, in effect doubling that
resistance to analysis. Like other souvenirs and keepsakes, snapshots
offered consumers the means to "preserve" their memories. Yet their
status as commodities—objects that sought to commodify beauty,

10 ◇ pleasure, and innocence—also ensured that such a perception was in part an illusion. By exponentially increasing the moments that could be captured and thus remembered, one might argue, Kodak advertising guaranteed that the "memory crisis"—the erosion of traditional modes of apprehending the past that Terdiman describes—would only get worse, and that the past that informs the present would be forgotten.

And as one might expect, according to Terdiman's analysis, it did. He goes on to argue that "the flux of reality in the postmodern world has become so inexpressibly dense that even if only such information as could be reduced to digital expression were recorded, all the memories that could accommodate such registration would fill up and overflow in a moment" (17). In order, then, to maintain some kind of circulation between present and past that allows us to function, according to Terdiman, we must dispose of our memories as we stock up new ones, making them as insubstantial as a digital image. The memories we keep, as any glance at a snapshot album informs us, are those that convey beauty, pleasure, and innocence.

Terdiman's study, then, offers a bleak history of modern memory, and while I find it provocative, I am also reluctant to accept it fully. Like many other writers on memory, Terdiman views nostalgia as a condition largely synonymous with forgetting, denial, retreat, and sentimental weakness.[13] To summarize Terdiman's argument, we might say that nostalgia thrives in modern Western culture because memory cannot. While I do recognize the dangers and limitations inherent in nostalgia, however, I also see nostalgia as a potentially valuable mode of feeling—one born not necessarily out of delusion or escape but out of necessity, resistance, even hope. Ultimately, I find it to be much more valuable than harmful.

In this sense, I follow in the analysis of such critics as Stuart Tannock, Maurice Halbwachs, and Leo Spitzer.[14] In *Hotel Bolivia*, for example, Spitzer writes of the snapshots taken by his Jewish refugee family immediately after they fled Nazi-occupied Austria and during the ten years they remained exiled in Bolivia. Initially puzzled by the consistently cheerful expressions and events that the photos presented, Spitzer came to realize that these snapshots efficaciously served to establish familial and national identity amidst the most violent of all possible extirpations:

In preserving the European albums, they [Spitzer's family] maintained a tangible connection with—and a kind of pictorial control over—the world they had been raised in and were now ex-
cluded from. They retained ownership of a visual memory of life,
place, and cultural engagement that subverted the alienation the
Nazis had tried to force on them. At the same time, the old and
new albums testified to my parents' faith in the future. They
showed familial experience over time—they were family documents intended for viewing in the present as well as in the future, not only by those alive at the time but also by those yet to
come. (9)

As Spitzer so poignantly demonstrates, the nostalgia exemplified
by the uses of photography does not necessarily entail retreat; it can
equally function as retrieval, as a means of reclaiming the past and
even of shaping the future. If nostalgia does misrepresent the past by
imagining it as more stable than it was, it also makes the present bear-
able, usable, even triumphant. As Stuart Tannock argues, it allows for
a "continuity" that can "replenish one's sense of self" even in the face
of terror and loss (455). Kodak recognized this dimension of nostalgia
and turned it into its best selling point.

The Lens

Some readers may wonder why I spend relatively little time discussing
the relation between Kodak marketing and other such strategies of the
time period. Such an approach, typically undertaken earlier by advertising historians, tends to treat advertising as a culture all its own, depicting advertisers as magically in tune with Western desire, or even
the exclusive manufacturers of that desire.[15] While I do discuss some
of the major transformations in American advertising during this time,
I do not propose to discuss specific agencies or personalities.

Even if I had wanted to take such an approach, I would have found
Kodak a difficult case study. As we shall see, the company prepared
most of its own advertising until 1928, when Kodak signed with the nation's leading advertising firm, the J. Walter Thompson agency. The in-
ternal communications of Kodak's advertising department—memos,
notes, minutes of meetings—interest me much less than the way the

12 company sought to communicate with its public. To explore this ques-
◇ tion, I examine not only individual advertisements but a range of Kodak literature that includes periodicals, bulletins, books, pamphlets,
and press releases. All of this archival material I then read against the
larger cultural formations that are spotlighted in the chapters ahead.

In an effort to make clear the ways in which Kodak transformed photography, I occasionally read its strategies and developments against older photographic practices and discourses. Chapter 2,
for example, provides a brief history of amateur photography before
the emergence of Kodak. In chapter 3 I highlight the serious formality of Victorian studio photography in order to emphasize how insistently Kodak ads promoted snapshot photography as a form of play for
children. Chapter 5 provides a brief account of the postmortem and
spirit photograph (both of which I define as "relic"), illustrating how
these images testify to an earlier willingness to include in the space of
the domestic photograph what is painful as well as what is celebratory.

As this description may indicate, I have not tried to write either a
comprehensive or strictly chronological account of Kodak advertising.
A comprehensive history of the advertisements that also sought to locate them within a cultural framework would have been nearly impossible, given the prodigious variety of inventions and advertising
strategies that distinguish this period. A strict chronology would also
have proven difficult, since the patterns that can be found in these ads
(as well as the ones I do not discuss here) recur and overlap rather
than begin and end in distinct time periods. I have included, however,
a brief and largely descriptive profile of key moments in Kodak advertising in chapter 1, recognizing that there are certain facts about Kodak's history and the history of American advertising that I wanted to
draw attention to but could not find occasion for in my more themati-
cally based chapters.

More important, I have organized this book in such a way as to
posit my own reading of Kodak's evolution during these forty-four
years. My key argument is that a crucial shift occurred in the company's promotional focus between 1888 and 1932, when photography
ceased to be a form of *play* and became a form of *memory*. Before its
advertising department realized that the preservation of domestic
memories should be advertised as Kodak's raison d'être, Kodak first
sold the fun of taking pictures: photography as play rather than as visual aide-mémoire. This evolution was neither abrupt nor absolute;

indeed, it resists an easy imposition of specific dates or time frames. Nevertheless, it seems safe to say that between 1888 and 1900 Kodak paid very little attention to promoting photography's mnemonic capabilities. During those twelve years, the sheer pleasure and adventure of taking photographs are the main subject: the delight of handling a diminutive camera, of not worrying about development and printing, of capturing subjects in candid moments, of recording travel to exotic places. Concomitantly, the ads spotlight outdoor settings, exotic locales, trips abroad. After 1900, with the invention of the Brownie camera, the focus starts to shift toward the importance of home and the preservation of domestic memories, but these subjects still remain subordinate to the promotion of snapshot photography as leisure activity. The real turning point—though again not an absolute one—was World War I, when Americans, as I argue in chapter 6, desperately needed photographs to perform as confirmations of family unity.

One disappointingly prosaic explanation for this shift lies in Kodak's steady improvement of indoor film; by around 1915, amateur photographers could take high-quality photos indoors with special equipment, and a wealth of literature (including such publications as *At Home with the Kodak*) and advertisements extolled the value of home as a "bountiful source of charming activities waiting for the snapshooter." But the roots of this transition also lie deeper, in what I see as a gradual tendency in Kodak advertising toward promoting photography as privatized memory. Certainly such a tendency reflects Kodak's response to the increasing importance of the nuclear family in American culture. My interest here, however, resides less in the issue of how snapshot photography participated in modern reconstructions of the family—a subject that has been extensively addressed by a range of critics, including Patricia Holland, Jo Spence, and Marianne Hirsch—than in how snapshot photography was transformed from a leisure activity—which, like all forms of play, celebrates freedom, spontaneity, and the pleasures of the present—to an obligatory act of preserving memories as defense against the future and as assurance of the past.[16]

Turning to the advertisements themselves helps clarify such a complex history. In figure 4 a young woman exudes sheer ecstasy as she holds her camera up high in a gesture that symbolizes the freedom embodied by play. Her youthful figure, summertime costume, and flushed face all reinforce the ad's promotion of photography as an

Figure 4. Kodak Girl poster, 1913. (Reprinted courtesy of George Eastman House)

activity rooted in the present. The setting is outdoors, with the open   15
expanse of the sea straight ahead of the photographer.   ◇

Compare this advertisement with one I will discuss at more length
in chapter 3, which is dated roughly ten years later and features a
visibly older woman, her body effaced by the dark shadows inside her
home, standing near an open door that leads to her backyard (plate 3).
The message here is clear: snapshot photography belongs to the private world of home and family. The woman no longer seeks the adventure of the outdoors; she finds her subjects in her children, her
camera now held down at her side as if the act of taking the picture is
secondary to the nostalgic sentiment that prompts the photograph.
Whereas the earlier ad conveys photography's participation in the
pleasures of the present, this ad's melancholy aura suggests that snapshot photography functions most importantly as a defense against
time. What used to be spontaneous play has now been transformed
into the obligatory act of preserving childhood on film, and the young
liberated woman has now become safely situated within the confines
of her home. Her children play; she watches.

Commencing this account of Kodak advertising's evolution from
play to memory, chapter 2 describes how the company first associated
snapshot photography with the world of leisure (particularly world's
fairs and automobiling) as it sought to redefine amateur photography
in terms of ease and simplicity. Embodying Kodak's image of the
leisurely amateur photographer was the "Kodak Girl," whose youthful
body and extraordinary vitality accentuate the sheer pleasure of taking
snapshots. Chapter 3 focuses on the 1900 invention of the Brownie,
the first camera designed exclusively for children. This chapter extends my investigation into Kodak's early promotion of photography as
a form of play by demonstrating how Kodak promoted the Brownie
camera as a *toy*. Chapter 4 spotlights fashion, which is also about
play—about the aesthetic reinvention of identity through representational plenitude. By associating its products with contemporaneous
notions of fashion, Kodak marketed snapshot photography as a medium through which consumers, particularly female consumers, could
invent new modes of appearance and thus new identities.

The first part of this book thus considers how Kodak capitalized
on youth, novelty, and the pleasures of the present as a means of selling photography. The second part, focusing on Kodak's promotion of

16 photography as a mnemonic practice, demonstrates how its advertise-
◇ ments extolled the value of the past. Chapter 5 was originally inspired
by that day in the antique store. What struck me then was the recognition that in photographs, as in so many of the objects we call "antique," a very fine line exists between value and disposability, between
pricelessness and worthlessness. We cherish now what was once
classified as relatively insignificant, willing to spend hundreds of dollars on an eighteenth-century napkin, thousands of dollars on a Victorian footstool.

Nothing more than paper and yet everything more than paper,
photographs are *instant antiques,* objects that condense to nothingness the increasingly small amount of time required to make something old into something cherished. The term "instant antique" captures the two moments of Kodak's self-presentation, play and memory,
on which I concentrate. The antiquing of experience in Kodak's ads repeatedly bundled photography with nostalgia. "Formerly confined in
time and place, nostalgia today engulfs the whole past," claims David
Lowenthal (6), so that nearly everything that can be distanced as
"past"—from Art Deco alarm clocks to platform shoes—has become
an object of tender regard or curiosity. Such accelerated nostalgia,
Lowenthal argues, is a relatively recent phenomenon: "Once the men-
ace or the solace of a small elite, nostalgia now attracts or afflicts most
levels of society" (11). Chapter 5, then, explores how Kodak marketing
came both to engender and to epitomize this modern condition, a condition seen in such phenomena as the rise of the antique industry
around the turn of the twentieth century.

Kodak's increasingly self-conscious promotion of photography as
a form of memory culminated, I argue in chapter 6, in a campaign that
flourished during World War I called "Let Kodak Keep the Story." In
more than two hundred ads linking photographs with "stories," this
campaign capitalized on the use of narrative as a means of organizing
experience and thus suggested that the collection of photographs
could provide a more effective means of recording, remembering, and
interpreting events than a consumer's own fallible memory.

Such a promise seemed particularly appropriate for a culture
about to enter World War I. As we shall see, many of the ads produced
under the "Story Campaign" urged wives and mothers to buy "Autographic" cameras (a 1913 invention that allowed the photographer to

write any information she wished on the negative) so they could send
photos of "life back home" to their absent husbands and sons. In these ◇
ads, attention is always on the family, never on the war or its brutal disruptions. Ads in the Story Campaign thus promised a photographic history that could displace memories of absence and separation with memories of familial bliss at a time when the solidity of the family was most severely threatened. Snapshot photography had thus been given its most important mission to date; no longer merely the sport of the leisured adult, innocent child, or fashionable young woman, it was vital to the memories of family and nation, to what Kodak ads called "the home version of history."

Even in war, then, Kodak advertising insisted on a nostalgic view of the world. From this time forward, Kodak's accent on memory intensified, creating a culture of amateur photographers who cared much less about the play of photography than about its capacity for mnemonic labor. From this time forward, Kodak systematically urged its consumers to view photography—and the world it recorded— through the lens of nostalgia. The culmination of this progress, as I argue in the coda, is the "Death Campaign," which Kodak initiated in 1932 but never carried into print. The idea of basing an advertising campaign on death rather than pleasure is remarkable in the way it brings the trail of Kodak marketing full circle without seeming to notice the difficulties of selling pain as opposed to momentary pleasures or the more complex pleasures of nostalgia.

Still, in making death a vehicle for advertising, Kodak underlined the complicated relationship between play and memory I pursue throughout this book. Or more precisely, it underlined the relationship between experience and memory, since play is a form of experience that the apocalyptic seriousness of death can in no way embody. Indeed, the campaign's abortion rested precisely on the fact that advertising cannot, as it were, play with death. Advertising sets forth commodities as playthings, so that not only photos but leisure, clothing, and even memories and stories can be commodified and played with; death—even and especially the mechanized death of the First World War—cannot be commodified.

In any case, the relationship between play (experience) and memory is captured, I believe, in the definition of the snapshot as an instant antique. In the course of Kodak's redefinition of the values of

18 ◇ leisure and memory for our culture, the company was able to teach consumers that the ephemera of snapshots in the form of commodities could enrich their moments and substantiate their histories. Death, in embodying the opposition between past and future, also accomplishes the marriage of experience and memory that governed Kodak's project to make photography part of everyday life, but only if experience excludes play. Death stands as the archetypal experience, common to all and unique in each occurrence, but, or perhaps therefore, it resists commodification and play more than any other experience. Once dead, of course, the human body immediately becomes memory, relic, antique. The fact that death embodies this contradiction between experience and memory, and that it does so in a manner congruent with the larger trajectory of Kodak advertising, blinded the most powerful and successful ad agents of the century to the black-humor absurdity of a Death Campaign.

In this book, then, I pursue the work of Kodak in shaping the ethos of our culture, an ethos based on the seeming self-contradiction of valuing the present moment and valuing a past that seems fully lost. Kodak taught us how to live with such a contradiction by holding it in the single image of a snapshot.

I

A Short History of Kodak Advertising, 1888–1932

IN A 1905 article titled "Kodak in Advertising," a writer for the nation's leading advertising journal, *Printer's Ink Monthly*, described Kodak's reliance on advertising this way: "It is an undoubted fact that the most important part of the policy of the Eastman Company has been its interminable pursuit of publicity. The finger of the company never leaves the pulse of the buying public" (7). The doctor-patient metaphor, soon to become an advertising cliché, not only claims that Kodak sedulously maintains interest in its customers; it also insinuates that the company actually sustains the life of the American public by supplying its needs, as if those needs somehow preexisted the marketing that in fact did so much to create them. Such encomiums on Kodak appeared frequently in *Printer's Ink* during the time period I cover here. Clearly the company had achieved an international reputation, even as early as 1905, for the effectiveness of its advertising.

The person initially responsible for Kodak's "pursuit of publicity" was George Eastman, who instinctively grasped what others in the photography industry came to realize much more slowly: that advertisements would, by reaching out to potentially millions of readers and viewers, help create an amateur market for photography faster and more effectively than any other single force. It was Eastman's original commitment to advertising, in addition to the financial backing of the entrepreneur Henry Alvah Strong, an old friend, that determined Kodak's rapid triumph over competitors.[1] In 1900, more than fifty major camera manufacturers existed in the United States, several in

20
◇
Rochester alone. Some of these companies, such as Seneca and Century, produced hand-held cameras and roll film of similar quality at comparable prices.[2] None of them, however, are familiar to us now, their obscurity largely a result of their inattention to selling photography as both a pleasurable and a necessary component of modern life. As one Kodak employee explained in 1918, "Mr. Eastman realized fully that it was the *charm of photography,* not merely his little twenty-five dollar black box, that must be sold to the public."[3]

During the first four years of the Kodak company's existence, Eastman handled virtually all of the promotional details himself. And he had a talent for promotion, what his biographer Elizabeth Brayer calls "an almost innate ability" (134) to write simple, memorable slogans and design illustrations, as a 1890 advertisement testifies (figure 5). At a time when ads were still generally cluttered with text, this advertisement's simple line drawing of hands holding a camera implies that the Kodak camera's distinguishing feature is its small size and light weight, the hand brilliantly portrayed here as the new measure of the camera. In the fall of 1888, readers of *Scientific American, Youth's Companion,* and several other magazines would have been among the first to see the ad.

Eastman also coined the name Kodak, which he registered as the company's trademark on September 4, 1888. "Few acts in the establishment of a commercial entity or the launching of a new product," writes the advertising theorist Henri Charmasson, "are as consequential for the success or failure of the enterprise as the assignment of the name under which that entity or product will be known in the marketplace" (3). Such an observation may strike today's consumer as commonsensical, almost natural, but in 1888 neither the nascent advertising industry nor its audience had yet to recognize the full importance of this basic tenet.[4] With his uncanny sense for advertising, however, Eastman foresaw the role a distinctive brand name would play in determining his company's success. According to tradition, he hit upon the name while playing anagrams with his mother—an ironic beginning, in view of my observation that Kodak's first ads promoted photography as a form of play. Eastman liked the letter *K* because it was "strong and incisive," and he intuited that a name that had no previous meaning and could not be translated into any other language would stick in people's minds more readily.[5]

"What in the name of all that is photographic is the *Kodak?*" asked

Figure 5. Advertisement for the Kodak No. 2 camera, 1890. (Reprinted courtesy of Eastman Kodak Company)

one writer on photography roughly a month after the Kodak camera appeared on the market.[6] The name sounded so peculiar that comments of this sort resounded throughout the first several months of Kodak's existence. Yet within two years the name Kodak had become familiar throughout the world, as an 1890 article in *Photography* makes humorously clear:

> Originally the arrangement [of the letters in "Kodak"] was absolutely without meaning; it has now acquired the dignity of a word with a very definite and precise meaning. . . . The word will very likely develop verbal, adjectival, and adverbial forms as "I am going to Kodak," "This is a Kodak negative," "This picture looks kodakky," and possibly we shall have abbreviations and compounds such as "I shall dak this morning," "This is a dak picture,"

a "dakotype," or "dakograph," for to such compounds the word very readily lends itself. . . . In years to come expert philologists might declare the word to be of Burmese origin, and confidently trace it through imaginary stages were it not that this paragraph in *Photography* will inform the world of the true origin and meaning of this interesting though impudent word, which almost without an effort has forced all civilised languages to adopt it without a murmur. ("Spirit of the Times" 577)

The writer's prediction that "Kodak" would soon transmutate into a variety of uses and forms proved correct; by the early 1890s, "Kodak" had been culturally rewritten as a verb, an adjective, and an adverb, emerging as a synonym for photography at a time when consumers were being bombarded by names and products of all sorts. Thomas Richards notes that in late nineteenth-century culture "there were so many new things, and so many new words naming them, that it was impossible to keep them all straight, and a new class of words came into being to describe things in general—words like gadget, dingus, thingamajig, jigger" (2). "Kodak," however, people remembered. Dozens of fiction writers appropriated it in the 1890s and early 1900s for such children's tales as *Captain Kodak* (a boys' adventure novel) and *Kodak Kate* (a dime novel published serially in 1891, featuring a female investigator whose ability to detect is, as the title implies, as accurate as a camera's). Amateur poets wrote such works as "Kodak True" and "Kodaktyl." Even newspapers sought to use the name in their mastheads, hoping to persuade readers that their reportage aspired to photographic fidelity.[7]

As one might expect, early Kodak ads consistently extolled the value of the Kodak name. "There is no Kodak but the Eastman Kodak" appeared in advertisements beginning in 1898, assuring consumers that Eastman is the good family name, the blueblood of the photographic industry. While testifying to Kodak's superior status, however, the caption also alerts us to the company's anxiety over its trademark. Kodak's success was so immediate that other companies were soon using its name to sell their own (supposedly inferior) goods. In many ways, Kodak courted this dilemma by publishing advertisements that invested the word with commonplace meanings, thus fulfilling the *Photography* article's humorous prediction (one of the company's most popular slogans advised consumers to "Kodak as You Go," for example).

When a word is allowed to play within the ambivalent shades of varying contexts, though, it is no longer the possession of its originator but bases its authority instead on use. This dilemma has haunted the makers of many products (Xerox, Kleenex, Q-Tips), but few companies have been as insistent as Kodak on exerting control over the use of its name, and thus of its meaning. One striking 1891 advertisement issued a "warning" to both the photographic trade and the public, citing the various dates of its patents and thus forcefully asserting that Kodak was buttressed by new laws and legal precedents in its exclusive claim to the name:

> We deem it our duty to notify the trade and the public that roll-holders, and cameras containing the same, are now being offered to the public, which are infringements of our said Letters Patent, and that we shall begin suit against the manufacturers of the same on account of said infringements and prosecute the same as vigourously as possible. . . . We warn all persons from selling or using these roll holders, and cameras containing the same, as sellers and users are liable to suit for infringements as well as the manufacturers of the same.[8]

But such legal challenges still do little to prevent what defines the biggest problem faced by corporations that wish to maintain exclusive rights to their names: popular use. No matter how many advertisements Kodak produced warning the public and photographic industry not to mistake the brand name for an "inferior" product, people continued to link "Kodak" with photography in general well into the 1920s. The phenomenon testified on the one hand to the company's astounding monopoly of the photographic industry and, on the other, to the way a trademark can linguistically sabotage its own company.

Kodak's rapid popularity commands particular attention when we consider that the company actually sold relatively few cameras during its first several years. The Kodak No. 1 camera cost $25 in 1888, the equivalent of roughly $400 in the early twenty-first century and the average yearly income of a farm laborer then. The camera was thus out of the price range of most Americans. Anticipating that the initial high

24
◇

cost might limit its marketability, Kodak produced only 3,250 No. 1 cameras in 1888 and 1889, and roughly 7,000 No. 2 Kodaks in 1890. These production figures increased exponentially with the introduction of the $5 Pocket Kodak, which was produced in shipments of 25,000 each year from 1895 to 1900. Still, it wasn't until the invention of the $1 Brownie camera that snapshot photography truly reached a mass market. Kodak's early popularity thus far exceeded its actual use, testifying to advertising's ability to create an illusion of universal acceptance even as a particular product remains in the hands of the relatively rich.[9]

No longer able to keep up with all the demands of his rapidly expanding company, Eastman relinquished sole responsibility for handling Kodak's advertising in 1892. In March of that year he hired Lewis Bunnell Jones as manager of Kodak's recently established advertising department. Jones's role in shaping Kodak's image was extraordinary, for he almost single-handedly controlled all of Kodak's promotional campaigns until he became vice president of sales and marketing for the company in 1926. A former newspaper reporter and lumberyard bookkeeper who "had a flair for light verse,"[10] Jones wrote most of the company's early slogans and copy himself.

One legendary account tells of how Jones, always accustomed to getting Eastman's approval of his designs before submitting them to Frank Seaman, Kodak's magazine broker between 1892 and 1928, took matters into his own hands once when Eastman was on a business trip and sent the ads directly to Seaman. When Eastman returned, he called Jones into his office and expressed his surprise over the novelty of the ads produced while he was gone. "These ads are better than anything you've done before. What changed?" Jones admitted the truth: "The other ads I did for you. These I did for the public." From that day forward, Jones never had to get Eastman's approval of his designs again.[11]

Under Jones's autocratic supervision, Kodak's advertising department devised some of the company's most legendary campaigns and strategies, including the 1893 introduction of the Kodak Girl in magazine ads and posters; the Traveling Kodak Exhibitions that toured the country between 1905 and 1910; the famous "yellow box" packaging in 1905; and even the radio show *The Kodak Hour* (widely known as "On the Front Porch"), which ran once a week in the mid-1920s and featured photographers who recounted their own photographic experiences and answered audience questions. According to John Brummett, the show was designed to "get people in the mood for picture taking during the weekend. To that end, the music—both orchestral and vocal—was nostalgic as well as 'reputable' [not jazz] and tended to suggest the flight of years, and the value and importance of a camera as the chronicler, a means of stopping time in its tracks—momentarily" (76–77). Hosted by Angelo Patri, a syndicated columnist on child development and parenting, the show extolled the value of photography as both a family activity and an indispensable tool for the preservation of important family moments.

Jones even came up with the "Kodak Electric Winkler," a neon sign invented in 1908 that read "Take a Kodak with You," which store owners who carried Kodak products could rent from the company for a nominal fee. Jones also capitalized on the still novel idea of using testimonials by celebrities as endorsements of products. In 1892, Robert E. Peary, not yet an admiral, returned from his Arctic expedition with more than two thousand photographs produced by a Kodak camera and was featured in several advertisements (figure 6). So was Rudyard Kipling, who journeyed to Africa with a Pocket Kodak in 1898. And in 1899 Jones began to advertise in the *Saturday Evening Post,* which was enjoying one of the fastest-growing circulations in the United States at the time.

By the end of the 1890s, Jones was spending $750,000 a year on advertising, the largest advertising expenditure at the time.[12] "Jones' Advertising Department," wrote John Brummett, "was practically an advertising agency in and of itself; it did everything any contemporary agency did, and did it well" (110). Like Eastman, Jones knew that the success of Kodak advertising would depend on sentiment, not facts. He consequently minimized descriptions of individual products, focusing instead on the "*idea of photography* as a practice which harmonizes with all aspects of one's life."[13] If photography was promoted only as a hobby, the danger existed that customers would tire of it and move on to yet another hobby. "As it is," Jones explained to an interviewer, "they may shift from one recreation to another a dozen times, and the Kodak fits into every one" ("Kodak in Advertising" 112).

What Jones did not write or design himself, he mainly left to those who worked in his department. All Kodak employees, in fact, were encouraged to submit slogans, designs, and photographs for the periodic contests the company sponsored, which often awarded prizes of $500

Figure 6. Advertisement featuring Lieutenant Peary, 1892. (Reprinted courtesy of Eastman Kodak Company)

to the winners. Such contests were part of Kodak's larger ambition to include employees at every level of company business, a goal repeatedly expressed to employees in official memos. "We want each one of our employees to feel vitally interested in the business of this Company, to feel that its success and his success are bound up together, and we will be very glad to receive suggestions from you and to pay you for any which are adopted," claimed Eastman in one such memo.[14] In 1897 the company also began to sponsor national contests for the "best amateur photograph," to be featured in its advertisements. More than 25,000 people competed in the first contest for prizes totaling over $3,000. In 1907 Kodak awarded a first prize of $1,000 to the best photograph, more than it had ever paid for a painting commissioned for an advertisement. Kodak even sponsored contests for children after the invention of the Brownie camera in 1900, awarding cash prizes of up to $300 for the best photograph.

All these contests played a vital role in the company's promotion of snapshot photography, for they cultivated a sense among Americans that their "amateur" photographs could in fact attain a quality high enough to sell the practice of photography to other Americans. These contests also exemplified Kodak's oft-repeated claim that what Americans wanted and realized from snapshot photography was precisely what Kodak endorsed.[15]

Much of the company's early marketing success was also due to the volumes of promotional literature Kodak produced for amateur photographers, salesmen, and dealers. For amateur photographers Jones and his department published such popular books as *Do I Want a Camera?* (1913) and *At Home with the Kodak* (1922), which offered simple suggestions on such topics as lighting, composition, and choice of subject matter. The *Kodakery*, a monthly magazine founded in 1913, included such suggestions as well. Also among Kodak's periodical literature was the *Kodak Trade Circular*, founded in 1899, which Eastman and Jones started in order to provide dealers with the "inside story" on new products, services, and advertising strategies. While the *Kodak Trade Circular* presupposed a relatively knowledgeable audience more interested in facts than in entertainment (even the general appearance of the magazine, with its lack of illustrations, testifies to its no-nonsense approach), articles in the *Kodak Salesman*, first published in 1915, were generally intended to indoctrinate its audience in the basic ins and outs of the photographic business while at the same

Figure 7. Cartoon from *Kodak Trade Circular*, July 1916. (Reprinted courtesy of Eastman Kodak Company)

time keeping them amused through anecdotes, lively descriptions, colorful suggestions, and even cartoons (figure 7).[16]

However ingenious the advertising strategies of Jones and the employees who worked under him, the company also owed much of its advertising success to sheer timing. Those early years of Kodak marketing coincided with the professionalization of American advertising. When Eastman patented his Kodak products in 1888, he entered a field dramatically different from what it had been only a few decades before. The self-legitimating apparatus of professional advertising— copywriters, art directors, account executives, marketing experts, brand names, labels, packaging—had just begun to be formed.[17] In the early to mid–nineteenth century, advertising in the United States was generally considered déclassé, a practice evocative of double dealing in shabby offices, patent medicines, and blaring overstatements printed on cheap handbills and circulars.

A businessman might succumb to the need for advertising, the cultural historian Stephen Fox explains, but usually with some degree of embarrassment, as it suggested that his product lacked the integrity to sell itself. What's more, until roughly the beginning of the 1880s, neither the newspaper and magazine industry nor the few advertising agencies that did exist took much professional interest in the honesty or appearance of the ads:

> Advertising was considered an embarrassment—the retarded child, the wastrel relative, the unruly servant kept backstairs and never allowed into the front parlor. A firm risked its credit rating by advertising; banks might take it as a confession of financial weakness. Everyone deplored advertising. Nobody—advertiser, agent, or medium—took responsibility for it. The advertiser only prepared the ad, but did not place it; the agent only served as an errand boy, passing the advertiser's message along to the publisher; the medium printed it, but surely would not question the right of free speech by making a judgment on the veracity of the advertiser. (Fox 15)

By the 1880s, however, the field of American advertising was working every minute to shed its dubious inheritance, catalyzed by the lightning-like development of a mass consumer culture after the Civil War and the recognition of advertising's potential to occupy a central

30   position in that culture. Advertising, agents began to recognize, could
◇   be designed in ways that would appeal to the new and dramatically expanding middle class, whose members enjoyed rising incomes and
more leisure time. And so the once disreputable ad man, a kind of
trickster figure, was transformed into an agent of trained intelligence,
part of the newly emergent managerial and professional class.

Before an occupation can become a profession, as Magali Sarfatti
Larson has established, the public must be willing to accept and le-
gitimize the superiority of a "professional's" knowledge and skills.[18]
Not surprisingly, then, by the early 1890s a series of journals for
advertising professionals began to appear, the most notable being
Printer's Ink.

These journals stressed repeatedly the value of a respectable image to both the advertiser and the agency he employed. Advertisers
were now advised to show "tasteful" images and illustrations accompanied by short, simple captions. "The newer advertising successes,"
Fox explains, "sold through pitches that were quieter, more believable,
even charming" (25). The emphasis was on credible understatement.
Hard-selling, detailed copy did not work, according to *Printer's Ink's*
editors, because it overloaded the public's attention span and taxed its
credulity. Advertising's shift from excess to uncomplicated, unadorned
copy conveniently paralleled Kodak's own emphasis on the simplicity
of its cameras and photographic "system." As the company explained
to dealers, "Simple ideas, simply expressed. That has been the key to
every aspect of our business, from the products themselves to the ads
that promote them" ("Brevity in Advertising" 2).

Eastman first advertised the Kodak No. 1 camera in the August 1888 issues of *Harper's, Century, Scribner's, Scientific American,*
and *Puck,* deliberately timing the introduction of the camera to coin-
cide with the beginning of fall because he wanted to "catch the Christmas trade." Each of these magazines had only recently begun to run
advertisements, largely in response to the efforts of J. Walter Thompson. By the late 1880s, Thompson was attracting such companies as
Kodak, Mennen, and Prudential Insurance by flourishing a "Standard
List" of thirty magazines under exclusive contract to his agency. Once
dismissive of ads, these magazines were now growing exponentially because of them; indeed, many historians describe the period between
1890 and the late 1920s as the "golden age" of magazines.[19] When
Thompson and Eastman began their partnership, however, the maga-

zines' circulation and profit were modest in comparison with what they would boast a decade or so later: in 1887, *Century* led all American magazines with a circulation of 222,000, followed by *Harper's* at 185,000. They carried, at most, about $30,000 worth of advertising per issue (Fox 33). In 1885, only four general magazines could boast a circulation of 100,000 or more readers. Two decades later, twenty such magazines existed, with a combined circulation of nearly 25 million. "The magazine world," Fox explains, "had been transformed: a revolution prodded, celebrated, and paid for by advertising" (35).

An article in a 1902 issue of *Printer's Ink* testifies that by that time American advertisers viewed magazines as their most important forum. Here, however, the writer betrays his predilection for magazines of a special kind: the "first-class" tier of periodicals written expressly for men and women whose lifestyles provided sufficient leisure to read about the expensive products available to them:

> Years ago it was discovered by advertisers that a first-class magazine was valuable because it was the companion of the hour of rest. If you wished to reach people with minds free from business cares you could do so in these periodicals—on grassy banks, stretched at full length, magazine in hand; in parlor car, traveling leisurely across the continent, turning over the pages of the latest monthlies; in the sand by the seaside, on a month's vacation, a magazine as companion; on winter's night snugly ensconced by blazing fire, turning over the newest "Harper" or "Century," while the wind howls without and snow piles up. As the magazine is peculiarly the companion of leisure hours, when the mind is free to accept new impressions, it follows that persons having words worth saying to the public find in these advertising pages a sure access to a large class of busy people who can be reached in no other way. (Walker 491)

As Susan Strasser has also noted, both Eastman and Jones targeted the "best" magazines right from the beginning, aiming to attract readers whose incomes ranged upward from $1,000.[20] By 1920, these titles had expanded to include most prominent national magazines, among them *McClure's, Cosmopolitan, Ladies' Home Journal, Munsey's Magazine, Woman's Home Companion, Youth's Companion, Country Life in America, Saturday Evening Post, Harper's Bazaar, Field and Stream,*

32 *National Geographic,* and *Outing Magazine.* According to a 1915 issue
◇ of the *Kodak Trade Circular,* ads were prepared and placed in publications with aggregate circulation of 35 million during each month of
that year.[21]

As their titles indicate, most of these magazines can be classified
in four categories: family magazines, outdoor magazines, women's
magazines, and children's magazines. Family magazines such as the
Saturday Evening Post advertised Kodak products extensively, most often with images of family gatherings and celebrations, particularly at
Christmas. Women's magazines, especially the *Ladies' Home Journal,*
provided Kodak with its most profitable advertising arena. According
to the historian Jennifer Scanlon, readership of women's magazines
grew from over 13 million per month in 1914 to a peak of almost 20 million in 1930.[22] Intuiting that women would constitute the largest
group of consumers for Kodak products because of their supposed
sentimentality, Eastman encouraged Jones to advertise extensively in
these magazines, urging the female consumer to see photography not
only as a necessary component of domestic life but as an integral part
of the world of fashion and feminine beauty. Outdoor and recreational
magazines, such as *Outing Magazine* and *Illustrated Outdoor World
and Recreation,* promoted the Kodak camera as a necessary part of
every vacation or outdoor excursion. And children, the newest group
of American consumers at the turn of the twentieth century, viewed
advertisements for the Brownie camera in such magazines as *American Boy* and *St. Nicholas.*

Much of the reason for the proliferation and success of these
magazines had to do with the transformation in image reproduction
engendered by such new photo technologies as the photogravure process in 1895 and the improvement of the halftone process in 1890,
which allowed magazines for the first time to reproduce photographs
with startling clarity of detail.[23] By 1900, most of the major magazines
were profusely illustrated, obeying the dictates of the advertising professionals, who argued that good illustration would be an invaluable
aid in attracting the public's attention, obtaining its sympathy, and im-
proving their own credibility. Quality illustration, advertisers claimed,
would be an indicator of the refinement and good taste of the advertiser, the product, and the purchasing public.

With his finger always on the pulse of advertising improvements,
Jones began around 1900 to devote a significant portion of Kodak's ad-

vertising budget to commissioning illustrators for Kodak ads. Indeed, as I go on to discuss in chapter 4, Kodak produced its most artistic advertisements between 1900 and roughly 1915, a period when noted illustrators such as Frederic Remington, Jessie Wilcox Smith, Edward Penfield, Maxfield Parrish, Blendon Campbell, C. Allen Gilbert, Fred Pegram, and Elizabeth Shippen Green were hired by most leading companies in the United States—including Kodak—to create designs for magazine displays, streetcar signs, and posters.

Part of the reason for Kodak's deployment of these illustrations rested on what the advertising department perceived as the limitations of photographic reproduction. Kodak began using photographs in its advertising in 1901, when further improvements in halftone technology finally resulted in reproductions clear enough to satisfy Eastman and Jones (although photograph reproduction was possible beginning around 1890, neither man thought the resultant images "clear and bold enough for a photographic company"). Convinced, however, that color images sold products more effectively than black-and-white ones, Kodak's advertising department attempted to color its photographs beginning in 1903. But the resultant images were distorted and consequently deprived of their credibility. The use of photographs was thus reluctantly curtailed until roughly 1915. This is not to say that photos disappeared from Kodak ads until 1915; on the contrary, black-and-white photos account for the bulk of quarter- and half-page ads during this period. But for the prestigious full-page and back-cover advertisements—those ad spaces, in other words, that clearly command the most attention—Kodak used color illustrations exclusively.

In 1915, technological improvements enabled realistic reproduction of colored photographs for the first time. And with these improvements, the company switched to photographs for almost all of its advertisements, so that by the mid-1920s, roughly 90 percent of Kodak ads incorporated photos. Beginning in 1921, Kodak also began publishing full-size color photographs in the rotogravure sections of thirty-five U.S. newspapers. The full-size newspaper offered a space unit larger than anything Kodak had used in previous campaigns. Consequently, as Jones explained in *Printer's Ink* that year, "the opportunity for the reproduction of beautiful photography is much greater" ("Kodak's Fighting Front" 15). John Brummett has also pointed out that "the rotogravure, with its excellent reproduction of photographs, was in itself promotion for Kodak goods and services" (65).

34 But the promotion worked in reverse as well; Kodak selected its most
◇   "artistic" photographs for the rotogravure section, and judging by popular responses to these ads, the reading public viewed them as a fitting
climax to the section's overall stunning visual effects.

With its near-exclusive reliance on photographs after 1915, Kodak's
ads differed dramatically from those produced by other major companies, which shied away from using photography with any real
frequency until the late 1920s. Leery of photography's realism—of
what one advertising theorist called its "vulgar, half-witted literalness"
(quoted in Johnston 67)—the advertising industry originally viewed
photography as too matter-of-fact a medium for the selling of fantasy.
As Patricia Johnston explains, "Although the technical qualities of
photography greatly impressed advertising professionals, the medium
was adopted slowly because the agencies doubted its ability to trigger
the imagination; photographs were considered too real" (86).

By the end of the 1920s, however, this perception had shifted dramatically; photos now dominated advertising pages precisely because
of their implied documentary quality, due in part to the advertising
work of such gifted photographers as Edward Steichen. Advertising psychologists began advising companies that the photograph's
supposed realism would convince viewers of the product's integrity.
Photography's associations with documenting truth, they maintained,
would authenticate images and the ideologies behind them, encouraging viewers to see the human subjects in ads as "real people" just
like them. Consequently, the use of photographic advertisements in
magazines increased by over 40 percent between 1920 and the mid-
1930s.[24] Ironically, these photos tended to glamorize upper-class life at
the expense of middle- and working-class concerns just as illustrations
in watercolor and painting had done, allowing consumers to believe
that products could transform them into ladies and gentleman of
leisure.

The photographs Kodak employed for its advertising—even the
elaborate color images for the rotogravure sections—differ profoundly in composition and effect from those produced by other corporations, however. While companies such as Jergens employed photographers as eminent as Steichen and Anton Bruehl to construct
highly stylized photographs, Kodak's images were increasingly designed to appear not only realistic but amateurish: in other words, they

were meant to perform as snapshots. As one writer in *Printer's Ink* explained, the advertising photos "often have a happy spontaneity about them which proves—or would seem to do so—that they are not the more or less labored product of the professional studio" (Bliven 112). John Brummett reiterates this observation: "Kodak advertising's most potent humanizing influence was the unsung amateur camera user. His unpremeditated, unstaged, unsophisticated snapshots helped to make carefully contrived studio work look phony" (40).

Experimental techniques such as close-up composition, dramatic depth of field, and soft focus were rare in Kodak advertisements. Instead, Kodak's images were increasingly designed to replicate the ordinary snapshot. Some of these photographs did represent the work of actual amateurs, who received a substantial cash payment along with the joy of seeing their snapshots appear in the ads. But the majority of these advertising photos were produced by professional photographers working with models, who would often spend an entire day taking pictures in order to get one "unsophisticated" photograph, as Brummett calls it (44).

Kodak's staged use of snapshot photography, perverting as it did the medium's connotations of spontaneity, naiveté, and intimacy, evokes for us the positively Baudrillardian dimensions to its advertising history. As in all advertisements, the simulacrum masquerades here as the real; the crucial difference is that it now promotes a product whose cultural authority resides precisely in its claim to the real. Just as important, Kodak's incremental reliance on staged snapshots provides further evidence of the promotional shift from play to memory I chart throughout this book. Between 1900 and roughly 1915, as we shall see, Kodak was much more willing to allow a range of media—watercolors, oil paintings, even cartoons—to function as surrogate photographs. By the time of World War I, the company had come to rely much more exclusively on photos, amateur-looking photos that increasingly depicted "realistic" views of home and family. In this sense, Kodak banished play from its advertising. No longer invited to imagine a multitude of meanings for photography as they considered its relation to other media such as watercolor and oil, viewers now came to photography by way of photography. And the photographs they saw depicted an ever-narrowing world—a world more and more shaped by nostalgia.

2

"Vacation Days Are Kodak Days"

Modern Leisure and the New Amateur Photographer in Advertising

JUNE 1907. The latest issue of the *Ladies' Home Journal* has just appeared on the doorstep of over a million American homes. On the cover a young woman swinging her tennis racket (lawn tennis, invented in the 1880s, had evolved into a fashionable sport for women by 1907) prefigures the theme of the issue: "How to make the most of summer weekends and vacations." Readers who skimmed through the magazine would have seen twenty-four articles and close to a hundred advertisements coaxing them, as one ad puts it, "to let life assume a different rhythm when away from the obligations of home or office." Among the articles listed in the table of contents one finds "A Fourth of July without Fireworks," "Summer Organdies, Lawns, and Dimities," and "How to Be Comfortable in a Tent." In the issue's advertising section, quarter- and half-page ads for train excursions abound, most of them illustrated with photographs of the destination being promoted. The Northern Pacific Railway advertises trips to Yellowstone National Park, which by 1910 had attracted over 5 million visitors.[1] The Union Pacific Railroad exhorts its readers to "Give the Tired Society Girl a Summer in Colorado" with an illustration of a droopy young woman surrounded by suitors. An advertisement for Oso hammocks portrays a reclining female smiling with almost lascivious pleasure—an amusing image, especially when one learns that the hammock's recent commercialization had sent at least one American into raptures at the possibility of "sleeping outdoors in the middle of the day, and in full view of your neighbors to boot!"[2]

Printed on the back cover of the magazine (the costliest position for a magazine advertisement in 1907) and the only ad reproduced in color, an advertisement promoting the Kodak Tank stands out among all the others (plate 4). The Kodak Tank Developer, invented in 1905, enabled amateur photographers to develop their own film without the need of a darkroom.[3] Painted in rustic shades of green, gold, and brown by the noted illustrator C. Allan Gilbert, the advertisement capitalizes on Americans' recent fascination with camping and the outdoors, catalyzed in part by the widespread formation of back-to-nature organizations such as the Appalachian Club (1876) and the Sierra Club (1892). The rhetoric voiced by these organizations stressed that couples in isolated natural settings would find relief from the artificiality and confinement of the city and attain a more "wholesome" life by communing with nature.[4] Certainly the couple depicted in this Kodak ad look robust and relaxed: witness their rolled-up sleeves, the man's unbuttoned shirt, and the casual, even "unladylike" pose of the woman.

The salient aspect of this image is Gilbert's depiction of photography as a naturalized part of the camping experience: the various components of the Tank that lie on the ground (metal bowl and canister, wooden box, film reels) look more like camping equipment than photographic equipment; the Kodak camera itself is slung on the branch of a tree in the left background, and the man holds the film as casually as he might a fishing line. The advertisement thus assures its readers that they can enjoy this product even in the most primitive of situations.

Indeed, Kodak contextualizes film development here within the popular rhetoric of the back-to-nature movement, the ad implying that consumers who use the Kodak Tank are self-sufficient (as opposed to dependent on factory expertise), resourceful, and, since the development can be done in daylight, eager to perform all aspects of snapshot photography in the great outdoors. As the caption guarantees, "Development is at your convenience. . . . It's all by daylight, as simple as 'pressing the button,' and the experts say that it gives better results than the dark-room method."

The contents of the *Ladies' Home Journal* show that leisure constituted one of the circumambient worlds of early Kodak advertising. Contemporary notions of what constitutes leisure—the development

38 ◇ of the paid summer vacation, for example—have their roots in late nineteenth- and early twentieth-century culture, as a wealth of literature on the subject has explained.[5] This commercial dissemination of leisure reflects a sea-change in the United States and parts of Europe during the second half of the nineteenth century regarding the nature, organization, and perception of work. When industrialism seemed to deplete labor of all vestiges of creativity and freedom as it mechanized an employee's performance (whether that employee was a factory worker, a clerk, a businessperson, or a professional), the early nineteenth-century emphasis on the ennobling value of work was displaced by a modern emphasis, culminating in the 1920s, on the value of play as an end in itself.[6]

The major distinction between work and play, declares Johan Huizinga, centers on the perception that play constitutes an activity in itself, whereas work (that is, the kind of mechanized labor characteristic of industrialized cultures) privileges the end result over the process.[7] Earlier Kodak ads enticed consumers to see photography as a form of play—to indulge in the adventure of performing photography rather than, as they would be conditioned to do in later years, engage in the work-driven act of taking pictures primarily to secure recorded memories.

Vivifying this accent on play are the leisure locales and activities that pervade early Kodak advertising: parks, tennis courts, fishing streams, campgrounds, sailboats, picnics, beaches, fairs, and automobiles.[8] This attention to outdoor scenes and pastimes invites special attention, given Kodak's emphasis on domestic settings after 1917, in keeping with its intensified focus on familial memories. The world seems to shrink with the evolution of Kodak advertising, moving more and more inward toward the home and family. But for now, parks, beaches, oceans, foreign countries, and world's fairs are all promoted as playgrounds for the amateur photographer. As one of Kodak's early slogans pronounced, "All out-doors invites your Kodak" (figure 8). Adventure predominates in these ads; family reigns later.

Gold-plated adventure, that is. Anyone looking at Kodak's leisure ads will immediately notice that models always play tennis in designer apparel, that the luggage they carry boasts monograms and Moroccan leather, that the automobiles they drive are not Model T Fords but Studebakers. As Thorstein Veblen so famously argued, the emergence of leisure as a value-laden concept in modern culture hinged on its

All out-doors invites your Kodak.

Let Kodak keep a picture record of your every outing. There's a new pleasure in every phase of photography—pleasure in the taking, pleasure in the finishing, but most of all, pleasure in possessing pictures of the places and people that *you* are interested in.

KODAKS, $5.00 to $100.00.   BROWNIES (*they work like Kodaks*), $1.00 to $12.00

EASTMAN KODAK COMPANY,

Catalogue free at the dealers or by mail.

ROCHESTER, N. Y., *The Kodak City.*

Figure 8. Advertisement featuring the Kodak Girl in sailor suit, 1911. (Reprinted courtesy of Eastman Kodak Company)

40 ◇ confluence with conspicuous consumption.[9] While Americans gradually came to perceive leisure as the right of every citizen, it was still—and largely remains today—the privilege of the middle and upper classes. This is not to say, of course, that avenues of leisure did not open for the working classes during this period; as such historians as David Nasaw and Peter Bailey have elucidated, significant reductions in the number of work hours by the early 1900s enabled wage earners gradually to enjoy evenings, Saturday afternoons, and Sundays free (it was not until the 1940s that most Americans could claim the entire weekend as free time).[10] Amusements such as dollar theaters, concert saloons, dime museums, nickelodeons, arcades, and dance halls, as well as various spectator sports such as boxing, football, and baseball, flourished in the latter half of the nineteenth century and were specifically designed for the entertainment of the working and lower middle classes. But these are not the forms of leisure represented in Kodak ads, nor are they the forms of leisure most often represented in advertising or tourist literature in general. The kinds of leisure activities depicted in Kodak ads—sailing, automobile touring, travel abroad—could be enjoyed, of course, only by those whose incomes registered far above that of the average middle-class American. Despite all the ways in which American capitalism had managed to provide leisure for the working classes even as it also sought to increase their productivity, representational conventions in advertising continued to consolidate leisure as the privilege of the wealthy.

Before Kodak could merchandise its cameras as accessories for luxury automobiles, however, it had to assure customers that its new method of amateur photography was easy: a difficult task, given photography's notorious reputation as a messy, time-consuming, and cumbersome activity. Selling the simplification of amateur photography thus became Eastman's primary goal. A secondary goal, as we will also see, was to feminize it.

A New Breed of Amateurs

In eliminating the darkroom component of photography, Kodak targeted those amateurs interested in "keeping a personal record of their everyday life, objects, places, or people that interest them," but hardly interested in (or capable of) processing the result. In the world of Kodak advertising, "amateur" thus quickly came to designate anyone (even a child by 1900) who could aim straight and "press a button." As ads guaranteed, the "entire process as well as all the simple ins-and-outs of the equipment can be learned in half an hour."

Before the advent of Kodak, the amateur photographer—generally male, relatively well educated, often extremely wealthy, and eager to justify his leisure time through a conspicuous demonstration of seriousness of purpose—would now metamorphose into a middle-class person who might well be a woman, someone interested in a hobby that required little or no technical expertise or intellectual effort. Unlike earlier amateur photographers, Kodak promised, the "Kodaker" would easily find abundant photo opportunities. The camera's readiness (its light weight, compactness, relatively fast shutter speed, and roll of 100 exposures) guaranteed this assurance. Simple and efficient, snapshot photography augmented the pleasure of other leisure activities (in 1895 Kodak even marketed a camera called the Kartridge Kodak, designed to fit squarely on the bar of a bicycle). Most important, Kodak pledged to the new amateur photographer its assiduous expertise.

In an essay on Kodak's near-instant popularity, one writer for the *Chicago Tribune* remarked in 1891 that "the [Kodak] craze is spreading fearfully. Chicago has had many fads whose careers have been brilliant but brief. But when amateur photography came, it came to stay" (quoted in Brayer 70). Everywhere one went, it seemed, "Kodakers were out in droves."[11] As I noted earlier, this perception of Kodak's "instant" popularity is misleading, given the moderate number of cameras produced and sold between 1888 and 1900. But by 1905, five years after the invention of the $1 Brownie camera, the company had broadened the field of amateur photography to encompass roughly one-third of the United States' population (at the end of 1905, it had sold over 1.2 million cameras).[12] Such mass production of snapshooters, however, came at a price. It entailed a shift of emphasis from knowledge to simplicity; the establishment of ownership (rather than skill or knowledge) as a primary criterion of the amateur photographer; the commercialization of amateur practices and conceptions; and a persistent alliance between technological simplicity and femininity. In other words, the transformation of amateur photography into a commercialized leisure activity also meant its exile from a world (albeit a largely masculine one) characterized by commitment, exertion, erudition.

42
◇

This reinvention of the amateur photographer reflects a much larger cultural shift in the United States and parts of Europe in the ideology, practices, and popular perceptions of amateurism.[13] By the 1880s, "amateur" had become a hotly contested word. On the one hand, it was jealously guarded by people who professed a passionate commitment to a given field and who saw themselves as following a noble legacy of early nineteenth-century "gentleman amateurs." Eclipsing this relatively small group of amateurs, however, was a formidable rank of middle- and upper-middle-class men and women who now enjoyed increased leisure time, given reduced work hours as well as a surfeit of new appliances that freed housewives to organize their family's recreational life.

This new body of amateurs flourished especially in the first two decades of the twentieth century, when the average workweek continued to plummet until it had reached an all-time low of 52 hours by 1920 (compared with an average of 70 hours in 1850).[14] Cultivating what they often called a "playful" interest in activities such as gardening, cycling, and sailing, these amateurs expected amusement from their hobbies, not enlightenment. By the 1880s, they had already been tagged with the label of "dabbler" by those "true" amateurs who wished to preserve "amateur's" original associations with devotion and industry (amator, "he who loves"). "Dabblers," argued their opponents, "are those whose active involvement, technique, and knowledge are so meager as to barely distinguish them from the public of which they are a part" (Stebbins, *Amateurs: On the Margin* 23). Indeed, the only criterion that demarcated "dabblers" from the larger public was their possession of the necessary equipment for their hobbies; in other words, ownership, rather than skill, qualified them as amateurs.[15]

Eastman, of course, was not alone in recognizing the commercial possibilities of targeting this newer and much wider group of amateurs—an observation borne out by the sheer number of magazines and books published in the 1870s and 1880s that bore the word "amateur" in their titles—*Amateur Gardening, Amateur World, Amateur Athlete, The Amateur Musician, The Yankee Amateur, The New England Amateur, The East Boston Amateur,* and even *The American Amateur Photographer.* Although some of these magazines were directed toward the more "serious-minded" amateur, most of them clearly aimed at an audience that wished to spend only a fraction of its time on a selected hobby. The subject matter of these magazines generally remains at a superficial level, the writing in nonintimidating, even elementary language.[16] A survey of the table of contents of one issue of *Amateur Gardening*, for example, alerts us to the rudimentary level of discourse and subject matter found in many of these magazines; articles for the April 1882 issue include "Why Roses Smell So Good" and "How to Arrange a Bouquet in Three Easy Steps." These titles should also indicate that, while most of these magazines profess an interest in both sexes, they generally target a female readership presumed to value simplicity of language and subject matter.

The topic of amateurism had become contested enough by the 1880s to warrant a host of popular essays on the subject: "What about Amateurs?"; "The Noble Art of the Amateur"; "A Nation of Amateurs"; "A Plea for Knowledge."[17] The most striking aspect of these essays is their reflection of a cultural ambivalence about the meaning and value of amateurism, an ambivalence that eventually led to what Robert Stebbins describes as the "annoying imprecision in both everyday life and sociological thought" with which the term "amateur" is now used (*Amateurs: On the Margin* 21). Clearly, mass amateurism as well as the rise of professionalism contributed to this ambivalence, resulting in the "serious" amateur's increasingly marginal position in society.[18] One would expect most writers on the subject to lament the fact that the ranks of "serious-minded" amateurs were now dwindling considerably, but a surprising number of them express precisely the opposite view.

In a sententious article titled "The Amateur Spirit" in the *Atlantic Monthly*, an anonymous writer argues that in comparison with the professional's commitment to his field, the amateur's seems excessive and impractical: "he [the amateur] is unskillful because untrained; desultory because incessant devotion to his hobby is both unnecessary and wearisome; ineffective because, after all, it is not a vital matter whether he succeed or fail" (271). After these censorious comments, he celebrates the professional's sense of purpose and "intense industry," characteristics acquired for the obvious reason that the professional's livelihood and reputation, unlike the amateur's, depend on them. While possessing a "charming" combination of "versatility and enthusiasm" (272), he argues, the amateur must give way to the

44
◇
professional, who recognizes the value of specialization in an increasingly competitive culture. Nothing less than the nation's welfare is at stake:

> Ours must be, not a "nation of amateurs," but a nation of professionals, if it is to hold one's own in the upcoming struggles,— struggles not merely for commercial dominance, but for the supremacy of political and moral ideals. Our period of national isolation, with all it brought of good or evil, has been outlived. The new epoch will place a heavy handicap upon ignorance of the actual world, upon indifference to international usages and undertakings, upon contempt for the foreigner. What is needed is, indeed, knowledge, and the skill that knowledge makes possible. The spirit with which we confront the national tasks of the future should have the sobriety, the firmness, the steady effectiveness, which we associate with the professional. (276)

Clearly, the United States can no longer afford the amateur, whose pursuit of personal development the author subtly aligns with the country's misguided xenophobia. This is not to say that Americans should not have hobbies outside of their professions, the author hastens to say, but these pastimes should warrant only the "lightest and easiest of interests . . . a desire to fill a Sunday afternoon or weekday evening" (278). In other words, hobbies should be relegated to one's spare hours and performed mainly with the intent to rejuvenate oneself before turning once again to professional work. Otherwise, as he boldly implies has been the case in Britain, the United States faces the prospect of harboring too many "unmanly" men, whose energy and intelligence clearly dissipate without the ballast of professionalism.

In simplifying photography to the extent he did, then, George Eastman answered the desires of a culture in which mass amateurism (that is, amateurism that required no serious commitment) had already undergone commercialization, and from the viewpoint of some writers, at least, appeared more "practical" than the British breed of amateurism, which diverted energy and time away from one's professional work. Fifty years earlier, in 1839, photography had been born into a much different climate in the United States and particularly in Britain, when a rhetoric of industry circumscribed the scope of ama-

teurism. Of course, photography's early complications (the long exposure time it required; the camera's notorious inability to capture movement; the impossibility of mass reproduction of photographs until
1851) demanded patience, resourcefulness, and exertion.

Today's consumers are by now so accustomed to thinking of amateur photography as an effortless pastime that it is hard to imagine an
age when the experimental nature of the medium required that amateur photographers be reasonably well educated, have some knowledge of chemistry, and enough leisure time (and money) to master the
skills involved in taking pictures—that photographers, in short, *work*
at their hobby.

As Grace Seiberling has documented in her extensively researched
study on the subject, amateur photography in the 1840s and 1850s
gained much of its currency from the notion of the "gentleman," a
figure whose financial independence freed him from the necessity of
working for his living.[19] The gentleman amateur represented leisure as
it was practiced by the upper classes in the early nineteenth century;
that is, when leisure signified the superiority of the privileged few
rather than, as it does now, the antithesis to work as an economic
function.

To serve the purposes of reputability, as Veblen argued, leisure
needed to leave a "tangible, visible result" that could be put in evidence and measured against the accomplishments of other members
of the upper classes (49). Gentleman amateurs thus directed their
leisure time toward the cultivation of such academic or artistic interests as landscape painting, drawing, musical performance, collecting,
the study of archaic languages, and even photography. These upper-
class enactments of leisure were often described as "rational recreation," a term that alerts us to how firmly early nineteenth-century
forms of leisure were bound up with Victorian seriousness of purpose
and abhorrence of idleness: leisure within a relatively rigid and mor-
alizing framework.

William Fox Talbot, one of the two men generally credited with
the invention of photography in 1839, represents the paradigmatic amateur. Independently wealthy, he pursued studies ranging from mathe-
matics, chemistry, and astronomy to Assyriology. In what is now considered one of the most important early treatises on photography, *The
Pencil of Nature* (1844), Talbot writes for an audience clearly assumed

46
◇
to comprise gentleman amateurs, men willing to devote considerable time and effort to learning the wonders of chemistry and who possessed an interest in art and architecture, in collecting objects, and in literature, as he did. In the two decades ahead, as Seiberling elucidates, the majority of British and American amateur photographers followed Talbot's precedent, foregrounding in their writings their educational and social background as well as their serious interest in scientific, technical, and artistic matters.[20]

Given Britain's social structure, the gentleman amateur was a much more potent figure in England than in the United States. Still, Talbot's emphasis on education, commitment, and good taste largely governed the field of amateur photography in the United States as well during photography's first few decades. Take, for example, Henry Snelling, founder and editor of the *Photographic-Art Journal*, an American nineteenth-century periodical devoted to promoting scientific and artistic advances in photography. As the title indicates, Snelling aimed to advance photography as a serious rather than merely commercial enterprise, one worthy of the respect of both the artistic and scientific communities. His first editorial forcefully expresses this hope:

> At the present day it [photography] is viewed, too much, in the light of a mere mechanical occupation to arrive at any high degree of excellence. In too many instances men enter into it because they can get nothing else to do; without the least appreciation of its merits as an art of exquisite refinement, without the taste to guide them, and without the love and ambition to study more than its practical application, neglecting the sciences intimately connected with it, and leaving entirely out of the question those of drawing, painting, and sculpture, sister arts, a knowledge of which must tend to elevate the taste and direct the operator into the more classical and elegant walks of his profession. (1)

With its emphasis on cultivating good taste and pursuing a scholarly interest in the medium, the passage suggests that what is key to becoming a successful photographer is all that defines a "gentleman." Amateurism is here conceptualized in terms of its root meaning—one who loves an activity, or rather pursues many different activities with enthusiasm, ease, and confidence. In this description, moreover, the absence of any mention of the camera reveals a desire to deflect attention away from the supposedly mechanical nature of photography and toward the training, talent, and enthusiasm of its practitioners.[21]

During photography's first few decades, amateur clubs, societies, and journals established to promote the free exchange of information and knowledge flourished in both England and the United States. As Seiberling describes, "The letters reveal the readers as men and women of wide-ranging interests, willing—perhaps too willing—to try out any new idea, and excited by the medium, despite their numerous failures" (14). Indeed, failure flourished, given the notorious delicacy of the two principal forms of early photography, daguerreotypy (which used silver plates for negatives) and calotypy (which used paper), neither of which was capable of reproducing an image that could be duplicated. In 1851, the wet collodion process not only enabled infinite reproducibility for the first time but produced negatives that were easier to prepare, more transparent, uniform, sensitive, and stable than the earlier plates. The process remained popular in the United States until the early 1880s. Even with all its advantages over earlier methods, however, the process was messy, time-consuming, and, if pursued outdoors, required the transporting of an arsenal of heavy (and easily breakable) equipment. As Robert Taft explains in his pioneering history of American photography,

> It is surprising, when one recalls the difficulties of the collodion process, that amateurs in any number were attracted to its practices. The amateur had to prepare his iodized collodion, flow it on the plate, allow the film to "set," bathe it in the silver sensitizing solution, and then expose and develop it while it was still damp. Photographic trips and excursions to remote and picturesque scenes were favorite pastimes of these early amateurs, but such trips added still another difficulty, for the dark room, of necessity, had to be carried with them. (207)

Among the equipment a photographer needed to convey were the camera (which often weighed as much as fifty pounds), lenses, dark tent, tripods, collodion, silver nitrate, alcohol, iron sulfate, filters, nitric acid, developing and fixing trays, scales and weights, glass plates,

48
◇ and bottles of various sizes: enough equipment, in other words, to weigh down even the most lighthearted of amateurs.

By the early 1880s, wet collodion plates had been replaced by dry gelatin plates, Eastman's first area of specialty before he patented the Kodak camera and roll film in 1888. Manufactured as already sensitive to exposure, dry plates eliminated the need for the photographer to prepare his own plates, so that he no longer had to transport all the equipment that on-site development required. Dry plates also reduced exposure time from $\frac{1}{6}$ to $\frac{1}{12}$ of that required of wet plates. Still, dry plates were expensive, large, and relatively heavy. Recognizing that even this improvement still limited the amateur market because of the plates' cost and relative size, Eastman began experimenting with a "roll holder" by the mid-1880s. The roll holder would allow sensitive film to be wound on a spool, much as it is in today's cameras, thereby providing a far greater supply of material in a far more compact form. Eastman's original roll holders, invented in 1885, were designed as auxiliary parts of the camera, to be loaded in the darkroom and attached to the camera.[22]

Even this invention, however, did not expand the amateur market as widely as Eastman envisioned. He still needed a camera that could be carried easily and inconspicuously on journeys. Such a camera, moreover, would have to contain the roll holder as an insular rather than auxiliary part of its apparatus, so as to ensure the most compact product possible. Most important, Kodak needed to shelter the amateur photographer from the mess, complexity, and technical difficulty of development, promising that such troublesome details would now be taken over by company experts. By the spring of 1888 he had perfected his system, and by September he had patented both the roll film and original box camera under the name of Kodak, its swift, modest sound meant to convey the simplicity of the process it represented.

Along with her camera, the amateur photographer in 1888 would have received *The Kodak Primer,* a twenty-page manual that included a set of simple instructions on how to use the camera and a brief description of the "Kodak system." This publication provided consumers with their first extensive introduction to snapshot photography, a circumstance that explains Eastman's impatience during the four months it took to compose it. He had originally hired a New York advertising writer and cousin named Kilbourne Tompkins to design the *Primer.* The twenty-one letters exchanged by Tompkins and Eastman

between January and April 1888 reveal Eastman's growing frustration
with Tompkins's failure to emphasize the revolutionary simplicity of
both the Kodak camera and snapshot photography as strongly as Eastman thought he should. "I have been obliged to pretty much rewrite
the whole thing," he wrote to Tompkins in April. "The main objection
to the last copy was that it was not forcible enough and did not make
clear enough the difference between old and new methods."[23] In fact,
Eastman did rewrite the *Primer* entirely, and the job that apparently
had plagued his cousin for four months took him a total of five hours
to complete: according to tradition, he sat down and rewrote the
entire copy in the afternoon stretch between lunch and dinner, two
days after winning a court battle with Tompkins, who had sued him
for refusing to pay the "excessive" bill he had tendered for professional
services.

Starting with its name, whose meanings include a "schoolbook for
elementary children," the *Primer* stresses throughout its pages the
"revolutionary simplicity" of the Kodak system. The Kodak system, the
booklet announces, has removed all need for labor and photographic
knowledge for the first time in history, transforming photography into
an activity that requires nothing from the consumer but "sufficient intelligence to point a small box straight and press a button" (2). After
the photographer finishes her roll of 100 exposures, the *Primer* proceeds to explain, she sends the camera back to the Kodak Company,
which will develop the film and return the camera with a fresh spool
installed for $10. "For a novice to be able to make a photograph of *fair*
quality in this way and by these simple instrumentalities and this division of labor would have been a remarkable feat; but to make the finest
quality of photographs in this way is wonderful" (*Primer* 5).

Eastman thus assured his consumers that there was now little
chance for error, since the most troublesome and labor-intensive aspect of photography would now be taken over by the factory. "When
you have finished the simple part allotted you, in making the hundred negatives, we will relieve you of the burden of completing them
and fill the Kodak with another band of sensitized film, to be repeated as often as you like" (*Primer* 11). Eastman's use of language (his
direct and familiar appeal to the consumer, the paternalistic portrayal
of the factory, the emphasis on consumer desire and the omission of
any description of the actual processes that take place in the Kodak
factory) reflects what Jackson Lears has described as the increasing

50

◇ acceptance of the "hegemony of the modern corporation as inevitable and beneficent" (113). As the *Primer* makes clear, the factory had already begun to emerge as the benevolent center of a new service economy, simultaneously mystified and personalized to the public through advertising.

In contrast to the results of earlier amateur photographers, the Kodak snapshot would not be indebted to the labor or even the talent of the photographer. Rather, its existence would be due to an easy cooperation among photographer, subject, and company experts. At the center of this triangle was a camera "no larger than an ordinary field glass," a camera that embodied unprecedented portability, compactness, and automation. Even when mishandled, the *Primer* explained, the Kodak camera would produce a "fine quality" picture. In the fairy tale world of the *Primer,* as in the ads and other publications that would soon follow, Eastman guaranteed satisfactory results and abolished all possibility for error—the damaged plates, the unfocused pictures, the misjudging of light and composition that kept so many people from practicing photography before.

"The Kodak system removes from the practice of Photography the necessity for exceptional facilities, so that *anyone* may take photographs without need of study, experiment, trouble, dark room, chemicals and without even soiling the fingers" (*Primer* 2–3). Eastman's last phrase commands particular attention, since the image of soiled fingers often appears in nineteenth-century photographic literature as a visual marker not only for photography's chemical and scientific aspects but for its associations with labor.[24] Like the dirty fingernails and callused hands of the common laborer, the stained fingers of the early photographer implied the necessity of engaging in unpleasant activity. In an age that fetishized the white, soft hand as a measure of gentility, these stains would have been a serious impediment to the practice of amateur photography, especially for women.

Reading through the *Primer,* the amateur photographer would undoubtedly note the attention Eastman gives to the camera itself. He points out, for example, that it "is covered with dark Turkey morocco, nickel and lacquered brass trimmings, enclosed in a neat handstitched sole-leather case with shoulder strap" (2). He also accentuates its small proportions so as to impress upon readers how much less cumbersome it is than most cameras: "It is no larger than an ordinary field glass, and you can carry it with you from your house to your store or office" (4). Like the *Primer,* Kodak's other promotional material published between 1888 and roughly 1905 repeatedly highlights the sizes of cameras. Weight and dimension become highly important; ads provide surprisingly detailed information about both. During its first decade, in fact, each camera Kodak manufactured was smaller than the one before, so that by 1898 its line of cameras resembled a set of Russian nesting dolls. Kodak's original box camera weighed approximately two pounds. In 1895 the one-pound Pocket Kodak Camera appeared on the market; in 1898 it was followed by the half-pound aluminum No. 1 Folding Pocket Kodak Camera, which could literally be folded in a vest or coat pocket. For the first time in history, Americans were encouraged to view the camera as a kind of toy, a promotional strategy that underscores the close relation between toys and modern commodities.

After publication of the *Primer,* a vast library of Kodak literature written expressly for the amateur photographer soon developed.[25] Each year the company produced dozens of books and pamphlets designed to advise the novice and more advanced amateur photographer on fundamentals of photography. Among the most noteworthy of these publications was *Kodakery: A Magazine for Amateur Photographers,* a monthly periodical, first published in September 1913, to which photographers could subscribe for a yearly rate of 50 cents. Starting with its colloquial name, the magazine approaches its subjects and readers with notable familiarity. The first issue begins with an article titled "Because This Is the First Number," which explains Kodak's intention to give top priority to the consumer's needs and desires: "There is a purpose behind *Kodakery* just as there is behind the Kodak itself. In both cases the purpose is to put something into your hands that will interest you—that will be of use in pleasant and practical ways—that may establish an easy, companionly relation with you" (September 1913, 1).

Compare this opening with the introduction to a contemporaneous book on amateur photography whose author, dismayed by the fact that Kodak has conditioned a "fascination with photographs as readymade articles," urges the beginning photographer not to be daunted by the prospect of difficulty:

> Photography cannot offer any exception to the rule that all beginnings are difficult. But still, a modicum of attentive study so

52
◇

planned as to be carried on intelligently and to master principles, coupled with the desire of doing really good work, will soon surmount the initiatory troubles. The technique having been acquired, the field will open in ever-widening circles to the more essentially artistic kinds of work. The man of a mathematical turn of mind will find much to interest him in the optical department, just as the experimentalist will in the deep and obscure chemical problems of the dark room. (Wallace, *Amateur Photographer* 9)

Obviously, this author's amateur (someone fascinated by optics, undaunted by chemistry) represents a whole different species (and sex) from Kodak's. Even the vocabulary indicates that this book is for the amateur who means business.

Kodakery was written for the amateur who meant fun. The magazine flourished during its first few decades precisely because it seemed so charmingly simple. To begin, it resembled a picture-book for children much more than it did a photographic manual. Only 6″ × 4″, it contained far more photographs than text. In one typical issue, fifty-two photographs accompany only five articles. Second, it minimized technical matter and approached all its subjects in a conversational, simple manner. "The editors and contributors are men who not only know about photography," promised Kodak, "but who know how to write about it in a simple way that the amateur can understand" (*Kodak and Kodak Supplies* 1).

Out of any ten articles, only one might be on a technical subject such as "Backlighting" or "Taking Pictures in a Storm." When such subjects do appear, moreover, the magazine's treatment of them is much too simplistic to be of any substantial value. A survey of some key titles from 1914 clearly indicates the magazine's approach: "A Camera in a Commonplace Town," "The Charm of the Simple," "Little Histories of the Younger Set," "A Stands for Album," and "My Kodak Is My Friend." After 1914, many of the articles were written by Kodak subscribers, who were invited to share their photographic experiences with others.

Women, not their husbands, brothers, or fathers, constituted the principal readership of *Kodakery*. Virtually every issue between 1913 and the early 1930s, in fact, features a young female photographer on the front cover—a peculiarity that alerts us to just how prominent women had become in the field of mass amateur photography by

this time.[26] Women's enthusiasm for taking snapshots is hardly surprising when one considers how Kodak advertising catered to the
supposed desires of its female audience. In the Kodak Girl the company provided women with their own idealized image of youthful femininity and exuberance, the joy they could expect to attain through
photography.

Superheroes in Skirts

Having created a camera and photographic system so revolutionary in
its simplicity, Eastman needed a new image for his amateur photographer. By 1892, in a letter to George Dickman, managing editor of Kodak Limited in England, he had named her. His new photographer
would be the Kodak Girl, a woman whose pretty face and stylish costumes would contextualize photography within contemporaneous discourses on fashion and feminine beauty, as we shall see in chapter 4,
and whose youthful image would signify the ease, pleasure, and freedom of snapshot photography. First appearing in advertisements in
1893, she functioned as Kodak's primary sales model for nearly eighty
years, appearing in posters, shop displays, cutouts, and magazine and
newspaper advertisements up through the early 1970s, when Cybill
Shepherd even posed as her.[27]

In Kodak's campaign to reinvent amateur photography as princi-
pally a woman's hobby, the Kodak Girl was naturally invested with all
kinds of meaning, her young body the site of symbolic excess. Debut-
ing amidst all the flourish engendered by the "New Woman," the Kodak Girl reflected her culture's tangled web of opinions about female
behavior and capabilities. On the one hand, she represents advertising's troublesome yet prevalent association of femininity with technological simplicity. Her adolescent look, for example, visually reinforces
the female photographer's status as amateur (see figure 8). Measured
against the man she can never become, the Kodak Girl is frozen at a
liminal, intermediate stage of womanhood. As such, she can never
achieve the status of professional photographer, her position forever
remains that of a novice, dependent on technological simplicity.

Jackson Lears, writing on the relationship between images of
young women and the factory, argues that advertising in the latter half
of the nineteenth century was purged of its decadent—and liberating—value once it became the cornerstone of corporate business. "As

54
◇

rhetorical constructions, [corporate] advertisements did more than stir up desire; they also sought to manage it—to stabilize the sorcery of the marketplace by containing dreams of personal transformation within a broader rhetoric of control" (10). Lears locates advertising's roots in the open-fair atmosphere of the seventeenth- and eighteenth-century marketplace, a site infused with the carnivalesque and miraculous, where a subversive discourse of abundance celebrated the corpulent and exotic, the mysterious and talismanic, the fecund earth and the fleshy woman. Toward the end of the century, this excess of skin, of body, was being rapidly streamlined into what Lears calls an "exaltation of industrial efficiency" as advertisers both slimmed and tamed their women (18). A new iconography developed: factory and machine emerged as the new sources of abundance, and young women became "bearers of good news from the deus ex machina of the factory system" (120). No longer the formidable maternal figures of early nineteenth-century advertising, women now appeared as girlish, unsophisticated, and reassuringly dependent on corporate expertise.

Lears's astute observations nicely contextualize the Kodak Girl, alerting us to how the image of the Kodak factory gained its aura of benevolence and paternalism (qualities for which it has always been notorious) with the aid of sweet young women. Still, such a tight-laced reading confines the cultural importance of the Kodak Girl. Though she clearly conveys youth and sweetness, her athletic body, apparent independence, and sense of adventure are not to be ignored. Kodak profited by associating the revolutionary simplicity of its roll film and camera with the modern freedoms represented by the New Woman.

Alone, adventurous, and unencumbered by heavy equipment and a male companion, the Kodak Girl *is* the New Woman in many of these advertisements, the "epitome of modern, confident womanhood" (Harding 12). In fact, the earliest ads (especially those between 1893 and roughly 1920) depict her as remarkably independent. They generally picture her outdoors, frequently on her own or in the company of another Kodak Girl, never in the company of a man (figure 9). Sunburned, with hair flying in the wind, she travels in a canoe, on a steamship, in a motorcar; she walks, rides a bicycle, plays tennis, journeys to Japan. If one of the rewards of leisure is an opportunity to enjoy personal freedom, the Kodak Girl is amply rewarded as she

Figure 9. Publicity postcard featuring the Kodak Girls, 1914. (Reprinted courtesy of Eastman Kodak Company)

56 revels in an ideal leisure that is beyond the reach of most American
◇   women.

In 1910 the poster artist John Hassell created a dramatic new element in the representation of the Kodak Girl by clothing her in a blue-
and-white striped dress that would soon become her signature costume. Indeed, after that date she most frequently appeared in that
outfit. As Alison Lurie notes, "blue-and-white stripes have long been
associated with the romantic freedom of the sea" (51), which of course
served to accentuate the Kodak Girl's connection with nature and
travel. Just as important, the costume's summertime look signified its
wearer's association with perpetual youth and energy.

The Kodak Girl's extraordinary vitality also exhibited what advertisers were conveniently calling "aliveness."[28] In the first two decades
of the twentieth century, companies presented many of their products
as keys to sustaining the vitality of a busy, energetic people. This
campaign seems to have emerged from what Anson Rabinbach has
identified as the Victorian obsession with fatigue. The late nineteenth
century, Rabinbach observes, exhibited a "widespread fear that the energy of mind and body was dissipating under the strain of modernity:
that the will, imagination, and especially the health of the nation was
being squandered in wanton disregard of the body's physiological
laws" (6). Rabinbach makes a wonderful case for modern culture's obsession with preventing fatigue at all costs. Among scientists, physi-
cians, psychiatrists, and virtually everyone else, it seemed, the central
question was how to make the human body as efficient as a machine.
Looking at Kodak advertisements, one might think that the best cure
was to hand a pallid woman a camera. Certainly, there was no slowing
the Kodak Girl down. Like the mechanical camera she carried, she
was slim, compact, and fast.

Significantly, the first illustration of the Kodak Girl depicted her
at the Chicago world's fair in 1893 (figure 10). This advertisement
would be the first of many to feature international expositions as promotional backdrops for Kodak products. As Julie K. Brown notes, a
surprisingly high percentage of the estimated 50,000 amateur photographers who attended the exposition were women—a fact that points
up Eastman's rapid success in enlisting women as his new market.[29]
The most noteworthy aspect of this advertisement is that these women
are depicted on their own, apparently away from the center of things.
The artist represents them as active and curious participants, appar-

THE KODAK GIRLS AT THE WORLD'S FAIR.

Figure 10. Advertisement featuring the Kodak Girls at the Chicago World's Fair, 1893. (Reprinted courtesy of Eastman Kodak Company)

ently on the verge of taking a photograph, which, judging by the seeming remoteness of their location, will depict a subject that most of the other participants will not be privileged to see.

Kodak Girls are always featured outdoors, most often in natural settings such as a beach, a park, or the countryside. No Kodak advertisement that I have seen, in fact, pictures her within a home environment, even though homes were among the most popular settings

58

◇

for Kodak ads. In fact, one of the primary functions of the Kodak Girl was to promote snapshot photography as an enhancement of vacations and such leisure activities as bathing, tennis, and golfing. As the historians Dorothy Brown and Martha Banta have made clear, leisure and sports offered one of the most important avenues for women in the late nineteenth and early twentieth centuries to assert their independence.[30] In fact, in the most stereotypical representation of the New Woman, she is wearing bloomers and riding a bicycle. American women, as yet unable to pursue careers in any kind of systematic and aggressive way, turned to sports and leisure as a means of establishing a sense of independence and freedom. Beginning in the late nineteenth century, magazines such as the *Ladies' Homes Journal* featured articles informing women on the details of planning a trip to the country, to the seaside, to New York City and Chicago.[31] Alongside these articles, essays on swimming, golfing, and tennis emphasized the importance of female fitness.

American magazines also capitalized on the association between independent women and the freedoms of the camera. On the covers of three issues of the New York–based magazine *Truth* in 1898, for example, young women carry box cameras as they travel independently. The most striking example depicts a woman resembling a Gibson Girl holding a travel bag in one hand and her box camera in the other as she strides from a train (figure 11). The image clearly conveys her autonomy: she dresses practically, walks purposefully, and apparently requires no man (only her female servant) to help her with her luggage. *Truth* earned a notorious reputation in the 1890s for its "spicy" features that often focused on actresses and other female professionals. In light of this fact as well as a host of literature testifying to the "improper uses" of the camera on beaches and in other public places, we can safely assume that by 1898 the Kodak camera evoked for some Americans behavior that was not only playful but risqué.[32]

Always traveling or engaged in other recreational activities, the Kodak Girl represented boundless pleasure and independence, a freedom that came from being away from home and family—the freedom that came, in short, with being single. By the early 1920s, however, Kodak had tempered the Kodak Girl's independence. In advertisements such as the one reproduced in plate 5, she observes a domestic scene set outdoors, holding her camera as she watches a family at play. Here the Kodak Girl stands off to the right as a young family welcomes a father traveling uphill for a picnic, one of the most common leisure

Figure 11. Cover of *Truth* magazine, 28 September 1898

60

◇

settings for Kodak's advertisements. The implication is that she, too, will someday participate in the scene she now only witnesses, an observation visually reinforced by her resemblance to the mother in the advertisement, whose features, hairstyle, and even facial expression mirror the Kodak Girl's. Uncomfortable, perhaps, with the implications of always depicting her alone or traveling in the company of another young woman, the company used this motif extensively in the 1920s, domesticating her at a time when, not coincidentally, American women were enjoying greater sexual freedom than ever before.

Leisure and Abundance: Kodak at the World's Fairs

The ad shown in plate 6 spotlights the Kodak Girl at her most triumphant moment as she stands high atop a vista in Paris, promoting the recent invention of Verichrome film and the upcoming 1938 Paris Exhibition, one of the last international fairs of its kind. Radiant, she looks to the heavens, holding her camera as the Statue of Liberty holds her torch. And like the Statue of Liberty a few decades earlier, she joins an impressive array of women who have personified a new social order, revolutionary avatars whose beautiful presence both masks and manifests their association with climactic change. She is no longer part of the scenery; she dominates it. And the future she advertises is defined by an abundance of representation and pleasure— more images, more joy, it seems, than even the photographer herself can bear. Indeed, the world is too much with the Kodak Girl. She cannot hold all her rolls of film, so they spill down to the world below like seeds, seeds that will sprout into endless pictures for a modern world. Indeed, the most striking aspect of this advertisement is the way it foregrounds the mechanisms of representation (photographer, camera, boxes and boxes of film) and presents the real world as an abyss, dramatizing what Thomas Richards calls the "phantasmagoria of commodity culture" (18). This excess of film embodies the very logic of consumption itself. To consume means to use up—and therefore to need to replenish. As we make images and consume them, we find ourselves making more images, and still more. It is not incidental, then, that the advertisement showcases a world's fair. Like the mass production of snapshots, fairs represent a commodity culture awash in representation, a world that projects an image of surplus.

Now generally viewed as remnants of an earlier age—costly cu-
riosities whose ambitious scope seems both wondrous and naive to   ◇
most of us now—world's fairs achieved an almost institutional status
during the age of Kodak's early development.[33] Between 1876 and 1925,
notes Reid Badger, hardly a year passed without at least one major
international exhibition, and no other country produced as many of
them as the United States (xvi). During Kodak's first two decades, in
fact, the United States hosted six world's fairs: the Columbian Exposition in Chicago (1893), the Atlanta Exposition (1895), the Tennessee
Exposition (1897), the Omaha Exposition (1898), the Pan-American
Exposition in Buffalo (1901), and the Louisiana Purchase Exposition
in St. Louis (1904). Millions of visitors attended these fairs; the Chicago exposition alone drew an estimated 21 million. With his usual
acumen, George Eastman intuited that these events, particularly the
one held in Chicago, would provide Kodak with an important promotional opportunity.

World's fairs offered a special kind of leisure activity for its visitors,
generally middle- and upper-middle-class sightseers with a new interest (cultivated mainly by the recently organized travel agencies) in visiting cities for their vacations. By the 1890s the city's diversity was
being widely promoted as a tourist attraction, with guidebooks, travel
magazines, and tour guides underscoring the city's range of ethnic
populations, its parks, shopping districts, building styles, and neigh-
borhoods. In visiting a world's fair, tourists were told, they would
see the attractions of its host city as well, at a time when the urban
landscape was "being reconceived as a place of play as well as of work"
(Nasaw 65).

More relevant for our purposes, by striving to present every imaginable spectacle and site of interest, fairs conditioned visitors to see
the act of viewing as a form of consumption, and thus to identify
leisure with an abundance of visual sensations, distractions, and
mobility in an era characterized by a never-ending stream of mass-
produced goods and amusements.

Fairs thus offered the perfect promotional backdrop for a method
of photography that exponentially increased the number of snapshots
a photographer could take in one session. By offering rolls of film containing 100 exposures, Kodak effected a transformation akin to that
undertaken by world's fairs, converting commodities into a myth of an

62

◇

abundant society. And both Kodak and the fairs that it so actively promoted conditioned consumers to see this abundance as a defining feature of leisure, leisure here equated with the sensuous experience of material abundance.

In order to deliver an abundance of photographs, of course, the Kodak camera had to be capable of both simple and instantaneous operation. As James E. Paster notes, the ads that introduced the first line of Kodak cameras emphasized two features: the ease with which consumers could learn snapshot photography and the camera's capability of taking "instantaneous" photographs.[34] This capability did not originate with Kodak, however; Edward Muybridge's sequential photographs of horses in motion, published widely in 1878 and 1879, represented the first publicized photographs of fast-moving objects or events. In the early 1880s, dramatic improvements were made in exposure time, the invention of dry plates reducing the length of exposures to roughly two or three seconds per plate. What *was* new with the invention of the Kodak camera and roll film was the simplicity with which one could take such an abundance of "instant" images: movement could now be divided into moments, literally 100 moments on just one roll of film.

The "snapshot"—the term had originated a few years before Kodak marketed the box camera and roll film but it soon became permanently associated with the company[35]—offered a style of photography that was relatively rapid, serial, and instantaneous, in contrast to the individual plate exposures and carefully constructed tripod images that had characterized both amateur and professional photography to that time. Writing of the Chicago world's fair in 1893, Julie K. Brown explains that "coping with the visual chaos that was the multilayered experience of the Exposition was the problem of the spectators as a whole, and photography provided amateurs with a tool for doing this. The world through the viewfinder was a precise, bounded, often controlled instant in time before the world dissolved again into the confusion of everyday life" (21). True enough, but with its simplicity, speed, and abundance, the Kodak system of photography allowed for greater control than any other method of taking pictures, as the ads aggressively claimed.

The Chicago world's fair was the first international fair to be held in the United States after Kodak's invention and, luckily for the com-

pany, the first to truly solicit the participation of the entire world. Intuiting that associating Kodak with what promised to be the grandest
fair ever made good business sense, Eastman initiated in July 1891
one of his most aggressive advertising campaigns to promote Kodak
products as ideal accompaniments to the exposition.[36] To begin, he re-
named the Kodak No. 4 camera the Kolumbus Kodak. One advertisement for the camera read: "What's worth seeing is worth remembering. There will be so much worth both seeing and remembering at the
World's Fair that you'll forget the best part of it. But you can faithfully
preserve each scene if you'll just 'press the button.'" In the opening
line we see one of the first representations of the Kodak camera as an
indispensable aid to memory, and it depicts vision as something that
must not be wasted: everything that falls under the visual scope of the
visitor needs to be saved and recorded. Nothing is dispensable. Vision
thus assumes the immediate value of memory. While reminding consumers of the abundance of sights available at the exposition, moreover, Kodak also gently reminds them of memory's inevitable failure,
the fact that they are doomed to forget the "best part" of the experience. The caption thus promises that the experience of the fair, by nature ephemeral and overwhelming, can be both regulated and recorded
through the simplicity of Kodak's system of photography.

Eastman's efforts to promote Kodak products as an integral part of
the fair extended far beyond advertising. Between the spring of 1892
and the summer of 1893, he aggressively petitioned the fair's administration to establish not only a Kodak exhibit, showcasing products
and photographs taken with Kodak cameras, but to sell film on the
premises and to set up a free darkroom so that visitors could buy and
reload their film. Eastman immediately faced what seemed like insur-
mountable obstacles, however. In the spring of 1892, the fair's administration imposed an elaborate set of restrictions designed to curtail
the use of amateur photography in order to ensure that visitors would
purchase their photographs instead from the fair's Department of
Photography. First, the board charged $2 per day (four times the daily
admission charge) for a permit to photograph on the fairgrounds; second, it prohibited cameras that used negatives larger than $4'' \times 5''$ and
third, it enforced a complete ban on stereo cameras and tripods. The
intention behind all these restrictions was to outlaw all large cameras
that could take professional photographs and to impede the use of

64 hand-held cameras on the premises. The board also flatly refused East-
◇ man's request to sell film on the fairgrounds.

Eastman, however, proved indefatigable. He and L. B. Jones created a line of advertisements that capitalized on the compactness and
portability of the Kodak camera in comparison with other cameras:
"The Kodak is the World's Fair camera. As neither glass plates nor
films will be sold on the Exposition grounds, the photographer must
carry his ammunition with him. This the Kodaker can easily do. His
roll of film capable of taking 100 pictures weighs but a few ounces. His
out-fit is self-contained—no bulky glass plates and holders with a lia-
bility of breakage. Kodaks are compact, strong, simple." As this ad exemplifies, Kodak capitalized on the board's initial refusal to allow the
sale of amateur film on the premises by reminding customers that Kodak cameras already came loaded with 100 exposures. The Kodak camera could thus take many more photographs than most other cameras,
since users of glass plates could not possibly carry 100 plates without
serious difficulty and likelihood of breakage.

Still, Eastman remained dissatisfied. He and the head of the Gus-
tav Cramer Dry Plate Company petitioned aggressively for exclusive
permission to establish both a darkroom and concessions for their
products. Eastman visited Chicago in March 1893 and then again in
May to present his application for a concession and accompanying
darkroom facility. Finally, on May 16, well after the exposition had
opened, Eastman achieved what he wanted: Cramer would have an exclusive concession for glass plates and Kodak for cameras and film.
Eastman wasted no time in alerting the public that Kodak film would
be available on the premises. An advertisement first published in
June 1893 trumpeted: "Having seen the superior work done on our new
Kodak films, the World's Fair authorities have decided to sell no other
film on the grounds."

Located close to the Department of Photography, the Kodak
building contained eighteen stalls for the convenience of customers
who wished to change their film and a showroom where people could
rent Kodak cameras and buy rolls of film for several Kodak models.
Among the rolls of film they could purchase was a specially designed
"Columbian" spool that held 250 exposures, advertised with the caption "To get value received the amateur must take a large number of
pictures in a day." In light of the current prevalence of the 24-exposure
roll, often used to record more than one event, the manufacturing of

250 exposures testifies to the perception of the fair as a site of un-
limited abundance.[37] Ads for the Columbian spool also promised that
photographers could "bring home the fair experience on just one roll,"
verifying that snapshot photographs were already being promoted as
metonyms of experience itself, the fair's abundance duplicated in the
collection of photographs.

As amateur photographers walked around the fair snapping their
pictures, one of the sights they saw was an exhibit of the world's first
automobiles. At that time, only a handful of visitors could have guessed
that the automobile would become available to hundreds of thousands
of Americans in just over two decades and change forever the shape
of leisure and tourism. If fairs constituted one of the most popular leisure subjects for Kodak advertising, automobile travel soon
emerged as another of its recurring motifs. And if fairs emphasized the
abundance to be had with snapshot photography, automobiles reinforced the mobility—and thus the romantic sense of freedom—-that
Kodak also wished to associate with its products.

Leisure and Mobility: Kodak and the Automobile

In 1922, L. B. Jones ordered several teams of Kodak advertising employees to drive along the country's most traveled roads and scout out
particularly scenic areas. Acting on their recommendations, Kodak's
advertising department erected nearly 6,000 signs along the roads to
tip off motorists that a scenic view lay ahead.[38] Composed simply of
black lettering against a plain white background, the signs read "Picture Ahead! *Kodak as you go.*" This moment in Kodak history foregrounds several issues central not only to the development of leisure
and tourism but to snapshot photography as well. First, it provides an
overt example of the capacity of mass tourism to determine the modern consumer's experience of travel. Designed and written like a traffic
sign, "Picture Ahead! *Kodak as you go*" deliberately plays on the authority of state regulations, directing motorists to obey its commands.
In so doing, it betokens how Kodak, and the larger tourist industry
in which it participates, constructs what John Urry has called the
"tourist gaze," which is "directed to features of landscape and town-
scape which separate them off from everyday and routine experiences"
and which demonstrates "a much greater sensitivity to visual elements
of landscape than is normally found in everyday life" (132). But such

66
◇

"sensitivity," Urry argues, is socially organized, packaged, and manufactured for the tourist by travel agencies and producers of brochures, posters, souvenirs, postcards, and travel books. Like all these other objects and institutions, photography has transformed the tourist into a semiotician—someone who, in the words of Jonathan Culler, sees everything as "a sign of itself": the roadside tavern as a sign of "local" American culture, the campsite as a sign of wilderness, the streets of New Orleans as a sign of French decadence (129). Kodak's placement of 6,000 signs across the country thus made visible photography's role in this semiotic approach to travel.

We also see here how Kodak capitalized on the burgeoning automobile industry to promote snapshot photography as a tourist activity.[39] As Gary Cross notes, "Probably no consumer product has shaped 20th-century leisure more than the mass-produced automobile" (*Social History* 184). The mass-produced Model T Ford, introduced in 1908, offered, according to its creator, "a motor car for the great multitude. It will be large enough for the family, but small enough for the individual to run and care for. . . . It will be so low in price that no man making a good salary will be unable to own one—and enjoy with his family the blessings of hours of pleasure in God's great open spaces" (quoted ibid. 185).

During the first decade of the twentieth century, automobility had already assumed an integral role in American life. The 450,000 motor vehicles registered in 1910 made the United States the world's foremost automobile culture. By the mid-1920s, automobile manufacturing ranked first in value of product and third in value of exports among U.S. industries. And by the end of the 1920s, the number of persons per registered motor vehicle in the United States had dropped from 10.1 to 4.5. Even working-class families skirted insolvency and sacrificed essentials for automobile ownership.[40]

Beginning in 1907, Kodak advertisements featured young women and men in touring cars enjoying the pleasures of the open road, and such ads proliferated as time went on. Between the first few years of the twentieth century and the late 1920s, a period historians generally identify as marked by the "first wave of mass car ownership," cars were used primarily for recreation—Sunday-afternoon drives in the country, visits to friends, vacation trips, frequently to visit national parks and go camping. What mattered most to the first and second generations of car owners was a sense of an independent journey through unfamiliar terrain, the adventure of seeing what had not been seen before, and doing it without the restrictions of the timetables and schedules that circumscribed public tourism. "What started out before World War I as an adolescent infatuation," writes Warren Belasco, "a passionate celebration of fresh experiences and unprecedented intimacies, developed by 1940 into a tamer, more restricted concern for comfort, efficiency, security, and privacy" (105). Discovering their own land's wide-open spaces suddenly became a key aspect of leisure that palliated discontent and frustration with modern life, particularly urban life—a romantic and antimodernist alternative ironically conditioned by a commodity that arguably epitomizes U.S. capitalism more than any other.

Promoting this romantic association of driving with freedom and spontaneity, a typical Kodak caption from 1917 reads: "Wherever the purr of your motor lures you, wherever the call of the road leads you, there you will find pictures, untaken pictures that invite your Kodak." The seductiveness of the language is matched by the glamorous image of a fur-coated woman holding her Kodak camera in a luxury automobile, a woman whose movie-star look recalls for us a time when Americans were in the throes of infatuation with Hollywood (figure 12). Here the uncharted territory traversed by the automobile falls as well under the scope of another machine with the ability to conquer space. In a perfect partnership, the car transports the motorist to new sites and places, and the camera, with its implicitly imperial powers, captures the landscape and reproduces it for endless consumption by the viewer. Kodak's promotion of the automobile thus linked the camera to the unbounded freedom and speed of the car and reinforced the ability of both to, echoing Marx, "annihilate space by time." Like the automobile, which could reduce a thousand miles to a few manageable days, the camera captures wide-open space with the lightning speed of its shutter.

The first Kodak advertisement featuring an automobile was published in 1907, at a time when a car cost several times the working person's annual income and required as much in yearly maintenance.[41] Though out of the price range of most Americans, however, in the popular perception the automobile had by 1907 already started to shift from its earlier status as a toy for the rich to a potential object of mass consumption. In fact, 1907 marks the first year in which this shift really began, as Peter J. Ling explains; motor vehicle sales increased

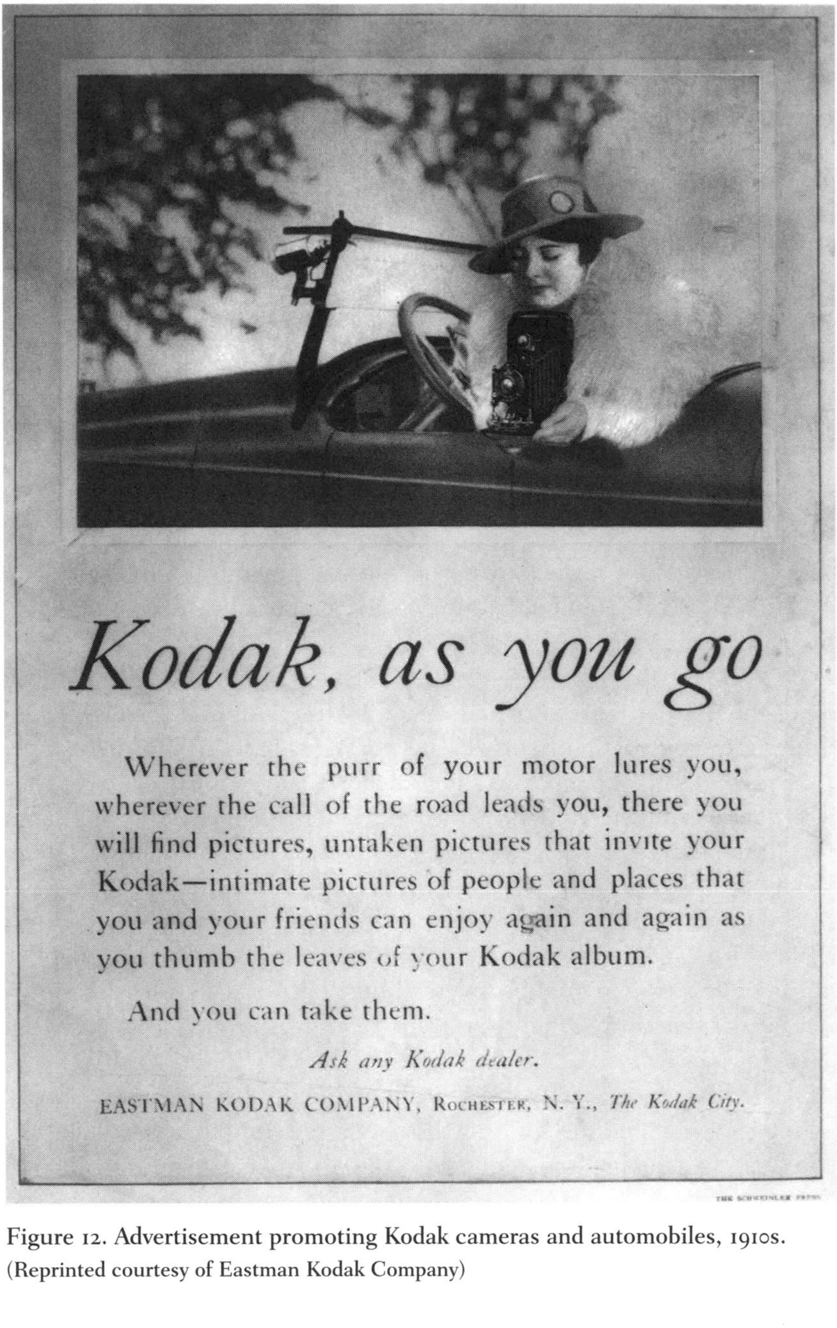

Figure 12. Advertisement promoting Kodak cameras and automobiles, 1910s.
(Reprinted courtesy of Eastman Kodak Company)

substantially that year despite a general business recession (1–11).

One Kodak ad produced in 1907 features a watercolor illustration by Blendon Campbell of a young couple with their Studebaker, she taking a picture of him with a folding Kodak camera as he repairs the car (plate 7). Featured in *Country Life* magazine, the ad exemplifies early romantic perceptions of the automobile as a vehicle of escape from the crowded industrial cities. Small country road, fauna in the foreground, a few trees in the background, clouds mottling the sky: Campbell invests his illustration with all the standard elements of the picturesque. The solitariness of the setting, moreover, emphasizes an intensifying desire among middle-class Americans for the privatized leisure so conveniently embodied by the automobile. Here it links this privatization with romance. The young couple, we may assume, are either newly married or engaged, a detail that points to the automobile's notorious role in courtship and romance. "Cars fulfilled a romantic function from the dawn of the auto age," claims David L. Lewis. "They permitted couples to get much farther away from front porch swings, parlor sofas, hovering mothers, and pesky siblings than ever before" ("Sex and the Automobile" 123).

The most striking aspect of this advertisement is the fact that what modern consumers now tend to regard as near-disaster—the breakdown of a car—here emerges as an appropriate subject for both the advertisement and the snapshot the woman will take. The man confidently repairs the car, his sleeves rolled up, serious intent on his face, tools neatly laid out on the ground. On the one hand, the ad's contrast of the car's malfunctioning with the working order of the camera accentuates the mechanical simplicity of the Kodak. On the other hand, repairing a car also seems to be represented here as a leisure activity, part of the pleasure of automobile ownership. As Ling notes, the early car "rewarded personal artisanship, particularly for those who bought early automobiles and had to do their own repairs and add their own accessories" (5). The simplicity of machinery thus provides the overall message in this advertisement, visually conveyed in both the man's seemingly effortless car repair and the woman's ease with her Kodak camera. Cars and cameras, the ad suggests, return consumers to simplicity rather than intensifying the pressures of modern life. As Ling argues, "just as automotive transport provided the means by which American capitalism could gear up for a more rapid cycle of capital accumulation, so the same technology in its social and recreational use

70 provided a therapeutic mechanism for individuals seeking to shift gears
◇ to a slower more relaxed pace, even when that relaxation had as its
preliminary the exhilaration of high speed" (5). The same argument
could be made about Kodak's representation of the camera. Promoted
as instantaneous, portable, efficient, and everything else that represented modernity at its best, the camera, by its continual representation in romanticized settings such as the countryside, encouraged an
alternatively nostalgic reading.

Although one of the major selling points of the automobile was
the claim that it could unite families by allowing them to vacation together, or by reducing the time members spent away from home, Kodak never pictured families in automobiles during this time period. Instead, ads invariably feature couples and single women, including, of
course, the Kodak Girl. In Kodak advertising, as we will see, the home
functions as the primary locale for the family; the road signifies individual freedom. Especially noteworthy are the many early Kodak advertisements that feature single women with their automobiles. Cars
had a special appeal for many American women, whose mobility was
so much more restricted than men's.

In an advertisement from the 1920s (figure 13), a young woman is
about to get into her automobile. We cannot see all of the car, though
the photograph draws attention to its license plate—a detail that reinforces the relatively large number of registered drivers by the early
1920s.[42] The composition of the ad conveys both movement and anticipation, focused as it is on the woman's descending a set of foregrounded stairs and walking into the car, its open door signifying an
invitation to adventure. As in other ads, the woman holds the camera
as she would a purse, the message being that her Kodak is slim and
compact enough to accompany her on this journey. Indeed, she carries the camera prominently in her right hand while tenderly placing
her left hand on the car, the photograph thus setting up an easy triangulation of camera, automobile, and her own body: all three represented as slim, sleek, beautiful, and apparently ready for adventure.

Even though cars had become signs of leisure's democratization by
the early 1920s, Kodak insistently linked automobiles with the privileges of wealth. No Kodak ad that I have seen conveys this appeal
to upper-middle-class sensibilities more vividly than the one seen
in plate 8, first published in 1917. The obviously staged and colored
photograph pictures a smiling and attractive servant (what Veblen

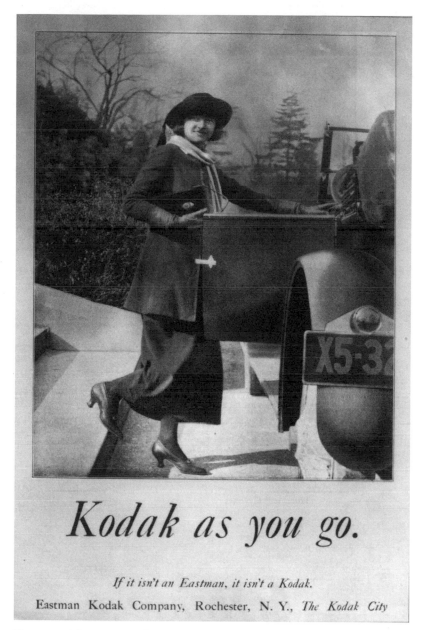

Kodak as you go.

If it isn't an Eastman, it isn't a Kodak.

Eastman Kodak Company, Rochester, N. Y., *The Kodak City*

Figure 13. Advertisement featuring young woman with camera and automobile, *Ladies' Home Journal*, 1920s. (Reprinted courtesy of Eastman Kodak Company)

72
◇

identifies as the "key appendage and symbol of class division" [55–56]), looking as if she has danced her way down the stairs to hand a Kodak camera to her employer, who is about to drive off in a car that looks preternaturally large, the implication being that the owner enjoys a social mobility denied to most of us. We cannot see the employer, only her arm reaching out for the camera, which establishes a triangulation among her, us, and the maid, so that we are placed in the position of desiring not only the product but the position of the woman being handed the product. Her invisibility only heightens her affluence, for though she isn't pictured, her chauffeur, palatial-looking house, and expensive car are. So, of course, is her sleek-looking Kodak, another of her accouterments as she embarks on one of her leisure trips.

Playing for Time

In all the ads in which Kodak promoted amateur photography as a form of play, time hovers at the edges like a specter out to ruin all the fun.

Leisure had emerged in the late nineteenth and early twentieth centuries as such a value-laden concept not only because it represented time away from work, or the fantasies of middle- and upper-middle-class consumption. As Johan Huizinga famously argued many years ago, leisure in modern industrial culture embodies the ideals of true individuality, creativity, and freedom (1–27). Joffre Dumazedier echoed such sentiments, arguing that contemporary leisure "is defined in relation not just to one's job, but to all of the ordinary necessities and obligations of existence" (14). Deprived of such affirmative feelings at work, many Americans have looked to their leisure time as the only part of their lives in which they can attain some level of personal satisfaction. This is why Americans invest so much emotional capital in the family vacation. Vacations represent the potential for a family to be brought closer together, while also promising a brief space of time in which life can be experienced as we idealize it—a space of time that, in Huizinga's words, "affords a pleasant expectation and recollection" (15). Huizinga's observation commands our attention, emphasizing as it does leisure's two tenses. Always ephemeral, leisure resists location within the present even while it purports to celebrate the present.[43] Thus leisure serves as the perfect abstraction

against which to sell snapshot photography, which has trained consumers to imagine the most meaningful experiences of time as those
we must anticipate and, conversely, those we can later cherish as a series of "pleasant recollections" captured in our photographs.

No advertisement more vividly illustrates how Kodak linked snapshot photography with the idealizing metaphysics of leisure than the
1904 watercolor advertisement seen in plate 9. Like many other Kodak
ads, this one uses the motif of a frame-within-a-frame to convey an actual moment's conversion into a snapshot souvenir. This framing technique invites particular attention because of the way it sets off the presumed reality represented by the snapshot from all that lies outside its
frame. A sensual border of magnificent chrysanthemums, long brush
strokes in pink and green watercolors, and a pagoda at the far left en-
circles the snapshot, each of its elements investing the ad with a notably Asian flavor. When we turn to the image that represents the
snapshot, however, we see a scene located in an American or British
countryside. By surrounding the Anglicized snapshot with markings of
Japanese aesthetics and culture, the ad insinuates that ordinary time,
once it enters the province of both leisure and photography, becomes
extraordinary time.

At stake in Kodak's idealized marriage of photography and leisure,
then, was nothing less than the reconception of time itself. According
to Kodak ads, all days could be vacation days with the aid of a camera.
In its ability to arrest moments, Kodak insinuates, photography can
enact what leisure only promises: the slowing down of time. And in
so doing, photography can prolong leisure, allowing consumers to "relive" their vacations and other pleasurable moments through snapshots (play transformed into memory). As most tourists will affirm,
this assurance is crucial to a modern culture in which leisure carries
such emotional weight.

The more leisure becomes separated from work and the routine of
daily life, the more it instills in us a sense of apprehension over its
(too brief) passage. Formerly associated with peace, timelessness, and
the antithesis of action, leisure now represents pleasure undertaken
within modern culture's most threatened resource of all: time. In this
sense, leisure does not represent play as much as it does the reconsti-
tution of work (that is, the perpetual effort to forestall the passing of
time) as something *resembling* play.

3

"Operated by Any School Boy or Girl"

The Marketing of the Brownie Camera

IN THE spring of 1898, exactly ten years after the original Kodak camera debuted on the market, Eastman asked Frank A. Brownwell, Kodak's camera designer and manufacturer and head of its "Camera Works," to invent a camera cheaper and easier to operate than any of its predecessors. The baronesque vision behind Eastman's request was such a sharp cut in the production and retail costs of this new camera that almost anyone would be able and willing to buy it. Brownwell completed work on the camera six months later, and by April 1900 it had appeared on store shelves across the country. It quickly became the most successful in Eastman's line of box cameras. Its name: the Brownie.[1]

Made of jute board, reinforced with wood, and covered with imitation leather, the Brownie came equipped with an inexpensive lens, a mechanically uncomplicated rotary shutter, and a red window indexing system. Loaded with a six-exposure cartridge of Kodak roll film, it produced $2\frac{1}{4}'' \times 2\frac{1}{4}''$ pictures that could be developed, printed, and mounted for 40 cents, with an additional roll of film included for 15 cents. In strong sunlight the camera's relatively small lens opening admitted enough light to expose film adequately and had enough depth of field so that all subjects from a few feet to 100 feet were in acceptable focus.[2] Distinguishing the Brownie from previous Kodak cameras, as Elizabeth Brayer so flatly puts it, "was its calculated averageness," designed as it was to "make average pictures in average light at average speed with film of average sensitivity" (205). The Brownie's only exceptional feature was its price: for $1, the price of a corset, two diapers, or a race ticket in 1900, anyone could now proclaim herself an amateur photographer.[3]

By the end of the year, the company had sold over 150,000 Brownies: 3,000 sales more than the Pocket Kodak, Kodak's previously most popular camera, had generated during six years.[4] Indeed, the Brownie's commercial success was largely responsible for the fact that roughly one-third of the U.S. population owned a camera by 1910. This phenomenal increase has prompted some historians to regard the Brownie, rather than the original Kodak camera, as the watershed invention in the history of amateur photography. The $25 charged for the No. 1 in 1888 had restricted the field of amateur photographers to middle- and upper-middle-class consumers; the Brownie's price of $1 (the rough equivalent of $20 today) enabled a much larger percentage of the American population to take photographs too.[5]

Adults probably purchased between one-third and one-half of all Brownie cameras produced between 1900 and the early 1930s,[6] but the ads focus exclusively on children as the principal owners of Brownie cameras. A 1906 advertisement (plate 10) commissioned by one of the most popular children's illustrators of the time, Elizabeth Shippen Green, features a tableau vivant of an elegantly dressed boy and girl at play, she with a Brownie camera, her brother with a toy sheep. The message here could not be clearer: Kodak simplicity extends even to children, their small fingers as adept at pushing a button, presumably, as their parents'.

If the Kodak Girl's amateur status rested in part on a traditional association between woman and child—on the presumed delicacy and tenderness of woman as the preservation of an infantile constitution—the logical next step in Kodak's evolutionary simplicity was to make a camera specifically suited for a young market. As snapshot photographers, children would confirm the truth of "Kodak simplicity." More important, the body of the child photographer and Brownie camera would lend material value to what had been, up to 1900, only a metaphorical means of describing the "play" of amateur photography. The Brownie's direct appeal to children thus legitimized photography as real play, children constituting the only social group whose status in modern culture rests on play's associations with innocence, spontaneity, imagination, and freedom.

76
◇

What distinguishes the world of childhood from the world of leisure is the degree to which it gains its shape from loss. Kodak's emphasis on leisure basically taught consumers to see photography as a
form of fun and adventure at a time when Americans were, in fact, experiencing more free time away from work than they ever had before;
Kodak's deployment of childhood encouraged a view of photography
as a form of innocence that could, in fact, never be experienced again.

In other words, the Kodak ads that feature children frequently
possess a melancholy aura absent from those that promote photography as a leisure activity, Kodak's accent on childhood insouciance continually haunted by the nostalgia that cannot help but appropriate
children as its subject. A central argument in this chapter, then, is
that advertising for the Brownie camera initiated Kodak's use of nostalgia, which always yearns, in a sense, for the child's return.

Picturing Childhood

Carol Mavor claims that "photography was invented hand-in-hand
with our modern conception of childhood. The child and the photograph were commodified, fetishized, developed alongside each other:
they were laminated and framed as one" (5). This observation certainly
does bear some relevance to the medium in its earliest decades, yet
children did not assume a salient role in photography until the advent
of Kodak. In the early to mid–nineteenth century in the United
States, no commercial culture of childhood yet existed, and an ideational one was still in its infancy.[7]

Consider the way children posed for the studio photographer during the 1840s through the 1860s especially: their awkward gestures,
buttoned-up costumes, and rigid expressions reflect their culture's basic perception of them as adults in the making. Indeed, to appreciate
how Kodak marketed snapshot photography as an activity suitable for
children, we must remember that before Kodak, most children's experience with photography was confined to the professional portrait studio. With its accent on formal dress and pose, studio photography
stands quite at odds—no matter how much the photographer may try
to make it otherwise—with the "natural" and uninhibited behavior
modern culture has come to imagine as characteristic of children.

This observation is especially apropos of portrait studios in the
first few decades of photography. In the mid–nineteenth century, when

the exposure time was long and the sitter had to remain absolutely mo-
tionless in a pose of impeccable posture, photographers had to go to
great lengths to photograph children. Props of all kinds were enlisted;
many studios were equipped with toys, candy, costumes, buggies, baby
bottles, even giant clam shells used as cradles. Parents would often
cover themselves with fabric and masquerade as chairs or tables so
that they could discretely hold their children in place, comic proof of
Gisele Freund's observation that within the space of the nineteenth-
century photographic studio, the "sitter himself seems to be nothing
more than a prop" (61). One early photograph actually shows a pair of
hands behind velvet drapes supporting a child by the ears.[8] With its
combination of palm trees, cushions, tapestries, and exotic furnishings, the Victorian photographer's studio might have seemed to a child
like a museum masquerading as playroom, or to use Walter Benjamin's
more lurid description, a "torture chamber masquerading as throne
room" (quoted in Rugg 167).[9] No matter what efforts a nineteenth-
century photographer may have undertaken to make his studio seem
comfortable to children, its artifice showed like the hem of a slip, stubbornly visible, I would imagine, to children, who sense the strangeness
of customs and behaviors to which adults have become inured.

Benjamin, incidentally, figured among the unfortunates who
posed before the studio camera as a child. His description of the
experience, recounted in his autobiography, *Berliner Kindheit um
Neunzehnhundert*, emphasizes the potentially objectifying power of
photography: its seeming ability to reverse the supposed order of
things by rendering human beings into objects and objects into something more than things. "Wherever I looked," Benjamin writes, "I saw
myself surrounded by screens, cushions, pedestals, which lusted for
my image like the shades of Hades" (quoted in Rugg 167–68).

Despite its obvious melodrama, Benjamin's description alerts
us to the undeniable theatricality and bourgeois pretensions of the
nineteenth-century studio, exemplified in its attention to such furnishings as velvet drapes, palm trees, statues, easels. Like Dickens,
Benjamin overweighs his recollection with such a detailed description of objects that they almost seem to live and breathe. And as in
Dickens's novels, the sheer force of these objects renders the child
absolutely passive, so much so that his consciousness becomes insep-
arable from them. Described this way, the photographer's studio becomes a space where what children both delight in and fear most

78 actually happens: the mastery of things, and the secrecy, forbidden
energy, and objectification such mastery entails. What distinguishes
the photographer's studio from the child's world of make-believe, however, is that these props are not enlisted for the child's fantasy; they
enlist him for theirs.

In the sixty-year span between photography's invention and the appearance of the Brownie camera, both photography and childhood
had lost their sobriety. Indeed, at least one writer has described the
period between the 1890s and 1920s as the "age of the child," [10] noting
an unprecedented ideational and commercial attention to the value of
children's play. By the 1890s, a look into any middle- or upper-middle-
class child's nursery would have revealed an array of games, toys, and
books specially designed for her consumption. Children had assumed
such social importance by the late 1890s, in other words, that they
were bound to influence the nascent industry of snapshot photography profoundly. And of course they did: to no small extent, snapshot photography gained its cultural currency from the promise that
children could demonstrate for the first time in photographic history all the characteristics—spontaneity, playfulness, innocence—recently discovered as uniquely their own.

It is by now almost a truism that adults in modern culture have
come to idealize the difference between childhood and adulthood, in-
ternalizing a vision of children promulgated by the Romantic poets. [11]
In the early nineteenth century, childhood started to emerge in literature and other cultural venues as a repository of qualities that had
disappeared in adulthood. As Hugh Cummingham observes, "the
more adults and adult society seemed bleak, urbanized, and alienated,
the more childhood came to be seen as properly a garden, enclosing
within the safety of its walls a way of life which was in touch with nature and which preserved the rude virtues of earlier periods of the history of mankind" (*Children of the Poor* 3). In this description, children
become objects in the world just as anxiety and its opposite—a remembered sense of wholeness, peace, and sanity—seem like objects
to be preserved, picked up, and played with, like an old photograph of
oneself as a child.

This nostalgic view of childhood did not flourish solely on the basis of Romanticism but was buttressed in the decades ahead by theories in behavioral psychology, child rearing, and education. Late nineteenth-century child theorists such as Ellen Key and William Shearer
argued extensively the need to preserve and extend the spontaneity of

childhood, promoting the value of amusement in an age that expressed
pronounced fears about the mechanization of modern life. By the turn
of the century, a wealth of advice manuals circulated extolling the
value of play. Elizabeth Grinnell advised parents to "let every child, before going to bed, hold a high court of revelry . . . devoted to romp, to
dance, to shout, to sing, to riot, and to play" (11).[12]

The upshot of their advice, according to Daniel T. Rodgers, was
that children were "isolated in an age-segregated world of peers and
social clubs, sports and Scout hikes, toys and games, from which the
exits into adulthood were by no means immediately obvious." He
explains:

> As mercantile capitalism gave way in the last third of the [nine-
> teenth] century to its industrial successor, and farms and shops
> were pushed aside by factories, machinery, batteries of clerks,
> and tighter work discipline, many of those nervous about change
> grew increasingly nervous about systematization itself. Drawn
> particularly to child matters, they turned their fears into idyls of
> pre-machinery childhoods where children's spirits had not been
> ground under by the drill of Gradgrindish schoolmasters or
> crushed by premature labor. . . . The result was a literature which
> served at once to train children and to enlist them in a web of
> adult fantasies—to project upon children, and thus lay bare,
> much of the covert restlessness and half-disguised anxiety within
> late Victorian America. As childhood was made over into the
> antithesis of the machine, one can watch the thrust of middle-
> class nervousness shift, towing children in its wake once more.
> (127–28)

As Rodgers so eloquently describes it, children had begun by the late
nineteenth century to serve their parents' psychological needs much
more than their economic needs. In the early nineteenth century,
working- and middle-class parents generally viewed children as sources
of family income, sending them out to fields or factories, or having
them perform household chores such as milking, sewing, and weaving.
By the 1870s, children began to assume another kind of quantitative
value, emerging as emotional assets that brought generosity, love, and
vitality to the home.

Beginning in 1900, Kodak produced dozens of ads each year illustrating this observation, ads not only for the Brownie camera but for

80 ◇ a variety of products specially designed for the amateur photographer.[13] Although images of children did not appear in Kodak advertising until the marketing of the Brownie in 1900, they gradually increased in number until they appeared in what I estimate to be over one-third of all advertisements produced between 1917 and 1932.[14] This incremental representation testifies to children's increasing symbolic value for Kodak once the company began to promote family and domestic life after the United States entered World War I.

In virtually every Kodak advertisement I have seen that features children, they look happy, occasionally impish, and always wholesome. Their presence in ads produced between 1900 and the early 1930s essentially performs four ideational functions: (1) pictured in or around the home, they reinforce the leisured world of the middle- and upper-class family; (2) pictured outdoors or engaged in some form of play, they embody the simplicity, adventure, and serendipity of snapshot photography; (3) depicted alongside adults or within surprisingly melancholic settings, they dramatize the distance between adulthood and childhood, reminding parents that they should take photographs of their children in order to "preserve what will soon be lost"; (4) portrayed as photographers themselves, they idealize the acts of seeing and remembering.

The first of these four functions predominates in advertisements that promote Kodak cameras as ideal holiday gifts. In the 1905 ad seen in figure 14, for example, an extended family gathers around the Christmas tree, the boy and girl in the lower right corner representing the nineteenth-century reinvention of Christmas as a children's holiday centered on gifts. With its attention to elegant home furnishings and expensive clothing, the advertisement, drawn by the illustrator Alonzo Kimball, clearly conveys middle-class comfort. Such attributes are of course reinforced by the ad's focus on the exchange of presents, which serves the double function of verifying the family's financial prosperity and at the same time sentimentalizing it.

As the anthropological work of theorists such as Marcel Mauss and David Cheal attests, gifts in Western culture are designed primarily to convey the sentiment, particularly at Christmastime, that objects can assume a highly intimate and expressive value. Gifts, especially children's gifts, thus moderate their own identity as commodities, drawing attention instead to the personal relations they supposedly embody.[15]

Figure 14. Christmastime advertisement illustrated by Alonzo Kimball, 1905. (Reprinted courtesy of Eastman Kodak Company)

82
◇

One noteworthy aspect of this advertisement is the way the father handles his new Folding Kodak camera with studious appreciation while his children examine their own present with similar intensity. The children, moreover, appear directly in the line of their father's vision, implying that his first snapshot will record them in a perfect Kodak moment: the opening and appreciation of a Christmas gift, which conveniently happens to be a Brownie. Overlying the camera's commodity status as well, then, is the suggestion that the Kodak camera will permanently record childhood pleasure while at the same time verifying parental generosity and affection.

This depiction of family unity within a generally overpadded world of prosperity pervades Kodak advertising, evoking for us the issue of how class informs modern constructions of childhood. In her book on representations of young girls in popular culture, Valerie Walkerdine asks whether "the issue of childhood innocence is actually about the protection and maintenance of a bourgeois and aristocratic world in which children grow up to be leisured adults and not workers, who are exploited before their time" (168). Despite its stridency, Walkerdine's question points to a crucial purpose behind Kodak's idealization of childhood. Looking at ads produced by Kodak between 1900 and the early 1930s, particularly ads for the Brownie camera, we can see how children and adults come together in a world of middle- and upper-class comfort, the play of children repeated in the seemingly leisured lives of their parents. The children in figure 14, for example, have received the same gift as their father and seem to handle and appreciate it in exactly the same way. The upper-middle-class world of which Kodak advertising is so enamored thus perpetuates itself through the image of the carefree, idle, and always well-dressed child.

A second purpose behind Kodak advertising's use of children centers on the suggestion that the simplicity of childhood finds its technological and representational counterpart in snapshot photography. Hundreds of advertisements from 1910 through the 1920s employ the slogans "All the child-world invites your Kodak" and "Where there's a child, there should the Kodak be." As these slogans indicate, Kodak aimed at naturalizing the relation between children and snapshot photography, the implication being that children's unaffected behavior is somehow mirrored in the simplicity, indeed the seeming naiveté, of the medium. Take the 1921 advertisement (figure 15) featuring a little girl serving tea to her doll. Strikingly minimal in content as well as

FROM A KODAK NEGATIVE.

Five-O'Clock Tea

Every day, in their little-world-of-make-believe, the children offer countless Kodak opportunities.   Mary, entertaining at five-o'clock tea or with
motherly solicitude putting Dolly to bed; little Jim, manfully mastering his
spirited wooden steed or in Indian garb carefully stalking a mountain lion,
impersonated by Tabby who is blissfully blinking beneath the hydrangeas—
such are the pictures that mean the most.

It is pictures of these every-day happenings that give to the Kodak
Album its intimate, human interest.   To-day, it is full of charm; to-morrow,
when the children have outgrown childhood, it will be priceless.

EASTMAN KODAK CO., ROCHESTER, N. Y., *The Kodak City.*

Figure 15. Advertisement featuring girl at play with tea set, 1921. (Reprinted
courtesy of Eastman Kodak Company)

composition, the image suggests that snapshot photography's predomi-
nant quality, like childhood's, is simplicity.

At the same time, the advertisement also exemplifies a third and
quite different purpose behind Kodak's employment of children: to in-
still in adults a vague apprehension over losing their children to the

84 passage of time. Aided by bittersweet images and captions such as the
◇ ones reproduced here, a surprising number of advertisements published after roughly 1917 capitalize on an imagined sense of distance between the worlds of adults and children. The caption for this advertisement implies, for example, that photographs of children assume greater emotional significance as the years advance precisely because their value depends on parental loss: "Every day, in their little-world-of-make-believe, the children offer countless Kodak opportunities. . . . It is pictures of these every-day happenings that give to the Kodak Album its intimate, human interest. To-day, it is full of charm; to-morrow, when the children have outgrown childhood, it will be priceless."

An obviously staged photograph despite its claims to the contrary, this image's attention to such details as the child's patent-leather shoes, neatly tied pinafore, and china set heightens the sense of exquisite loss the caption seeks to convey as part of parenthood. Consoling the parent in future years, however, will be the "priceless" photographs that have preserved the child as she appeared on the day they were taken. Unlike the actual child, photographs are represented as pure objects not taken up in the changing sphere of lived reality. Like the *idea* of childhood, as opposed to its reality, photographs remain complete, whole, timeless.

As James Kincaid morosely reminds us, children "grow up with the speed of darkness" (54). Only the camera, adds Carol Mavor, "can keep up with their velocity" (4). In this advertisement, a child presides over a world that appears artificially still, slowed down by the adult nostalgia that has supposedly determined the taking of the photograph. This association of children with a seemingly atemporal world constitutes a common trope in Kodak advertising, as the advertisement reproduced in plate 3 also exemplifies. Here a mother pensively observes her children, the ad inviting the viewer to look with her onto the radiant space in which they play.

Adult reverie assumes the shape of childhood as the female photographer (depicted here as far more mature and sedate than the Kodak Girl of earlier years) remains enclosed within the melancholy shadows of her home. Indeed, her wistfulness typifies later advertisements depicting women photographers observing their children, just as the ad's general air of melancholy testifies to Kodak's much more dramatic exploitation of nostalgia by the mid-1920s. We are encour-

aged to see the children as she does, as representatives of a realm that
she is no longer part of yet appreciates all the more because it is lost
to her. As in other Kodak advertisements produced in the 1920s, the
open glass door functions as a metaphor of passage between two
spaces, dramatizing the Hermes-like role of the mother, who mediates
here between the worlds of shadow and light.

Playing on the symbolic importance of darkness, this advertisement subliminally suggests that childhood, like photography, assumes
its shape and poignancy from death.[16] Childhood evokes nostalgia in
part because the vitality of children makes their preordained end in
death seem even more tragic, in much the way the constructed innocence of snapshot photography emphasizes its subjects' mortality. In
other words, the smiles, informal poses, and generally carefree world
we have come to see as characteristic of the snapshot mirrors the
world we have constructed for the child. And both arouse such profound nostalgia because their aura of cheerful naiveté makes them
seem so vulnerable.

Thus the child in Kodak advertising embodied family prosperity,
snapshot simplicity, and a nostalgic sense of loss. With the advent of
the Brownie camera, the image of the child was also enlisted to perform a fourth function: to idealize the acts of seeing and remembering. Perpetuating the sentiments of Romantic poetry, modern Western culture has depicted the child as possessing, despite her age and
naiveté, an almost preternatural ability to observe what adults' cynicism and propensity for distraction prevent them from seeing. The
child is constructed, writes James Kincaid, as the "great rememberer,
though it is the child being remembered. . . . Memory is constructed
from observation; the powers of observation are never so strong as
when we are young . . . thus we can remember childhood only by ask-
ing the child to do the remembering for us" (230).

With their Brownies in hand, children in Kodak advertising literally appear to be answering such a request. Indeed, one of the striking
aspects of Brownie advertising is how often children are depicted observing events or objects that might ordinarily escape the attention of
adults. They take photographs of their dogs at play, of their younger
siblings struggling with getting on their winter clothing, even of Dad
reading his paper on the front porch.

The most fascinating example of this observation may be found in

86
◇

one of the earliest advertisements for the Brownie camera. First published in 1902, the ad features a little girl of no more than five or six appearing as Kodak's latest amateur photographer (plate 11). Her exquisite features and costume not only evoke the fashion dolls so popular during this period but recall the Kodak Girl, whom she almost seems to replicate in miniature. Like her predecessor, the child presides over a setting constructed as beautiful, tender, yet aesthetically sealed off from the viewer by an ornate frame. We know, as we peer through the frame, that we must not approach this snapshot, or the child's world it represents, with vulgar mimetic or realistic expectations. If we are to enter at all, we must enter through a child's imagination.

The girl pictured here is about to photograph a brownie, one of the legendary elves popularized by the children's writer and illustrator Palmer Cox. It was his illustrations that inspired the name of the camera. As Cox explains, the brownie figures had always been represented in English folklore as invisible: "They work and sport while weary households sleep, and never allow themselves to be seen by mortal eyes" (vii). Cox's books were, in fact, supposedly the first publications to include illustrations of the brownies, which were undoubtedly what made them so popular. That a camera company in particular would capitalize on the visualization of the invisible suggests the possibility, which has always been part of the discourse of photography, that the camera can see what the human eye cannot, that it can open onto a larger, preternatural world—in this case, a world to which children seemingly have sole access.

Photographs of the invisible floated everywhere in the mid–nineteenth to early twentieth century, convincing many Americans that the camera could actually take pictures of ghosts and other numinous objects. In 1917, as hundreds of people believed, cameras apparently could also take pictures of fairies. Two young girls near Bradford, West Yorkshire, allegedly produced photographs between 1917 and 1920 that depicted themselves at play with fairies (figure 16).[17] Like the image in the Kodak advertisement, these photographs portray exquisite-looking children whose physical beauty reinforces their own innocence as well as that of the world they represent. In each, the child photographer appears as female, alerting us to the fact that the constructed purity of childhood also depends in part on its feminization.

Figure 16. Cottingley fairy photograph, 1917. (Reprinted courtesy of Brotherton Collection, Leeds University Library)

The resemblance between these two images, separated as they are by time, locale, and a range of historical contexts, suggests that the image of the child photographer reflects a larger cultural desire to privilege imagination over realism even from an invention that has been so clearly identified with the world of empiricism.[18] In both images, children's play is represented as possessing a special kind of imaginative truth. Such depictions of play suggest that what we desire most of photography, as of childhood, is the possibility of seeing and experiencing the world through the lens of imagination.

As Kodak advertisements testify, the child in the nineteenth and early twentieth centuries was always present and always lost, lost in the past of the individual as well as of the culture that sought so desperately to recapture her. Like the memories depicted in a photograph, childhood came to represent what was gone and yet waiting to be found again. In this way, the figure of the child embodied the interiority of photography, the wish to find an inner self and its "purer" history through photographs that idealize experience. As Carolyn

88   Steedman puts it, "The child is the story waiting to be told" (11). So,
◇   too, are the child's playthings.

Toy Stories

If we can call childhood a nineteenth-century invention, it seems
plausible to describe the toy (or more specifically the mass-produced
children's toy) as the brainchild of the early twentieth century. As children assumed greater emotional value in Western culture, toys began
to emerge as the most visible—and the most commercialized—measure of their social significance.[19] It should come as no surprise, then,
to discover that Kodak aggressively marketed the Brownie camera as a
children's toy. Although Kodak dissuaded customers from viewing the
Brownie as technically inefficient by claiming that the camera is
"much more than a toy—it is a practical and efficient instrument," the
images it deployed always situated the camera within the realm of
children's play. Kodak thus profited by sentimentalizing the Brownie's
toylike charm while simultaneously relying on textual authority to accentuate its mechanical efficiency.

Much of the original Kodak camera's appeal centered on its relatively small size and light weight. In making such a product, Kodak essentially transformed the camera into a toy for adults. The marketing
of the Brownie foregrounded this implicit transformation by squarely
situating the camera within the realm of children's toys. At stake in our
consideration of the Brownie's marketing, then, is a radical shift in
popular perceptions of photography as the camera shifts its original
materiality (that is, its materiality before the advent of Kodak) from a
studio-size box (often as heavy as sixty pounds) to a two-pound box
camera in 1888 and finally to a brightly packaged half-pound toy for
children in 1900.

Thanks to the work of such historians as John Tagg, Cathy Davidson, and Alan Trachtenberg, we now know that a plethora of material
exists testifying to Victorian anxieties about photography.[20] Judging
from written accounts as well as a range of visual material, much of
this metaphysical and epistemological apprehension seemed rooted in
the camera, which often figured as an enormous black box, a gigantic
signifier of the objectifying powers of photography (figure 17). In fact,
one of the aspects of early writings on photography that most commands our attention, particularly during the decades from 1840 to

Figure 17. French cartoon of man with camera, 1850s. (Reprinted from Braive's *The Photograph: A Social History*)

1860, is how often the camera gets cast as a huge black box invested with an almost predatory potential.[21] Like all gigantic objects, the camera in these stories and illustrations threatens to envelop the human figure, swallowing him in its immediacy. This popular perception was in all likelihood reinforced by the sheer size and weight of most studio cameras. Many studio cameras produced during the 1860s measured over five feet long, sported an enormous brass lens, and weighed over seventy pounds because of the need to accommodate large glass plates.

The representational size of an object often reflects public perceptions of it. In the first few decades after its introduction, the camera seemed to partake of the invasive and mysterious. Its size, large in actuality and exaggerated in representation, suggested that the photographic process, like the gigantic object that represented it, could be known or experienced only partially, abstractly, never intimately.

As Susan Stewart explains, "Our impulse is to create an environment for the miniature, but such an environment is impossible for the gigantic; instead the gigantic becomes our environment, swallowing us as nature or history swallows us" (89). Or, as I argue in chapter 5,

90

◇

as death swallows us. Stewart juxtaposes the gigantic with the miniature in her study of nostalgia, arguing that while the gigantic represents what cannot be understood or mastered because it so clearly
cannot be contained, the miniature calls attention to itself as total object and thus serves to create the illusion that it can be known and experienced intimately. In other words, the relation of gigantic to miniature might be compared to the relationship between, say, history and
nostalgia, relic and antique, or even adulthood and childhood.

This obsession with the camera's objectifying potential speaks to
the ways in which early nineteenth-century culture wrestled with the
implications of its new technologies. The first several decades of the
nineteenth century were the heyday of the machine and the concomitant mechanization of labor. Not surprisingly, this period witnessed
the production of a vast array of literature, some of it written expressly
for children, that anthropomorphized machines as terrifying sources
of havoc and destruction.[22] In the works of children's authors such as
Edward Wood, these animated machines foreground what Joseph
Schwarcz sees as a cultural desire to project onto children adult fears
over the social effects of industrial capitalism.[23] As several historians have noted, photography also generated a surprising number of
"coming-alive" narratives during its first few decades.[24] In these stories, the apparatus of photography assumes a life of its own; the photographer is either completely absent from the story or enslaved by the
camera's self-generating and often diabolical powers.

In this brief narrative of adult fears about photography, a narrative
that I see as ending with Eastman's invention of the Kodak No. 1 camera in 1888 and its ghost laid to rest with the invention of the Brownie
camera in 1900, we can recognize a confluence of two histories, the
history of cameras and the history of toys. Before the nostalgic recon-
struction of childhood in the mid- to late nineteenth century, toys in
popular American culture frequently emerged as sources of anxiety
and terror; by 1900, as the works of H. G. Wells and G. K. Chesterton
exemplify, they had been transformed into objects of tender regard.[25]
As Chesterton wrote with characteristic poignancy in 1913: "It is an old
story, and for some a sad one, that in a sense childish toys are more to
us than they can ever be to children" (quoted in Kuznets 46). The toy's
evolution from an object of anxiety to one of nostalgia may be mirrored
in the history of the camera.

In order to appreciate this point more fully, we might turn here to
the work of Bruno Latour, who argues that in order for a scientific in-

vention to be widely disseminated, it must first be "packaged" into what he calls a "cold, unproblematic" black box (3). Latour in fact repeatedly draws on the metaphor of the black box to illustrate how any scientific invention, if it is to enter the world of public use, necessarily involves an ongoing process of simplification so as to strip it of any possible exceptions, controversies, competitions, and technical difficulties. Whenever cyberneticians are faced with great complexity, he writes, "in its place they draw a little box about which they need to know nothing but its input and output. . . . That is, no matter how controversial, how complex their inner workings, how large the commercial or academic networks that hold them in place, only their input and output count" (2 3). The image of the black box thus provides the scientific community as well as the general public with a concrete, neat, simple machine that supposedly has debugged science of its controversies and failures while at the same time diffracting and shunting away discussion.

I bring up Latour not only because his interpretation of the black box seems relevant to my understanding of Kodak's transformation of the camera into a toy, but because the black box is made literal by the camera. Photographic history lends itself easily to Latour's argument—after all, the evolution of the camera might be visualized as a series of increasingly smaller black boxes, progressing from the room-sized camera obscura, through the "first" camera made by Nicephore Niepce in 1816, the first commercial daguerreotype camera in 1839, and the relatively tiny and portable box camera originally produced by Kodak in 1888, to the simplest of all black boxes in 1900, the Brownie.

Like Kodak's promise of a story through photographs, black boxes provide convenient narrative strategies; they give us a beginning and an end, but no complicated middle. Like the unconscious, neither the box nor the narrative should be opened, or else the disorder of science in the making subverts the orderly and rational pattern of science as ready made. I draw on this metaphor purposefully, for what is implicit in Latour's argument, though never actually stated, is the suggestion that black boxes allow us to forget history. When Kodak transformed the camera into a mass-produced commodity along with the photograph, the history of photography was, in a sense, completely swallowed by the corporation. As with all mass-produced commodities, the origin of Kodak's invention and its site of production were neatly, magically transferred to the abstract space of the factory.

Figure 18. Advertisement promoting Kodak research laboratories, *Collier's*, 15 February 1919. (Reprinted courtesy of Eastman Kodak Company)

And with the Brownie camera we have the logical, inevitable con-   93
clusion to this gradual erasure of photographic history. As an object   ◇
specifically designed for a child, the Brownie camera entered a world
that is profoundly ahistorical. Children have little sense of or appreciation for history; their world subsumes the past and present into the
immediate, the here-and-now. They make themselves into the illusory
creators of objects, ignoring any and all predecessors. No advertisement I have come across captures this situation more vividly than a
1919 ad that features "intent observers in a darkened laboratory" on
one side and a "little girl in the sunshine" with her camera on the
other (figure 18). We don't have to read the accompanying text to get
the message: Kodak researchers diligently work behind the scenes to
improve the photographic process so that the young girl, like her parents, may take pictures in blithesome ignorance, as if she were indeed
handling a toy. An archaic definition of the verb "to toy," interestingly
enough, is "to forget."

Brownie Cameras and the Commodification of Toys

Several years ago I visited a child's museum with an entire room devoted to toys that had been manufactured between 1900 and 1920, the
two decades in which the Brownie enjoyed its greatest popularity. I remember especially one English doll dressed in the red velvet robes of
a peeress, produced at the time of the coronation of King George V in
1910. She wore a white satin gown underneath her robes, which was
embroidered with blue stones that I initially mistook as sapphires.
Mounds of lace that looked delicate enough to have been made by
nuns in a convent rather than seamstresses in a factory lay underneath
the satin, extending her splendor in all directions. Down the shelf
from her stood a Cossack doll, his head tilted in her direction but his
face pointed knowingly at me—as if, despite his soldierly formality, he
wanted to say: "She's a beauty, isn't she?" He was made by a German
factory in 1914, and wore a lamb's-wool hat and had miniature bullets
in his pocket.

Seeing these two dolls, I knew before I had gone any further why
the toys of those decades had a room of their own. Like the rest of
the toys that lined the shelves and filled the cases of this room, these
dolls were amazingly intricate, especially in light of the fact that they
had been designed for middle-class American children, and especially

when I compared them with most of the nineteenth-century toys featured in another room, which suddenly seemed like a home for the dispossessed.

Toys enjoyed relatively little cultural importance in the United States before 1900. As the historians Stephen Kline, Karin Calvert, and Gary Cross have explained, the Victorian world of child's play was not a world of manufactured things. Up until the Civil War, toys had been reserved mainly for the wealthy and usually imported from Europe, particularly Germany, which until the First World War was the world's leading manufacturer of toys. Mechanical soldiers, ceramic dolls, and toy theaters were not for the ordinary child and not necessarily associated with childhood at all. As Kline notes, most American children in the first half of the nineteenth century played with objects such as discarded wheel hoops and sticks or handcrafted rag dolls and wooden blocks. Parents did not assume that their children needed a profusion of toys to mature, nor were most of them able to afford them had they thought so. Revolving mainly around school, work, and chores, the life of the typical American child in the early nineteenth century left little time for play, and any recreation took simple forms. Even if the technology had been available to make a product such as the Brownie camera in the first half of the nineteenth century at a cost comparably low, it is almost inconceivable that parents would have purchased such an intricate machine for their children.

In the years between 1865 and 1900, as Americans directed their energies toward rebuilding their families after the Civil War, manufacturers began to produce toys in somewhat larger numbers, often applying techniques developed in other industries.[26] Makers of wood, metal, mechanical, and print and paper goods produced miniatures of their "adult" products or used waste materials to turn out modest batches of cheap children's playthings for Christmas. Walking dolls first appeared in 1862; so did dollhouses, some even equipped with running water, gas-jet lighting, genuine silverware, and marble fixtures. The last decades of the nineteenth century also witnessed the advent of several toy companies such as Parker Brothers and the McLoughlin Brothers, both of which specialized in lithographed board and card games. By the turn of the century, 50 percent of the toys sold in the United States were produced nationally (as opposed to 20 percent before the Civil War). "The industrialization that transformed American life in the generation after the Civil War," Cross explains, "changed the material worlds of children. Those lucky enough to visit toy shops and the new department and variety stores after 1865 were the first generation to imagine owning any significant number of playthings" (*Kids' Stuff* 21). Toys had thus clearly emerged as a burgeoning new industry by 1900, transforming children for the first time in history into owners of mass-produced playthings.

But as most historians agree, the American toy industry underwent its most drastic transformation between 1900 and the early 1920s. Factory production lowered costs and increased distribution, thus enabling the basic lines of toys and games (such as Erector sets, Lincoln Logs, and electric trains) to be more widely and easily integrated into schools, clubs, and family leisure activities. By 1920, after a wave of national sentiment during World War I resulted in the boycotting of most German-made articles, 90 percent of American toys sold were being nationally produced, many of them bearing the stamp of the factory.[27]

One sign of this transformation, according to Gary Cross, was toy manufacturers' promotion of fantasy. Toymakers in the 1870s and 1880s generally treated playthings as sidelines and advertised them in hardware catalogs; now innovators gradually learned the importance of selling imagination and novelty in toys. Cross notes that by the turn of the century even vintage toymakers catered to the child's imagination by personifying their previously generic toys with fanciful names, such as "Whistler" and "Grand Duke," and by packaging toys in brightly colored boxes. Generic toys and dolls acquired name brands at the same time that soups and soaps did. The early 1900s witnessed the advent of such personified toys as the Teddy bear (1903), the Humpty Dumpty Circus (1903), the Polly Dolly (1903), and the Kewpie doll (1907), all of which were designed to foster a more intimate relationship between child and toy.

When the Brownie camera first appeared on store shelves in April 1900, it was packaged in a bright red, green, and yellow box that the *Kodak Trade Circular* described as "loud as a circus poster." Cavorting around all four sides of the box was a potbellied, googly-eyed elf, which most consumers in 1900 would have recognized instantly as one of Palmer Cox's mischievous brownies. Along with the poetry of Kate Greenaway, Walter Crane, and Randolph Caldecott, Cox's brownie books helped shape a new children's culture in the United States after the Civil War. Unlike early nineteenth-century authors

96   who invested their books with heavy didacticism and moral instruc-
◇   tion, these authors reflected the new association of children's culture
      with fantasy by peopling their books with talking animals, fairies, and
      sprites.[28] By appropriating the brownies as its ambassadors to the chil-
      dren's market, then, Kodak not only rode the coattails of Cox's well-
      established popularity but, just as important, placed its new camera
      within the realm of amusement, fantasy, and imagination.

          Kodak was certainly not alone in recognizing the commercial
      value of these little creatures. By the late 1890s, Cox's brownies pro-
      moted a range of novelty products, including horseshoe nails, bicy-
      cles, record players, egg cups, napkin rings, school supplies, and even
      cameras produced by other companies (Lothrop 7). This commer-
      cial exploitation of the brownies exemplifies what advertising the-
      orists now call "personality marketing." As in the much later cases of
      Tony the Tiger and Ronald McDonald, the well-established familiar-
      ity of the brownies enabled a psychological transference from persona
      to product, thereby promoting consumer loyalty—especially chil-
      dren's loyalty—by "personalizing" products. Children supposedly have
      too short an attention span to remember an abstract brand name, but
      they will ask for a certain brand, advertising theorists have argued ever
      since the turn of the century, if they identify it with someone they like
      very much. In the case of the brownies, Kodak could hardly have cho-
      sen a more popular personality; in 1900 the brownie books had sold
      over a million copies and made Cox one of the most successful chil-
      dren's authors in the world.

          Between 1900 and 1910, these legendary elves cavorted around
      dozens of advertisements for the Brownie camera (figure 19), their car-
      toonish figures investing the advertisements with childlike energy.
      One of the salient aspects of Kodak's appropriation of Cox's brownies
      centers on the fact that, as cartoons, these illustrations contrast in im-
      portant ways with photographs.[29] Cartooning is the art of overcharge.
      It connotes a kind of juvenile energy—what John Updike so aptly de-
      scribes as the "nervous glee of drawing" (80). Cartoons thus partake of
      the comic because they both exaggerate and, in their "nervous" en-
      ergy, seem to move. In this sense, they differ profoundly from pho-
      tographs, whose metaphysics and ontology depend on the literal ar-
      restment of movement. Unlike photographs, moreover, cartoons make
      no claim to accuracy; instead, they demand we see reality in their
      terms. Their figurative status, in other words, requires a new way of

Figure 19. Advertisement featuring Palmer Cox illustrations for Brownie camera, *Cosmopolitan*, December 1900. (Reprinted courtesy of Eastman Kodak Company)

98   looking. It is noteworthy, then, that these Brownie advertisements,
◇   like the watercolor posters of the Kodak Girl I will discuss in chap-
     ter 4, would draw on another medium so far removed from its sup-
     posed ontology. By exploiting the connotations and metaphysics of the
     cartoon, these ads effectively purged photography of its stillness and
     linked it with animation.

     This observation becomes clearer if we look at advertisements that
     actually integrate brownie figures into the space of the photograph
     (figure 20). By 1901, only a year or so after the Brownie's initial ap-
     pearance on the market, Kodak began to advertise the camera with
     black-and-white snapshots of children at play. This change was made
     possible by the dramatic improvement of the halftone photographic
     process that year, which revolutionized the iconographical matter of
     most magazines, displacing wood engraving, stipple and line engrav-
     ing, and chromolithography almost overnight. What it must have been
     like for Americans to see photographs reproduced in magazines with
     such unprecedented clarity is, of course, difficult to imagine. Even
     harder to imagine is how magazine readers may have reacted to images
     such as these. Although the figures pictured here are obviously not
     cartoons but "real-life" toys, they would have instantly recalled for
     contemporary readers Cox's actual drawings.

     By integrating these toys, with their cartoon aura, into the new ac-
     curacy of the reproduced photograph, Kodak achieves an optical illu-
     sion much like the one realized in *Who Framed Roger Rabbit?*—the il-
     lusion of animation entering the world of the human and living. The
     exaggerated space of the cartoon thus enters the "realistic" space of
     the snapshot, transforming the photograph's realism into fantasy and
     the cartoon's fantasy into realism.

     As advertisements between 1900 and 1910 make clear, Kodak tar-
     geted young children as the Brownie's market at first. Indeed, one of
     the striking aspects of these early Brownie ads is that they frequently
     employ images of children who are obviously much too young to op-
     erate a camera, thereby exaggerating the simplicity of the product. But
     this marketing ploy also suggests that the ads were designed mainly
     with parents in mind, testifying to the commodification of parenthood
     as well as of childhood. Until roughly 1910, merchandisers seem to
     have had little interest in motivating or addressing children them-
     selves. Their specific target was middle-class mothers, who presum-
     ably made most of the household purchases and who constituted the

Figure 20. Advertisement for the Brownie camera, *Youth's Companion,* 1908.
(Reprinted courtesy of Eastman Kodak Company)

majority of magazine readers. Advertisers banked on the assumption that these middle-class women also read child-rearing manuals, many of which argued that wisely conceived and chosen toys would encourage children to respect property, develop perseverance, and work well with others.[30]

Kodak capitalized on such theories about proper parenting, stressing photography's ability to offer youngsters both fun and education. One of the most popular slogans for the Brownie during this time was "Let the Children Kodak," which appeared in ads from roughly 1910 through the mid-1920s. Directed toward parents, the slogan implies that allowing children to photograph involves a liberation of creativity as well as an opportunity to demonstrate responsibility. "There's nothing that will give him more good wholesome fun, fun which at the same time teaches things that are worth while," claims another ad. Others even go so far as to advise parents that when they purchase a Brownie for their children, they are helping to alleviate "whatever nervousness, care, and ill-feelings enter their little world." In a remarkable *Kodakery* essay titled "The Kodak Cure," the anonymous author describes how a "white-faced, frail little chap" suddenly burst into robustness after a doctor prescribed a Brownie for him. Once confined to his bed, the boy now spends all his time outdoors, taking pictures of the woods near his house, his pet dog, and his new friends. "He's brown as a berry and putting on weight every day," the father proudly exclaims at the end of the article, advising readers that if they have a child who stays indoors too much, they ought to "run out and buy him a Brownie too" (4).

Kodak ads also encouraged parents to practice photography with their children, thus providing adults with a socially sanctioned reason to play. In another article for *Kodakery* titled "Every Family Its Own Camera Club," a father explains how photography has brought his entire family closer together: "You know, I'm just beginning to know those kids of mine. They are both older than I thought they were and they say I am a lot younger. . . . Kodaking is a common pleasure ground where you and the youngsters really meet as equals. That's the secret. Every family its own camera club" (5). Photography thus rejuvenates the father while instilling maturity in the child, its simplicity so basic that each derives equal satisfaction from it.

Between 1900 and roughly 1910, then, Brownie ads promote the camera for very young as well as older children. After 1910, however, the ads focus largely on children over ten.[31] Apparently the company realized around this time that it was no longer practical to market Brownies for very young children, since those below the age of eight apparently had difficulty focusing and lacked the necessary attention span to take a picture. Once older children emerged as the new market for the Brownie, moreover, the company began to advertise more extensively in such magazines as *Youth's Companion, St. Nicholas,* and *American Boy,* all of which were designed for middle-class children between the ages of ten and eighteen.

The last magazine title indicates another trend in Brownie advertising after 1910: the targeting of boys between roughly ten and fifteen as the principal users of Brownie cameras. Many ads feature boys photographing with their fathers. Men appear in Kodak advertising much less frequently than women, thus reflecting their marginal role in the maintenance of family life during the early twentieth century. Fathers *are* pictured constantly, however, in Brownie ads between 1910 and the late 1920s, actively participating in their sons' photographic enjoyment and learning. Ellen Seiter notes that ads for boys' toys, especially for such items as train sets and model airplanes, frequently picture a rejuvenated father brought closer to his family because he can participate in the activity. Certainly Brownie ads after 1910 support such an observation. In a 1923 advertisement, for example, father and son are poised in the middle of action as they examine the boy's new Brownie camera. The daughter, meanwhile, sits off in a corner, apparently happy just to watch (figure 21).

As the boy photographer assumed central importance in Brownie advertising, he became noticeably more adept with the camera. The *American Boy,* the largest-selling illustrated monthly for boys in the 1920s, with a circulation of almost 250,000, devoted an entire section of its back pages to a column titled "The Boy Photographer." Like Kodak, it sponsored contests for best pictures and published the winners each month. It also featured advertisements for cameras, manuals, and other photographic equipment. What's most surprising about this column is its level of technical language, its specialized rhetoric for boys who would have been, at the oldest, fifteen or sixteen, informing them of the newest developments in such areas as color photography, lantern slides, and lenses.[32]

Unlike the Kodak Girl, whose look, mannerisms, and appeal rested entirely on her status as amateur, the boy who used a Brownie

Figure 21. Christmastime advertisement for the Brownie camera, 1923. (Reprinted courtesy of Eastman Kodak Company)

Figure 22. Advertisement for the Brownie camera, *Youth's Companion,* 1924.
(Reprinted courtesy of Eastman Kodak Company)

camera was presumed to know about its technical features and opera-
tions. A 1924 advertisement (figure 22), for example, pictures him in
shirt and tie, not only reading about the photographic process but performing every step, from picture taking to printing to mounting. By
the late 1920s, the Brownie camera had thus been transformed from a

104 ◇ fantastical instrument represented by cute little elves to a semiprofessional one for young men. Now it no longer signified fantasy as much as it did adult behavior in the making.

The Brownie is thus a concrete example of a toy designed as a miniature adult tool, an object that gave children the illusion of participating in the "real" world of their parents. Like the Tinkertoys, Erector sets, and chemistry sets of the period, the Brownie attempted to minimize the barrier between the plaything and the real thing, teaching children to admire the technologies of the future as their parents did. More important, perhaps, this "adult" emphasis in toy manufacturing and promotion underscores the close relation between toys and modern commodities.[33]

It is this relation that constitutes one of the most salient aspects of the Brownie's advertising history. Ads for the Brownie increasingly positioned children as mature and appreciative owners of their cameras, alerting us to the fact that toys say as much about the nature of commodification as they do about childhood. As Dan Fleming observes, "Toys are a wonderful place to look at the complex interactions between the desiring individual and the massified demand. It's all so visible here—the child appealing for satisfaction and the market providing the very vocabulary for appeal" (8). Like all toys, the commodity isolates the user in a fantastical, fetishistic relationship with an object that seems to contain the complexities of modern culture. Just as material goods gave shape to modern adult consciousness and experience, so toys became the measure of the child, shaping his identity as well as adults' perceptions of him.

No clearer proof of this observation exists than the remarks propounded by advertising theorists during this time regarding children's "natural" propensity for consumption. Realizing that children's desire for immediate gratification made them, in a sense, the perfect consumers, advertising theorists began to stress the importance of "talking" directly to children rather than to their parents, who were bound to be much more conservative in both their tastes and their judgment. As one writer in *Toys and Novelties,* a national magazine for toy manufacturers and retailers, cynically noted in 1913, "an advertisement to a child has no barriers to climb, no scruples to overcome." Other advertising magazines echoed the same sentiments. "The nervous temperament of the average American child and the rapidity with which it tires of things [ensures] a continuous outlet in this country for toy sales" (quoted in Cross, *Kids' Stuff* 31).

That a child would be described as "nervous," a characteristic that for many people epitomized modern culture itself, profoundly undercuts the cultural tendency during this period to idealize children as free from the anxiety that seemed to be infecting adults, reminding us not only of advertising's duplicitous role in the construction of children's culture but of how closely children may have been mirroring the behavior of adults, despite the tendencies to see them otherwise.

In its eagerness for dealers to sell Brownies more aggressively to children, the *Kodak Trade Circular* soon featured accounts of how children, introduced to photography by way of the Brownie, go on to purchase more sophisticated cameras, the implication being that dealers will be well rewarded in the future with sales of more expensive Kodaks if they sell the cheaper Brownies now. "In one family," the magazine explains, "a boy buys a Brownie and becomes interested in amateur photography. In a week or two, he decided that he wanted a larger and more elaborate instrument; he bought a Kodak and gave the Brownie to one of his brothers" (May 1912, 2). What's most remarkable about this announcement is its lack of self-consciousness; a week becomes an acceptable—indeed, a desirable—lifetime for a Brownie, as if commodities had now become so disposable that even children, or especially children, desired a "better" object when they had barely used the original one. The charming appeal of the advertisement pictured in figure 23, for example, belies the commercial implications of its message: Kodak has literally made a camera for every children's age group, "from the little dollar Number One Brownie up to the 3A Folding, with its rapid Rectilinear lenses and pneumatic release shutter." When one child "grows out" of her camera, she simply moves on to the next and more sophisticated one, until she finally reaches the last camera, with highly specialized features that are described here, of course, in purposefully technical language. This ad thus reinforces the concept of a child's toy as the most disposable of all commodities, testifying to the power of consumerism to engender in people of all ages a guaranteed loss of interest in particular things, an ever-present desire for newer and better products.

By 1915, then, Kodak was aiming much of its advertising directly toward children, especially boys, and with a more aggressive campaign than any that had preceded it. Take, for example, this caption from a 1925 ad: "Your dad would give a lot for snap-shots of himself and his bunch that were made when he was a boy. Wonder if he knows you'd like a Brownie? It wouldn't do any harm to talk to him about it." Here

They Work Like Kodaks.

THE BROWNIE FAMILY
Provides a Camera for Every Boy and Girl

From the little dollar Number One Brownie up to the 3A Folding, with its Rapid Rectilinear lenses and pneumatic release shutter, they are well-made—every one. They are so simple to work that any boy or girl can quickly understand them—they are fully reliable, each one being carefully tested, and, especially in the smaller sizes, are by no means expensive to operate.

With a Brownie Camera you use light proof film cartridges that require no dark-room for loading or unloading. You can easily do your own developing and printing, also without a dark-room if you use a Brownie Kodak Film Tank or a Brownie Developing Box. Or you may merely "press the button" and let some one else "do the rest."

And there's plenty of fun in photography. The fishing trip, the ball game, the picnic party, the dog and the pony and even the dolls and Teddy bears, to say nothing of your boy and girl friends, all offer subjects that are interesting to take and in the months and years that follow, the pictures will always be a delight. There's no other pastime that "wears as well" as picture taking—because it always offers something new.

"The Brownie Book" free at your dealers or by mail, tells all about the eight members of the Brownie family, ranging from $1.00 to $12.00.

EASTMAN KODAK COMPANY,
ROCHESTER, N. Y., *The Kodak City.*

Figure 23. Advertisement for the Brownie camera, *Youth's Companion*, 1909.
(Reprinted courtesy of Eastman Kodak Company)

the private life of a child, like the lives of his parents, is being eerily transformed into a space that will be filled by commodities. But the caption raises another and perhaps even more disturbing problem, one that points to the obvious distinction between cameras and other toys. In cultivating child photographers through the marketing of its toy-camera, Kodak conditioned in boys and girls what had already become a determining factor in the lives of their parents: reliance on photography as a certification of experience and a substitute for memory. Hundreds of Brownie captions encourage the boy to see photography as a means not only of enhancing his pleasure but of confirming it. Even children, then, must learn to accept the unreliability of their memories, using their cameras in a way that signifies just the opposite of play. Play affords children a refuge from the consequences of both past and present events by providing them with a kind of atemporal environment, a world in which time seems almost suspended. In this caption, Kodak already inscribes past and future into the world of play, suggesting to its child consumers that play, like everything else that connotes family unity, leisure, and middle-class prosperity, exists in order to end up in a photograph.

Over Twenty-One

With his eye forever on the future, Eastman had predicted that if children could be instructed to operate a Brownie, he could promote them to increasingly more advanced cameras until they grew up into strong, healthy, free-spending customers. In regard to this vision, at least, the generally prescient Eastman failed. Although the Brownie continued to sell well until the 1950s, children never really caught on to photography in the way Eastman had hoped. Kodak went so far as to give away a free camera to every boy or girl whose twelfth birthday came within the calendar year of 1930, but even this spectacular promotion didn't result in more sales of Brownies.

The possible reasons for this indifference are worth pondering. Certainly the Brownie's technical requirements were simple enough for children over seven or eight. And the price was certainly affordable for both middle- and working-class parents. Photography, it would seem, should have appealed to children for all the reasons the advertisements provided: it sends them outdoors, allows them to express their interests and concerns through the production of a tangible

108   product, teaches them to validate their own world and the things in it.

◇   Perhaps one reason for children's growing indifference to photography lies in Kodak's success in replacing photography's playful qualities with its nostalgic obligations. Based as it is on loss, yearning, and the pain of experience, nostalgia is an adult's game, not suitable for players under twenty-one.

The history of the Brownie camera suggests that the same argument might also be made for photography.

Plate 1. Advertisement for the Pan-American Exposition, 1901. (Reprinted courtesy of Eastman Kodak Company)

Plate 2. Advertisement with man and woman on train, 1910. (Reprinted courtesy of Eastman Kodak Company)

Plate 3. Advertisement for Autographic Kodak featuring mother watching her children, early 1920s. (Reprinted courtesy of Eastman Kodak Company)

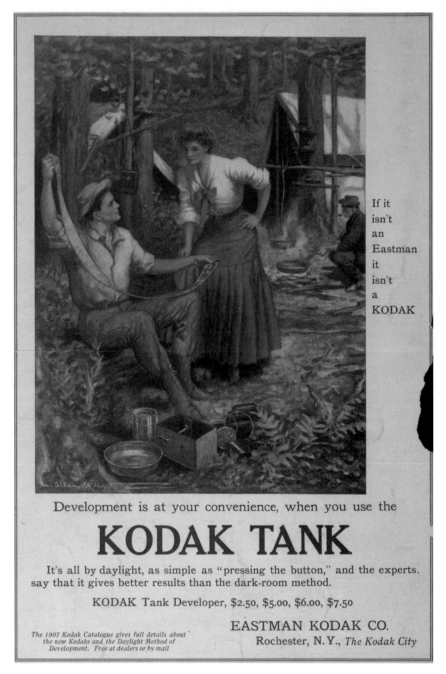

Plate 4. Advertisement for the Kodak Tank developer, 1906. (Reprinted courtesy of Eastman Kodak Company)

Plate 5. Poster featuring Kodak Girl and family picnic, Britain, early 1920s.
(Reprinted courtesy of Eastman Kodak Company)

Plate 6. Poster of Kodak Girl at World's Fair, France, 1934. (Reprinted courtesy of Eastman Kodak Company)

The Kodak Story

Of summer days grows in charm as the months go by—it's always interesting—it's personal—It tells of the places, the people and the incidents *from your point of view*—just as you saw them.

And it's an easy story to record, for the Kodak works at the bidding of the merest novice. There is no dark-room for any part of Kodak work; it's all simple. Press the button—do the rest—or leave it to another—just as you please. The Kodak catalogue tells the details. Free at the dealers or by mail.

Kodaks, $5 to $100
Brownies, $1 to $9

EASTMAN KODAK COMPANY
Rochester, N. Y., *The Kodak City*

Plate 7. Advertisement for Kodak with man repairing automobile, 1907.
(Reprinted courtesy of Eastman Kodak Company)

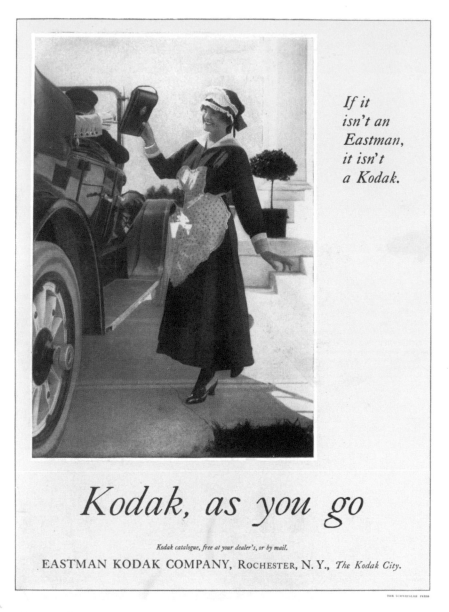

Plate 8. Advertisement with servant and automobile, 1910s. (Reprinted courtesy of Eastman Kodak Company)

Plate 9. "Vacation Days" advertisement, 1904. (Reprinted courtesy of Eastman Kodak Company)

Plate 10. Advertisement illustrated by Elizabeth Shippen Green, early 1900s.
(Reprinted courtesy of Eastman Kodak Company)

Plate 11. Advertisement for No. 2 Brownie camera, *Youth's Companion,* 1901.
(Reprinted courtesy of Eastman Kodak Company)

Plate 12. Advertisement for Vanity Kodak, 1928. (Reprinted courtesy of Eastman Kodak Company)

Plate 13. Advertisement featuring Kodak Girl in Japan, 1905. (Reprinted courtesy of Eastman Kodak Company)

Plate 14. Advertisement featuring Kodak Girl and family, early 1920s. (Reprinted courtesy of Eastman Kodak Company)

Plate 15. Advertisement with illustration of Kodak store, early 1900s. (Reprinted courtesy of Eastman Kodak Company)

All out-doors
      invites your Kodak

EASTMAN KODAK COMPANY, Rochester, N. Y., *The Kodak City*

Plate 16. Advertisement for Autographic camera featuring two women and a man outdoors, early 1920s. (Reprinted courtesy of Eastman Kodak Company)

4

"Proudly Displayed by Wearers of Chic Ensembles"

Vanity Cameras, Kodak Girls, and the Culture of Female Fashion

I N THE fall of 1927, just as American women were slipping into
dresses that exposed their knees for the first time, Kodak commissioned the well-known industrial designer Walter Dorwin Teague
to create a camera for the "style-conscious woman." The result was
the Series III Vest Pocket Vanity Kodak. Covered with embossed
leather and ornamented with an Art Deco metal design, the matching
camera and case came in five colors: Sea Gull (gray), Cockatoo (green),
Redbreast (red), Bluebird (blue), and Jenny Wren (brown). Using the
basic framework of the Folding Vest Pocket camera, Teague designed
the Vanity Kodak to be thin, sleek, and held like the flat "envelope"
purses popular during the mid- to late 1920s—that is, with one's
fingers slipped seductively underneath a strap.

Indeed, Teague modeled the camera entirely on concepts of the
modern handbag. For fashion-conscious women in the 1920s, hand-
bags were among the most important of accessories, their colors, lin-
ings, pockets, and clasps all carefully considered in the act of purchase. "The fair purchaser of this day," according to two fashion
historians, "inspected with concern the silk and suede lining, the
number of inner pockets, and the vanity accessories which must accompany every up-to-date bag" (Lester and Oerke 424). Generally
these accessories included a compact, lipstick case, and change purse,
a fact apparently not lost on Teague; when he issued the Vanity Kodak
Ensemble in the spring of 1928, it consisted of a color-coordinated
camera, lipstick case, compact, mirror, and change purse, "all nestling
among ripples of moiré silk" (plate 12). Kodak commissioned Richard

110 ◇ Hudnut Cosmetics to create the compact and lipstick, specifying in a letter to one of its designers that "the shades should be those which are in greatest demand and therefore suitable for the majority of complexions."[1]

"It is the ideal accessory—highly useful, highly ornamental and intensely personal in character," announced one advertisement. "As an addition to one's ensemble, it is nothing if not chic." According to the fashion historian Julian Robinson, "chic" emerged in the late 1920s as the operative word for describing everything the American public perceived as modern, in vogue, and exquisite, from bobbed hair to motor cars (78). Another advertisement even went so far as to proclaim the camera the hit of the fashion season: "Swagger . . . aristocratic . . . modernity at its best . . . those are words to describe what is probably the most momentous addition this spring to the correct ensemble." In this description, as in all descriptions of the Vanity Kodak, the language of fashion displaces attention to mechanical or technical considerations. What's obviously most important here is how the camera looks—how it coordinates with one's clothing, how it fits into one's hand. "Even before one snaps a picture, one carries a new and intriguing detail of costume-accessory exquisitely in key with the current trend toward color and novelty," claims another advertisement, implying that the actual taking of pictures is indeed an ancillary consideration.

Beginning in July 1928, the *Kodak Salesman* offered detailed advice on how to sell the Vanity Kodak. In one article written for the monthly column "Selling to Women," a "feminine authority on retail salesmanship" named Ruth Leigh proffers the following tips:

> Bright color, swagger style, chic effect, snappy lines—that's what interests Miss America today. Salesmen who sell to the modern woman must consequently adjust their selling talks and describe their goods in vivid style language.
>
> So with selling Vanity Kodaks to women. Regular camera sales talk is not spirited enough. You may have to jazz it up, make it snap with style. Forget that you're selling a piece of photographic mechanism. Sell a Vanity Kodak that's style, color, a chic costume accessory. (July 1928, 9)

An entire column dedicated to "selling to women" indicates Kodak's perception of female consumers as requiring a special kind of attention.[2] Anticipating that such fashion rhetoric may not come easily to the typical salesman, the writer proceeds with detailed instructions on what to say and even how to hold the camera. "Now these airy, feminine arguments may not fall lightly from your tongue, when you're accustomed to speaking glibly of levers, shutters, lenses, and focusing. You may have to practice opening up a Vanity Kodak gift box, and holding the case daintily (yes) before your debutante customer" (ibid.). The camera salesman here becomes reshaped into a fashion consultant; just as the gross materiality of relic becomes the immateriality of nostalgic image, as we shall see in the following chapter, so the salesperson who traffics in *things* becomes the expert on *appearances*.

Thus, among other qualities, he must have some knowledge of color, a matter that acquired unprecedented fashion significance in the 1920s as a result of advances in the dye and textile industries. Beginning in the early 1920s, colors such as bright red and yellow were refashioned into desirable signifiers of vibrancy and lightheartedness, as opposed to their nineteenth-century associations with garishness (Robinson 4). What's more, the new names used to describe them—such as the "Seagull" and "Jenny Wren" of the Vanity Kodak—were now equated with the subtleties of supposedly feminine moods and personalities, thus solidifying the modern phenomenon of using color to signify sexual difference. "Color is the characteristic to accent in your sales talk. To do this, select a color of Vanity Kodak that matches or harmonizes with the coat, suit, dress, or hat your customer is wearing. . . . By connecting the Vanity Kodak with a color worn by your customer, you make a strong personal appeal, and, when you talk of 'fashionable colors' that match what she is wearing, you flatter her a bit" (July 1928, 10). Indeed, judging by most of these columns, the necessity of flattery became one of the most frequently repeated tips to Kodak salesmen, implying that the sale of cameras to women rested on a kind of legitimized flirtation rather than the communication of practical information or knowledge.

The Vanity Kodak sold for only two years, ostensibly because women found it difficult to match the color of a camera with their clothing. This forgotten product marks the culmination of forty years of sustained effort to align photography with feminine beauty and fashion. The Vanity Kodak aestheticized the play of snapshot photography, its chic design testifying to the new importance placed on the look of a mass-manufactured object as opposed to its use value.[3] If the Brownie signified Kodak's reinvention of the camera into a toy, the

112   Vanity Kodak represented its evolution into a gadget. Like toys, gad-
◇   gets define our relationship with objects as playful rather than utili-
tarian. They symbolize a frivolous economy. Gadgets differ from toys,
however, in their association with both novelty and (short-lived) admiration. A toy can remain a beloved object for years, even generations; gadgets die young. And while toys can perform useful functions,
such as training children for certain adult activities, gadgets are "fab-
ricated not to be used but to be admired" (Richards 35). Gadgets thus
belong to the realm of fashion, embodying as they do the pleasures of
novelty, innovation, and a kind of defiant uselessness.

Fashion restricts itself, for the most part, to the universe of
women. It gives preeminence to—indeed, even makes sacred—the
concepts of feminine beauty and sexuality.[4] Through the image of
the Kodak Girl, Kodak thus charged its advertisements with an eroti-
cism that conflated feminine beauty with the attractions of snapshot
photography.

Anna Wintour notes the importance of snapshots in the twentieth-
century formation of fashion photography, which gains much of its seductive appeal, she argues, through "the illusion of spontaneity and
therefore absolute credibility" that snapshots provide (19). But ads
featuring the Kodak Girl also suggest that discourses on fashion may
have influenced early twentieth-century uses of the snapshot. At least,
it is clear that Kodak's advertising department intended such an
influence, for these ads clearly aim at encouraging female viewers to
see snapshot photography as a practice akin to fashion—as an activity that could enable them to constantly remake the images that purported to represent their lives, just as clothes allowed them to constantly remake their self-image, into objects of desire.

Like the world of leisure and childhood, then, fashion takes play
as its modus operandi. Its time, like that of play, is the present. Indeed,
fashion represents the tyranny of the present. Roland Barthes describes fashion as a discourse that vehemently denies the possibility of
any relation with its own past; he calls it fashion's "refusal to inherit"
(*Fashion System* 7). Fashion also promises the play of endless repetition—a never-ending story of beautiful clothes and styles—as opposed to narrative, whose attraction resides precisely in its promise of
an ending. By linking its products and models with contemporary
fashion trends, Kodak thus implied that photography would be a witness of glamour rather than drudgery, the amateur photographer an
expert on haute couture rather than lenses. More important, it sug-

gested that photography's ontology resided in the play of appearances. 113
If, as Jean Baudrillard argues, "the signs of fashion are free-floating
and not grounded in the referential" (*Jean Baudrillard* 97), then Kodak's use of fashion insinuated that snapshots, like beautiful clothes,
also played with the pleasures of surface, with the delectable viewing
of perfect appearances. Emphasis on fashion, then, extended Kodak's
promotion of photography as play, which, as Johan Huizinga argues,
"always has a tendency toward beauty" (4).

Romancing the Photographer

In *The Desire to Desire,* Mary Ann Doane rehearses an assumption
common in feminist critiques of consumer culture: that "woman's objectification, her susceptibility to processes of fetishization, display,
profit and loss, the production of surplus value, all situate her in a relation of resemblance to the commodity form" (22). Like commodities,
women have been shaped by consumer culture as teemingly seductive,
their allure as much a formation of consumer culture as that of the
commodity. Unquestionably, Eastman's original reason for deploying
the image of the Kodak Girl was that a "picture of a pretty girl," as he
so prosaically phrased it, "sells more than a tree or a house" (quoted
in Brayer 135). Eastman carefully envisioned the look of the woman he
would use for his products: beautiful but wholesome, "fashionably
dressed" but not "too unapproachable." In the advertisements that
would feature such a woman, Eastman imagined, her accentuated
characteristics—sophistication, attractiveness, and "simplicity"—
would duplicate the very qualities the company promoted as distinguishing its products from those of other manufacturers. Right from
the beginning, then, Eastman envisioned a female sales model who
would not only represent his vision of the new amateur photographer
but also function as an object of massified desire.[5]

Roughly fifteen years later, between 1900 and 1905, the use of
beautiful women to endorse commodities was the most frequently discussed topic in advertising journals. In a 1902 article titled "Beauty in
Advertising Illustration," for example, the writer even points to the Kodak Girl to show how the image of an attractive young woman can validate the quality of a product:

> What is the psychology of using a pretty face? The humblest that
> travels and reads will tell you that he is mysteriously inclined

to regard the mechanical adjustment of the covered apparatus which hangs at the charming young woman's hip as being of a highly superior order of merit because of the beauty of face and raiment. Certainly no young woman who can dress so cleverly and with such good taste would be guilty of carrying a camera not of the most skillful mechanical construction. (Walker 497)

The allusion here to "the humblest" of magazine readers anticipates a fundamental tenet of advertising, suggesting as it does that advertisers profit by appealing to an instinctive sexual response supposedly common to all male viewers (whatever their background or education) rather than to reason or judgment. Outside the realm of technical knowledge, but squarely situated within the sphere of fashion and beauty, the woman sells products effectively because she appeals to masculine desire.

More surprising, however, is the author's suggestion that the woman's fashion sense acts as an indicator of the mechanically superior products she endorses, as if an appreciation of mechanical efficiency requires nothing more than an attention to appearance. In light of this observation, we might note the author's use of the word "clever" to compliment the way the model dresses, an adjective often deployed to describe products that are "handy, convenient, and easy to use."[6] Hence a description meant to praise a woman's apparel conflates with the characteristics one ideally seeks in a camera, testifying even further to the confluence of women and commodities in consumer culture.

The first mention of the Kodak Girl in company correspondence appears in November 1892, several months after Eastman hired L. B. Jones as Kodak's advertising manager (Brayer 135). It is not known for certain whether Eastman or Jones came up with the idea of employing a beautiful young woman as Kodak's central advertising image, but it seems likely that the conception was Eastman's. In 1886 he used a line drawing of a pretty young woman in his advertisements for the Eastman-Walker Roller Holder, the first invention for which he launched a major advertising campaign. The woman's elaborate costume (complete with white gloves, no less!) is designed to suggest the facility with which the amateur photographer could develop her own film. In 1889 Eastman hired one of his employees, a secretary named Kitty Kramer, to pose with the No. 2 box camera (figure 24). Since the halftone process could not yet reproduce photographs with the kind of

Figure 24. Advertisement with Kitty Kramer, Kodak's first sales model, holding Kodak No. 2 camera, 1890. (Reprinted courtesy of Eastman Kodak Company)

clarity Eastman desired, this advertisement never appeared in magazines, but it was distributed widely in the form of posters, circulars, fliers, and pamphlets. It seems, then, that even though the official image of the Kodak Girl did not materialize until 1893, she was clearly in the making.

116   When two female employees did make an official appearance as
◇   the Kodak Girls at the Chicago world's fair, they showed up in tailored
dresses with mutton sleeves, a costume that represented the latest in
travel fashion because it allowed relatively unhampered movement.
The artist strategically posed them in front of the fair's Art Palace, a
building named for its architectural grandeur as well as the artistic
"masterpieces" it housed. Writing a year after the fair, one historian
described the palace in adulatory terms: "No structure among the
many which made up the White City commanded more universal admiration than did the Art Palace, wherein were displayed the triumphs
of artists from all over the world" (Weber 66).

    The Art Palace was among the buildings visitors lauded as "ma-
jestic," "stately," and "dignified" in the fair's White City district. As
David Nasaw describes it, this synthetic city was carefully designed as
an "urban utopia made possible through the judicious application and
administration of industry, technology, learning, and high culture" (67)
(as opposed to the fair's midways, which reputedly featured "tasteless"
forms of entertainment designed for working-class visitors). As the
showcase of the White City, the Art Palace thus provided the perfect
backdrop for accentuating the upper-middle-class beauty of these
young women while also linking amateur photography to refinement,
high culture, and good taste. Soon afterward, the resulting sketch was
used for worldwide advertising. In addition, framed copies of views of
the exposition featuring one of the two Kodak Girls were supplied as
promotions to some of the leading photographic journals.

    From this year forward, both Eastman and Jones devoted careful
attention to the process of hiring models (several of whom were Kodak employees), choosing their costumes, and selecting appropriate
scenery and settings for the ads that would feature them. In later
years, Eastman even consulted his female friends on the matter, inviting them for lobster dinners at his home, where they discussed, among
other topics, the latest fashions in *Vogue* magazine. By the mid-teens,
the Kodak Girl's striped summer dress had become so popular that the
"costumers" Mssrs. Fenwick of Bond Street, London, were advertising
"Kodak striped sun frocks in macclesfield crepe."[7]

    After 1900, Kodak's advertising department began to employ pro-
fessional photographers such as William Shewell Ellis, a wedding photographer, to take photos for the Kodak Girl campaign. Known especially for his portraits of young women, Ellis produced some of Kodak's

most artistic advertising photographs. These images reveal Ellis's penchant for soft focus and lighting, techniques designed to etherealize the face and figure of the model, as in figure 25. Here light falls on the slightly exposed shoulder of the Kodak Girl as she looks directly at the viewer in a way that suggests coyness as well as availability, or what one historian has described as "fashion's perpetual combination of the chaste and erotic" (Breward 15).

In all likelihood, Eastman and Jones gained much of their inspiration for the Kodak Girl from Charles Dana Gibson, the American illustrator who made a career of drawing beautiful young women.[8] In 1890 Gibson produced the image that became famous as the Gibson Girl, whom he fashioned as elegant, robust, well-bred, chaste, unchaperoned, and adventurous. Her hair swirled upward and her head held high, she reigned as the American standard of beauty in women until roughly 1915 (figure 26). She enjoyed her greatest popularity in the 1890s, when representations of the archetypal New Woman flourished. As critics such as Martha Patterson have argued, the Gibson Girl "legitimized, democratized, and commercialized" the New Woman (73). Her relative independence challenged assumptions of women's innate frailty, an argument frequently advanced to discourage women from pursuing such New Woman ambitions as a college education or a political career. And although this independence was manifested in the Gibson Girl's participation in athletic activities and choice of costume rather than a commitment to societal reform, many New Women adopted her image to legitimize their own reform efforts. Charlotte Perkins Gilman, in fact, extolled the Gibson Girl as "braver, stronger, more healthful and skillful and able and free, more human in all ways" (quoted in Banner 156).

Of almost amazonian height and proportions, the Gibson Girl's body was clearly that of the "natural" and not overrefined or dainty woman. Yet, as a figure who focused all of her energies on maintaining her image and acquiring a mate, a woman seemingly innocent in her sexuality, the Gibson Girl also contained the threat of sexual expression and freedom frequently associated with the New Woman. "Indeed," argues Patterson, "although Gibson seldom pictured her with offspring, the Gibson Girl promised fertility if not maternal devotion since she attended to men and the mirror rather than books" (74). Less threatening than most depictions of the New Woman and yet more liberated than other representations that still sought to

Its just great here. When
you come be sure to bring
your Kodak. The opportunities
for snapping the people and
places are keeping mine
delightfully busy.   Jane.

Figure 25. William S. Ellis photograph of Kodak Girl, 1910s. (Reprinted
courtesy of Eastman Kodak Company)

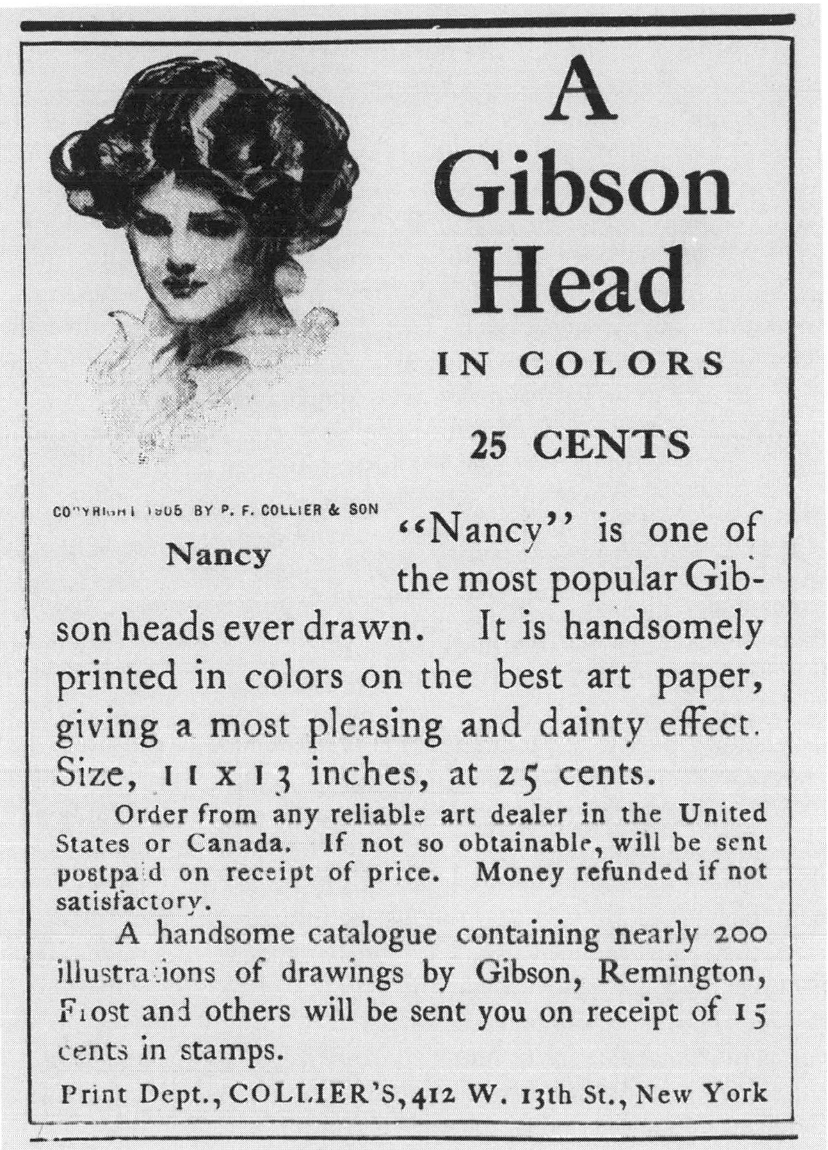

Figure 26. Gibson Girl advertisement, *Collier's*, 1905.

120 characterize American womanhood as "delicate," the Gibson Girl
◇   served to negotiate the intense debates over the value of female independence in the 1890s and early 1900s.

It is not surprising, then, that she emerged as the most popular of
all images of American womanhood in circulation during this period.
As Lois W. Banner notes, attempts to depict the American Girl were
quite common in the 1890s, with illustrators such as Harry McVickar
and S. W. Van Schaik capitalizing on a cultural desire to define a quin-
tessential American spirit through the spontaneity, wholesomeness,
and vitality of a young woman. These graphic artists controlled the
meanings and reception of images of American beauty during this
time because their art reached a mass audience and could thus realize the greatest commercial value. The Gibson Girl stood out among
other representations, however, because more than anything else, she
functioned as *image*. Not associated with one particular movement,
region, or philosophy, engaged in a continual metamorphosis through
her attention to gesture, pose, and fashion, she represented the fluid-
ity of image-making. "The Gibson Girl," argues Patterson, "proved
that one could become the image that one saw—an image of a desir-
ing/desirable subject, expertly managing the desire she evokes" (81).

In only a few years, her image appeared in popular magazines,
novels, and theatrical productions, and on pompadours, silverware,
chinaware, corsets, perfume, calendars, flasks, cigarette cases,
brooches, and more. All over the country little girls wanted to be just
like her when they grew up, no matter what their family situation,
though her look and surroundings clearly indicated an upper-class urban milieu. A glorious image, she justified the existence of the upper
class that had produced her. Through her image, Americans of all
backgrounds were invited to identify with a world of glamour and fantasy. In this sense, she embodied what Gilles Lipovetsky sees as the
democratizing value of fashion—the ability to unite people of all
classes, ages, and races through a desire (however hopeless it may be)
for a certain kind of appearance.

To participate in such democratization of desire, of course, one
must also participate in a consumer economy. And this point, perhaps,
gets at the real essence of the Gibson Girl's popularity. Always beauti-
fully dressed, engaged in constant travel and other costly forms of
amusement, she represented the new purchasing power of the female
consumer, reminding female viewers, no matter what their back-

ground and class status, that by consuming goods one could produce a better self. "Gibson Girl images embodied the values necessary to sustain a consumer-based economy—discernment, purchasing power, and insatiable demand—thereby harnessing and transforming the New Woman's desire for social and political change into a desire for new goods" (Patterson 74). And although this transformation obviously served to displace desire for intellectual and social freedom into the realm of consumerism, it also performed a liberating function for women. As Rita Felski has also argued, "the category of consumption situated femininity at the heart of the modern in a way that the discourses of production and rationalization previously did not" (61). Through consumerism, women could participate in the shaping of modernity, their status as consumers giving them an intimate familiarity with the rapidly changing fashions and lifestyles that were an important part of the felt experience of being modern.

Like the woman who possibly inspired her, the Kodak Girl combined independence with an air of charm, grace, and style. Just as important, she also represented the pleasures of consumerism, her beauty standing not only for Americans' new attraction to snapshot photography but for the enjoyment that comes with the purchase of consumer goods. While Kodak's male models are generally pictured as *taking* photographs, she is often represented as looking down at her camera, handling it with an obvious admiration and satisfaction that speaks of its status as a special commodity. Just as she desires the camera, moreover, the viewer is encouraged to desire her. On one level, of course, her beauty is designed to arouse the male viewer, the female labor of consumption explicitly mirroring his desire of the desiring subject. On another level, the beauty of the Kodak Girl as she "consumes" her camera is also designed to appeal to women, who presumably love to see attractive women in fashionable clothes because, as Iris Marion Young argues, such images "encourage fantasies of transport and transformation" (206). Appearing here as icons of consumption, their lovely, fashionably dressed bodies the specific sites of advertised spectacle, Kodak Girls invite the female consumer to see them as reflections of their own idealized selves.

In no set of advertisements does the Kodak Girl more clearly evoke the image of Gibson's creation than in those produced between 1901 and 1903 (figures 27, 28, 29). Her dark hair swept up in the prevailing pompadour, the woman who modeled for these advertisements,

Figure 27. Kodak Girl advertisement, 1901. (Reprinted courtesy of Eastman Kodak Company)

Figure 28. Kodak Girl advertisement, 1901. (Reprinted courtesy of Eastman Kodak Company)

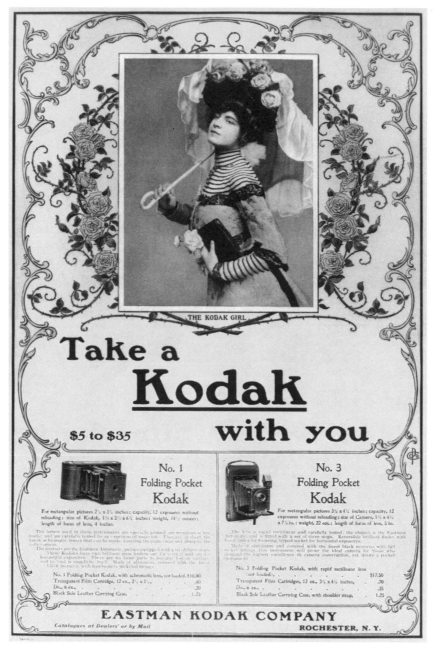

Figure 29. Kodak Girl advertisement, 1901. (Reprinted courtesy of Eastman Kodak Company)

Maude Marguerite McConnell, conveys the elegant imperiousness of the Gibson Girl herself. Like Gibson's creation, she lends these advertisements a kind of aristocratic grace, her pose and expression exuding self-possession bordering on haughtiness. And like the Gibson Girl, she seems to possess the ability to transform virtually any object she encounters into a fashion accessory; in these advertisements, as in so many of the ads featuring the Kodak Girl, her camera serves to complement her beauty as much as the stylish clothes she wears.

All three of these advertisements, in fact, demonstrate an almost fastidious attention to costume. In all three, for example, the Kodak Girl wears a gown that embodies one of fashion's most important tenets: adaptability to change. That is, each costume includes detachable trimmings: the high-necked yoke of heavy lace in figure 27, the chiffon scarf in figure 28, and the wrist-length sleeves in figure 29, which she could shorten to the elbow by unfastening several buttons. According to the fashion historian Christopher Breward, such accessories were meant to convey to women how easily they could transform their appearance with the help of a few relatively inexpensive items.[9] Other noteworthy items are the roses that adorn the Kodak Girl's parasol and waist in figure 29. Martha Banta locates a recurring visual formula in late nineteenth-century depictions of young women that she playfully describes as "roses at the breast" (71). A variation on the ageless convention that associates pleasing femininity with flowers, this formula was most often employed, Banta notes, for portraits of debutantes, the just-opening blossoms signifying their own recent development into womanhood. Although the flowers have shifted from breast to waist (no Kodak Girl ever exposed cleavage!), they still evoke the rose's traditional associations with romance and at the same time recall the more recent images of young society women in demure poses.

It was these three advertisements, along with roughly ten more produced between 1901 and 1903 featuring the same unidentified woman, that transformed the Kodak Girl into an international celebrity. Ms. McConnell's debut, in fact, marked the most extensive campaign to date featuring the Kodak Girl; in May and June 1901, she was featured on the back covers of the *Ladies' Home Journal* and the *Woman's Home Companion* and on the front cover of the *Saturday Evening Post*—at roughly $4,000 each time. Not coincidentally, these

126   were also the first photographic images of the Kodak Girl to be dis-
◇   tributed in magazines. Indeed, the amazing popularity of these ads
stemmed from the fact that they were photographs. "The ideal aesthetic pleasure clothes can give," writes Anne Hollander, "the sparks
of visual delight they can strike, are always largely in debt to the
ideal fictions the lens has created, the vivid images that give fashion
its true life" (46). Photography, that is, makes fashion come alive; no
wonder, then, that Kodak's advertising department paid such care-
ful attention to the Kodak Girl's clothes and general appearance for
this particular series of advertisements, for Jones and the others probably guessed that Kodak's introduction of the reproduced photograph
would direct a new kind of attention to its models and thus to all they
embodied.

     Between 1901 and roughly 1910, but especially during the first few
years of the century, the Kodak Girl inspired dozens of poems, love letters, essays, songs, musicals, and even an operetta, *The Girl from Kodak Town*.[10] "In the first years of her presentation," a former Kodak
employee observed, "Miss Kodak probably elicited more metric feet of
poetry than any publicly heralded beauty since Helen of Troy. And
while men responded to her more personal charms, fashion-conscious
American womanhood avidly awaited her next appearance in order to
see what she was wearing 'this time'" (quoted in "Kodak Girls" 1). In
virtually all of these texts, she emerged as locus of masculine desire,
her youthful body, fashionable costuming, and beautiful face standing
in metonymic relation to the newly constructed erotic qualities of
commodities in general and snapshots in particular.

     An article in *Cosmopolitan's* fashion column testifies to just how
significant a presence she had become in American culture by the end
of 1901:

> The ever lovely Kodak Girl appears in some new "fixins." What
> a wardrobe she has got, lucky girl! But the clothes are not the
> whole story by any means. The writer personally knows half a
> hundred swains who fell in love at the start before they were
> aware that she has more than one summer frock and a parasol. It
> is not violating any confidence to admit that down to the last hall-
> boy, the males in this office are on the list of the fatally wounded.
> That is, the unmarried males, of course. Since she began to mul-
> tiply costume upon costume it is hard to decide how we like her

best. Her latest is for such of us as admire simplicity with the touch of the antique—in apparel, not features. (Quoted in "Kodak Girls" 3)

The most salient aspect of this passage is the lack of attention it pays to photography; indeed, photography receives no mention here, subsumed as it is by expressions of romantic attraction and fashion curiosity.

The author's closing remark, in which he describes the Kodak Girl as combining "simplicity with the touch of the antique," also invites attention, for the phrase underscores the relatively conservative look of the Kodak Girl in relation to other feminine icons of the time. Beginning sometime around the turn of the century, advertisers expressed increasing concern over the danger of exposing too much flesh in advertisements. "At one period there was a disposition to indelicate drapings," notes one writer in 1901, "but in the course of time it came to be understood that good taste required that everything offensive should be eliminated, and that that advertisement was most effective which attracted all and offended none" (Walker 495). Kodak's advertising department apparently adhered to this tenet; in several of the ads featuring the Kodak Girl, she is costumed in clothing that, while clearly fashionable, remains somewhat quaint, as if the company were reluctant to associate its models with too much novelty. Even fashion, then, gets subsumed by nostalgia; that is, by the predilection for a kind of old-fashioned beauty she apparently represents.

Her face featured in full-page ads, posters, and billboards across the world, the Kodak Girl became a kind of precursor to the Hollywood star, a prima ballerina of photography, as this 1904 ditty by one of her devotees reveals:

THE WITCHERY OF KODAKERY

No wonder where the Kodak is
    A witchery is nigh;
For, see! the witch approaches,
    With enchantment in her eye.
And I feel the luring magic
    Of each dainty, rose-crowned curl

128

◇

As I view the pictured features
    Of the Ko-dak Girl.

With the neatest little,
    Fleetest little,
Sweetest little glance
    From sparkling eyes that under
Shyly drooping lashes dance,
    She comes—a breath of summer
When the finest flowers unfurl!
    Oh, the airy, fairy beauty
    Of the Ko-dak Girl!

I can read an incantation
    On the full and curving lips
I can feel her spell around me
    As across the page she trips
And I vow my sole ambition
    Through life's gay and giddy whirl
Is just to press the button
    For the Kodak Girl. . . .

                    ("Kodak Girls" 5)

The obvious flirtation with rhyme and metonymy in such poems—and there were many—mirrors the supposed desire of the author for his subject. The "restlessness of metonymy," as Ronald Schleifer says of the lyrics of Cole Porter, here conveys the speaker's unsatisfied yearning for the Kodak Girl. Here, as in fashion, style is meaning, and meaning is desire. The metonymic description of the Kodak Girl— eye, curl, lashes, lips—conveys how fully she performed in the popular imagination as object of mass vision and desire, her face and body— presumably those of a photographer—ironically subjected to the gaze of the camera and viewers. Indeed, like most people who wrote about the Kodak Girl, this rhymester never mentions her role as photographer; in fact, he closes the poem by articulating his desire to "push the button" for the Kodak Girl. Bordering on sexual innuendo, the phrase clearly displaces her role as photographer with her role as object of romantic attraction (her skill at "kodakery" is clearly secondary to her skill at "witchery").

Arguably, the overwhelming popular interest in the Kodak Girl stemmed in part from the company's decision to withhold the identities of its models. Judging by an article in the *St. Louis Post-Dispatch* in 1903 headed "The Romance and Mystery of the Kodak Girl," a national campaign almost seems to have been launched to track her down. "Who is the Kodak Girl? She is the best known girl in America, yet nobody knows her. Her face and form are familiar to the people beyond the seas, but her identity is a mystery as deep as those same seas. . . . Men have fallen in love with her picture and with a sort of hopeless hope have written to the Kodak company, requesting her identity" (18). Instinctively, it seems, Eastman and Jones knew it was good business to keep the names of their models a secret, that their models' anonymity would help ensure their status as icons of eternal youth. Identity assigns mortality, dooming the model to popular recognition of the eventual—and always too sudden—aging of her body.

This issue emerged as a key subject in women's magazines around the turn of the century, testifying to a growing awareness that photography required an almost prepubescent youth of its models: "Mature beauty is not worth a continental to the camera. Tiny lines that the eye would never observe are distinct upon a negative, and the photographer can not be bothered with retouching. A woman now in her late twenties is more beautiful than ever, but no longer in a girlish way; and the public has wearied of her face connected with every cosmetic on the market. . . . Some photographers put eighteen, some twenty, others twenty-two as the age limit. I have never heard of any older ones who were in demand" (Comstock 17). In contrast to the body we see on the page, the body of lived experience is subject to change, transformation, and, most important, death. The idealized body of the advertising model denies death—it participates in the realm of transcendence and immortality, a realm of the classic as opposed to the natural. And the Kodak model, who changed with the coming of every new year beginning in 1904, remained outside lived experience. Like the snapshots she took, she resisted the natural processes of time— frozen, it seems, in a beautiful world whose principal characteristic, like that of fashion, was its refusal to ripen.

Illustrating the Kodak Girl

Beginning in 1895, Kodak's advertising department began to employ such famous illustrators as Claude Shepperson, Dudley Harvey, Horace Rich, and Fred Pegram to "lend a painter's sense of grace," as

130   Jones described it, to the image of the Kodak Girl (quoted in "Kodak
◇   Girls" 3). Indeed, of all campaigns produced by the company during
these forty-four years, the series of advertisements featuring the Kodak Girl enlisted the greatest number of illustrators at the highest
fees. Fred Pegram, for example, was paid $1,500 for one of his paint-
ings of the model. Kodak increasingly deployed simple and seemingly
artless snapshots for ads promoting the attractions of home and family, particularly after 1915; the watercolor and oil paintings it commissioned were reserved largely for the Kodak Girl. And while photographs certainly attracted international attention to her image,
especially between 1901 and 1904, illustrations also played a pivotal
role in her popularity. No doubt such images were intended to convey
the Kodak Girl's associations with beauty and desire in a way that the
camera, because of its realism, could not.

As most art historians would agree, the decades between 1880 and
1930 were the golden age of illustration, a time when noted illustrators
such as Norman Rockwell enjoyed unprecedented authority in determining and shaping American responses to art.[11] Michele H. Bogart
suggests that we might see illustration during this period as "a new vo-
cation structurally bound up on the one side with fine art, and on the
other side with the development of national advertising and mass-
marketing publishing" (16). Illustrators thus inhabited two worlds,
bridging the gap between the exclusive and confined world of fine art
and the massified demands of the consumer public. By 1910, advertisements had become "bigger, bolder, and more calculatedly artistic,"
Bogart observes, as magazine publishers and advertisers came to realize that an illustration of high quality could indicate that both the
advertiser and the purchasing public were people of good taste and
cultural refinement (25).

Without doubt, Kodak advertisements—especially those produced between roughly 1900, when ads moved away from line drawings, to roughly 1915, before the war would put greater emphasis on
"realism"—aimed at an aura of artistic flair and style. One of Kodak's
most common techniques during this period was the use of an ornate
frame around the photos featured in its advertisements. Another strategy was to borrow designs and motifs from the Art Nouveau movement, noted for its efforts to transmute such everyday objects as lamps
and tables into things of seemingly organic beauty.

One of the most stunning illustrations of the Kodak Girl produced during this time features her in "fair Japan." Drawn by C. Allan Gilbert, it first appeared in magazines in the fall of 1905, the year of Japan's victory over Russia and the beginning of what many historians describe as the country's Westernization (plate 13). Advertisements depicting the Kodak Girl in foreign countries outside Europe are so rare that the choice of Japan as a setting invites questioning. Up until 1899, the year in which Japan's treaties with various Western countries were revised so as to allow increased travel, it was quite difficult for Western tourists to visit Japan. By 1905, travel had opened up considerably but the number of people who journeyed there was still quite small. It is precisely because of its isolation that Japan became such a locus of fantasy for Westerners in the nineteenth century. Known as a country of exotic beauties and of supposed diminutiveness, Japan was frequently described by Victorian writers as "toy-like." One traveler described it as a "world where everything is upon a smaller and daintier scale than with us—a world of lesser and seemingly kindlier beings, all smiling at you as if to wish you well, a world where land, life, and sky are unlike all that one has known elsewhere—this is surely the realisation, for imagination nourished with English folklore, of the old dream of a world of Elves" (quoted in Lehmann 45). Note what the Kodak Girl is presumably about to photograph. On the left side of the advertisement stands a lantern, which serves as a visual marker for a Japanese garden. She is thus about to take a snapshot of what late nineteenth- and early twentieth-century viewers might have seen as a metonym for Japan, the garden embodying all the exoticism and quaintness, the diminutiveness, that Western culture has invested in the country. Her tiny camera, representing one of the West's technological triumphs, thus becomes a perfect implement for seeing and representing this tiny country—a country that ironically has since produced photography's most avid practitioners, and that in 1905 was well on its way to the modernization the Kodak Girl represents.

The advertisement's focus on Japan is thus designed to accentuate the Kodak Girl's beauty, youth, and charm. Note how she is figured in relation to the Japanese man pulling the ricksha. On one level, her whiteness stands in sharp contrast to his darker skin and clothing. Whiteness thus seems to define and penetrate the Kodak Girl, as it does the image of the American Girl in general. Implicit in her representation is racial purity, the supremacy of the nation she represents over the country she visits and photographs. Such supremacy is

132   reinforced by the beauty and obvious expense of her clothes, the sheer
◇   whiteness of her chiffon dress and touring veil lending her body an al-
      most ethereal quality, particularly in contrast to the presumably time-
      worn utilitarian clothes of the man pulling her in the ricksha.

      But consider also her resemblance to the man who transports her
so slavishly. Gilbert paints both figures in profile, with their gaze in
precisely the same direction. The similarity of their expressions, poses,
and even facial features forms a stunning focal point for this advertisement, suggesting as it does the confluence of American and Japanese beauty. The confluence is reinforced by the advertisement's use
of watercolor, a traditionally Asian art form that became popular in
the United States in the late nineteenth century, to represent the aesthetic appeal of snapshot photography.

      Indeed, the use of watercolor invites particular attention, since it
was so frequently deployed for ads featuring the Kodak Girl.[12] In the
early twentieth century, watercolor remained in the popular imagination a somewhat "feminine" art, since it was the principal amateur
medium for leisured women in the late eighteenth and nineteenth
centuries (oil painting was generally considered too difficult for women
to manage successfully). If one of Kodak's aims was to realign the
practice of amateur photography with women, the exploitation of
watercolor illustrations visually reinforced such an association. Too,
watercolor had a traditional association with luxury; down through the
ages watercolors have been produced on such sensuous and expensive
materials as silk, ivory, and velvet (Koshkin-Youritzin 4).

      More important, watercolor is the art of atmosphere, its interest
directed toward mood and effect. Accurate representation of nature is
not critical in Japanese watercolor, for example; what matters much
more, as Frederick Wong phrases it, is a "successful realization of
the emotional impression of natural forms in their environment" (9).
In this sense, watercolor differs profoundly from photography, whose
metaphysics and ontology depend on the assumption of realism. By
associating snapshot photography with the medium of watercolor,
then, Kodak softened the harsh edges of the photograph, encouraging
viewers to regard it as the realization of feeling rather than fact.

      As Victor Koshkin-Youritzin notes, watercolor also lends itself to
intimacy: "While oil paint is suited to the slow, rich, three-dimensional
modeling often essential to history painting and other monumental
subject matter, watercolor, especially in its pure, transparent manner,

tends to be more suited to modest, intimate themes and to those that require intensely poetic handling" (13). In this sense, watercolor painting is kin to snapshot photography, both mediums having been constructed as suitable for the seemingly insignificant details that, within their metaphysics, become the sublime. Fashion, too, offers such a possibility in its power to transform someone's psychological state by such seemingly frivolous details as a silk lining or rhinestone button.

The End of Fashion

Kodak's association of its products with the discourses of fashion effectively ended with the Vanity Kodak, whose brief career underlines the growing difficulty of promoting snapshot photography as a medium that traffics in the novel and ephemeral. Even though Kodak models continued to grace pages of magazines for decades, they performed much less dramatically as fashion models, appearing more and more in the standard costume of the blue-and-white summer dress we saw in chapter 2, or in such athletic outfits as swimsuits and tennis clothes. Paintings of the Kodak Girl, moreover, all but disappeared by the mid-1930s, displaced by snapshots of her in generally conventional poses and settings.

Such an end has important implications when we consider that the histories of fashion and photography share a range of parallels, perhaps the most noteworthy one being their participation in the modern cult of individuality. "In essence," explains Lipovetsky, "haute couture substituted a multiplicity of styles for a uniform cut; it diversified and psychologized dress. It was pervaded by a utopian vision according to which each woman of taste had to be attired in a distinctive fashion adapted to her own particular 'type' and personality" (85). Until the nineteenth century, clothing was severely limited in its range of styles, fabrics, and accessibility, just as early photographic portraits were limited to a set of conventional poses, gestures, and props. By the 1880s, fashion had begun its entry into its present state—as a medium that allows for an endless repetition of seemingly individualized looks and performances, just as the abundance of snapshots occasioned by Kodak's establishment did. As Joanne Finkelstein argues, "fashion is not just about categorising and ranking culture; it is also about the manipulation of desire, pleasure and the play of the imagination" (37).

Seen this way, fashion liberates and democratizes. Seen this way,

134 the image of the Kodak Girl served an emancipating function for fe-
◇   male consumers. Beginning in the late nineteenth century, women
came to view fashion as one means of asserting both their individuality, however problematic such a notion was, and their participation in
the dynamics of modern culture. Georg Simmel argued that fashion,
with its emphasis on novelty and change, represented the essence of
modernity.[13] In his speculations on women's interest in fashion as an
expression of individuality and a symbolic articulation of a desire for
innovation and change, Simmel affirms a link between women and the
modern sensibility, which he sees as centering on the "shock of the
new" (303). Fashion thus emerges as one of the few avenues open to
women for participation in the shaping of modern culture. The preoccupation of women with fashionable dress, argued Simmel, relates
to the limitations they experience in other parts of their lives, and thus
is an ambiguous cultural phenomenon that may function as a form of
compensation and as an act of resistance.

Like most twentieth-century writers on fashion, Simmel recognizes the problems with such an argument, drawing our attention to
what many critics have since come to locate as fashion's inherent
hypocrisy: while fashion purports to accentuate individuality and personality, it bases its logic on convention. "Fashion," writes Simmel, "is
the imitation of a given example and satisfies the demand for social
adaptation" (296). Pressuring consumers to adopt an ever-changing
look, fashion encourages blind adaptation and reckless spending. It
provides the illusion of individuality, functioning as a semblance of or
substitute for much deeper desires. "Fashion always stands," Simmel
observes, "at the periphery of personality" (311).

What also complicates an affirmative view of fashion is its obvious
catering to the upper classes—a characteristic it shares with leisure
and antiques. "The very character of fashion demands that it should
be exercised at one time only by a portion of the given group. . . . As
fashion spreads, it gradually goes to its doom" (Simmel 302). This "select portion," Simmel makes clear, is composed solely of the wealthy.
Seen in this light, Kodak's discontinuance of fashion as a promotional
strategy possibly heralds a new democratizing strain in its advertising;
if fashion is indeed the amusement of the rich, its displacement by images and discourses of domestic life may point to an increasing desire
to appeal to a less exclusive audience, an effort to abandon Kodak's
hitherto unapologetic promotion of upper-class tastes and lifestyles.

Still, in curtailing its appeal to the uses and meanings of fashion, Kodak advertising also restricted our responses to photography in important ways. Simmel's discussion of how fashion may compensate for women's limited opportunities was based, as one might expect, on women's general restriction to household and family duties. Fashion, as Simmel viewed it, held the potential to draw women out of their private spheres and into the social world of exchange and novelty, stressing as it did adaptability to and tolerance of change. Perhaps more important, this shift from fashion to domesticity marks the end of Kodak's acknowledgment of photography's affinity for surface illusions. The ephemeral nature of fashion, coupled with the highly stylized illustrations that Kodak commissioned, promoted photography as mood, personality, style, desire. From the time ads became squarely situated in the home in the late 1920s, Kodak advertising purported to depict real lives in real settings. Playtime was now over.

5

"Kodak Knows No Dark Days"

The Disavowal of Death in Snapshot Photography and Advertising

To ENTER the archives of the George Eastman House, I must descend a stone staircase that winds me away from tourist traffic and into temperature-controlled stillness. At the foot of the stairs, I pass through a series of doors until I reach a room furnished, it seems, with only a table, chair, and mammoth computer. If I know the exact photograph I want to examine—say, Alfred Stieglitz's *Winter on Fifth Avenue*—a curator will retrieve it for me. Otherwise, I must search the computerized database, itself dazzling proof of the museum's ability to assemble and arrange the material evidence of human history. In the metonymic space of the computer screen, I can survey thousands of scanned photographs dating from the 1830s up to the present, each of them stamped with a digital number in the top left-hand corner. After I print out my selections, I hand them to a curator, who then withdraws to a room hidden from view. Several minutes later, he rolls out a cart stacked with the photographs, as if submitting bodies for an autopsy. I then slip white cotton gloves over my hands, ready at last to touch and dissect.

It is a curious experience to look at old photographs through digital technology, and to recognize that the photographs I am viewing, which may once have sat on someone's mantelpiece or nightstand, have now been numbered, catalogued, and ordered for history. But it is especially bizarre when the images are postmortem daguerreotypes—such as the one shown in figure 30—which by their very status as souvenirs of death resist all nostalgic overtures.

I inspect this one carefully. The child's emaciated face and frame,

Figure 30. Postmortem daguerreotype, 1850s. (Reprinted courtesy of George Eastman House)

her sunken eyes and aged look make me recoil. Like an optical illusion, this daguerreotype seems to produce two competing images, so that at one moment I see a child, the next an eighty-year-old woman. These death traces grimly undercut the immaculate aesthetic the photograph strives to achieve, with its attention to the child's delicate linen, the luxurious white pillow on which she rests, the obvious attempt to pose her as if asleep. Whatever "beauty" this image may have contained has withered, in fact is still withering, into dust.[1] Especially

138 because it has been housed in the mausoleum of the archive, this
◇   postmortem daguerreotype, representative of a practice that now
seems so alien to us, brutally disrupts and disclaims any connection to
the past. It does not invite us to enfold it into the present. I do not
want it in my home. Its place is there, in the archive, in the tomb. And
it is precisely because so much attention is given to preventing the
viewer from touching it that its meaning resides completely in its materiality. It offers physical remains that we can look at but never keep,
never want to keep.

One flight up, in the gift shop, visitors can also search through
a huge computer that for $5 will print out a reproduction of a photo-
graph in the museum's collection suitable for framing. It was in that
computer that I first encountered the advertisement seen in plate 14,
commissioned by Kodak in 1925. Although the image is actually a
watercolor illustration, it could not have looked more Kodak to me. No
occasion to mourn here: childhood in this "photograph" has been glo-
riously re-presented in springtime color, signifying not the frailty of
the past but its timelessness; the little girl in the far-right corner is
caught in the symbolic act of crossing a stream, resurrected, as it were,
from her previous entombment in the postmortem daguerreotype.

My immediate interest lies in the frame of this advertisement. The
apparent task of any frame is to draw attention away from itself and
toward the content it surrounds, endowing that content with significance, unifying its details, determining how they will be read. A
centralizing agent, the frame also serves to fragment and isolate. It
severs the image from the flux of the outside world, in this case even
from the advertisement that determines its reproduction, so that the
illustration is conveniently distanced from its own marketing.[2] Ornate
and ostentatious, the frame makes this particular image into an "an-
tiqued" representation, inviting us back through time with its mirrorlike aspect. Like Alice's looking glass, it transports us to the space of
nostalgia, into a still, bucolic world where Kodak cameras now keep
their fingers on the pulse of experience. In so doing, the advertisement
presents us with an image that, ironically, we have seen a hundred
times before, in our own family albums and those of our friends, in
photographs as recent as this year's. Memory here is bound up not in
the finality of death but in the idealized look of an archetypal past that,
like a piece of old china, provides the illusion of singularity even while
its duplicates sit in many dining rooms.

These two images, which differ so profoundly from each other in their representational aim and effect, represent two pivotal moments in the history of portrait photography and in the history of memory itself. With Kodak's invention, the portrait photograph was transmuted from relic to antique. In hundreds of radiant ads like the one in plate 14, the snapshot is rendered a thing of beauty whose most attractive feature, like that of all antiques, is its promise to facilitate a recollection of the good and a forgetting of the unpleasant. Bound as it is to nostalgia, which yearns for a prelapsarian experience untouched by pain and loss, snapshot photography as constructed by Kodak left no space for the kind of graphic and wounding representation exemplified by the postmortem daguerreotype.[3]

As a distinctly Victorian practice, postmortem photography signifies the pervasiveness of death as both reality and artistic subject in the mid–nineteenth century, when the average American adult could expect to live only forty years and when the accelerated rate of infant deaths, due in part to epidemics of cholera and tuberculosis, made children's connection to life seem especially tenuous.[4] Postmortem photography developed at such a surprising rate from the 1840s through the 1860s that it became a staple for many photographic businesses. Professional photographers even as late as the 1880s regularly specified in their advertisements "a readiness to make pictures from Corpses if desired" (quoted in Welling 61).

During photography's first few decades, in fact, people were more willing to pay $2 for a daguerreotype that memorialized a loved one's passing than they were to commemorate a marriage or birth.[5] Often they would commission a photographer to take pictures of the deceased only hours after he or she had passed away. These photographs would more than likely occupy a prominent place in the household, displayed on a mantelpiece or parlor table. One Victorian remarked of photos of his dead children thus exhibited, "The constant sight of them comforts me" (quoted in Jalland 290). The grim facticity of death thus enveloped early responses to photography just as it did everything else. Fearful of their mortality, many people embraced the new medium as a means of counteracting death. If their lives were to be short, their image at least could endure. If their lives had already been taken, the daguerreotypist could take a lasting portrait, preserving their bodies in the photograph's quiet and immobile world.

Just as important, postmortem photography points to a willingness to include in the space of the portrait photograph what is painful as well as what is celebratory. The fact that it was such a common

140
◇ practice testifies not only to the relative frankness with which people
confronted death in the nineteenth century; it reflects a culture still
experimenting with the uses of domestic photography and still willing
to be reminded that death awaits us all. This is not to argue, of course,
that photography before Kodak was not also enlisted to record scenes
of bright sentiment and events to be celebrated, but such uses constituted only one part of a range of practices and expectations for the
medium; while early and mid-nineteenth-century consumers would
visit a studio photographer to commemorate such occasions as the
birth of a child or a wedding, they also frequently requested his services to record not only the death of a relative but such other sorrow-
ful occurrences as the destruction of a house by fire or the loss of a
family pet. Snapshot photography, on the other hand, emerged as an
almost exclusively celebratory practice, as Douglas Collins has also
argued:

> From the beginning snapshots were intended to record events
> worth remembering mainly for the fondness of the happy
> emotional messages. To a large extent, the unexpressed and
> unexamined snapshot aesthetic of the early twentieth century
> overflowed with bright sentiment. Very few snapshooters, it
> seems, grabbed a camera for the purpose of recording times of
> sadness, family disruption, or personal disaster. What was worth
> remembering was worth remembering; what was not was not
> photographed. (121)

What, then, is worth remembering? The practice of photographing the
dead dramatizes photography's relation to memory before the advent
of Kodak advertising and the snapshot culture it produced. As Pat Jalland and other historians have made clear, one of the characteristics that so distinguishes nineteenth- and twentieth-century memory
practices is the relative willingness of the Victorians to indulge in
painful memories that sustained their grief. In the initial period of
deep grief, and often for long afterward, Victorian mourners sought
to keep the loved one's memory alive as vividly as possible through
paintings, drawings, photographs, busts, and death masks.[6] Their relation to memory was thus profoundly different from ours in this
sense, reflecting as it does a conception of memory as bound up in the
necessity, indeed the desirability, of mourning. Memory was widely
seen as a form of consolation for the bereaved, its painfulness desir-

able precisely because it seemed to keep the presence of the deceased
palpable.

As Matt Matsuda argues, memory should not be merely a theme to trace in texts or a convenient trope to impose generically upon material, but should be studied as a historical entity. "A truly historical project must be attentive to the ways in which 'memory' is not a generic term of analysis, but itself an object appropriated and politicized. Or, equally, nationalized, medicalized, aestheticized, gendered, bought and sold" (6). While it is not my intention here to undertake an extended analysis of the shifting meanings and uses of memory, I offer "relic" and "antique" as two possible ways of approaching memory as conditioned by domestic photography in the nineteenth and early twentieth centuries.

Bones, teeth, hair: this is the stuff we call "relic." Representing death in its crudest, most unadulterated form, the relic is that which remains after destruction or wasting away; it is remnant, residue. At least, it is this definition that primarily informs late twentieth-century thinking about relics. "'Relic' implies the idea of lifeless debris, of the dead shell of purposeful energy which has moved elsewhere," claims Susan Pearce. "But to an earlier age 'relic' meant the living dead at work amongst us, a voice from a past not left behind but entering into present life" (197). Pearce is simply articulating here what has by now become a truism—that a religious investment in relics was long ago dismissed by a secular age. The belief in a harmonious integration of the living and the dead as symbolized by the medieval relic now seems to most people like the remnant of a remote, naive, and almost make-believe age. Susan Stewart frames the transformation this way: "In contrast to the restoration offered by such gestures as the return of saints' relics, modern relics, such as the voodoo doll and the hunting trophy, mark the end of sacred narrative and the interjection of the curse" (140). If the appearance of saints in the Middle Ages indicated that grace still operated in the world, their scarcity today only confirms that modernity ushered in affliction without miracle. And in the absence of miracle, superstition assumes occupancy, furnishing magic in the empty spaces of ignorance. Ironically, then, when contrasted with an age that believed in the active presence of the divine because it had proof, modernity gets cast as irrational, sustaining rituals and the hope they embody without evidence.

With the introduction of evolutionary theory in the 1830s, the massive outbreaks of cholera and tuberculosis in the 1840s, and the blood

142

◇

spilled on the battlefields of the Civil War, many Americans in the nineteenth century may well have felt that the curse had come. Yet amidst all the anxiety about death and disease that characterizes so much of nineteenth-century American culture surfaced a renewed interest in the possibility that the dead might be walking happily among the living in the form of ghosts, animated objects, mediums, and, yes, even photographs, whose quasi-magical status seemed to promise communion with the otherworldly.[7] Nineteenth-century responses to the medium thus reveal an attempt to revitalize medieval notions of the relic, an attempt that was doomed to assume the form of superstition. In texts as wide-ranging as geologic reports, gothic fiction, and religious tracts, many writers explored the possibility that the photograph, as physical trace, could actually be invested with supernatural potency.

These writings and practices marked the final sustained effort to locate in the photographic image not only a deadly aura but a supernatural one as well. They constitute a relatively short-lived history, anomalous in the chronicles of a culture well known for its refusal of death. Some years ago the American historian David Stannard articulated what most of us vaguely recognize—that death in the United States has been "disguised, suppressed, and denied in a way unprecedented in the history of human culture" (28). This brief period—from roughly 1840 to the late 1880s—tells another story, one that expresses a cultural desire to keep the dead roaming comfortably among the living. After this, the "end of sacred narrative" returns with a vengeance, conditioning a modernized age whose principal characteristic is its systematic drive to anaesthetize us to death. After this, Kodak begins.

The "end of sacred narrative" is what allows for the beginning of nostalgia. In an age that reawakened but could not permanently revive a belief in the sacred relic, Kodak offered a new and comforting means of viewing the past, as it promised through its advertising the continuity of experience rather than the violent disruption of time signified by mere physical remains. Nostalgia provides a history informed by the aesthetics of the antique. It allows for the comfortable belief that we can somehow envelope the past in the present by commodifying, domesticating, beautifying it.

The Photograph as Relic

"Photographs state the innocence, the vulnerability of lives heading toward their own destruction," claims Susan Sontag (15). This observation has been echoed most famously by Roland Barthes, who argues in *Camera Lucida* that photographs enjoy the unique privilege of an illusionary indistinguishability from their referents: "It is as if the Photograph always carries its referent with itself, both affected by the same amorous or funereal immobility, at the very heart of the moving world: they are glued together, limb by limb, like the condemned man and the corpse" (6).

Such an observation may strike the contemporary photographic critic as true enough, but it makes most present-day practitioners of snapshot photography uncomfortable. Snapshooters generally use photography as a means of avoiding, indeed of denying, painful memories, including most notably the memory of a loved one's death. They take photos of almost exclusively happy moments, and then use those photos as a means of reconstructing their histories into narratives of "timeless" pleasure and affection, thus striving to secure a future that will remain untouched by pain as it looks back on what seem to be moments that have somehow escaped sorrow and loss. "However untidy or unsatisfactory the experience," Patricia Holland observes, "we can ensure that the picture will project the appropriate emotions into the future" (2). To hear that photographs testify to the frailty of life strikes the average American as odd, morbid, the self-indulgent work of the intellectual.

Such was not the case, however, in the early to mid–nineteenth century, when responses to photography were often framed within discourses on death and mortality. "Here is a genial, smiling, energetic face, full of sunny strength, intelligence, integrity, good humor; but it lies imprisoned in baleful shades, as of the Valley of Death; seems smiling on me as if in mockery. Doesn't know me, friend? I am dead, thou seest, and distant, and forever hidden from thee; I belong already to the Eternities" (quoted in Welling 55). Here Thomas Carlyle clearly sees in the photograph an almost mirrorlike reflection of his own mortality, photography's eerie technology mimicking the way death freezes a living subject into a corpse. And, as Alan Trachtenberg, Cathy Davidson, and Jennifer Green-Lewis have documented, his response to the invention was echoed by people of all classes and walks of life, creating a chorus of responses striking in its insistence on seeing photography's mechanisms as akin to those of death.[8]

While for many people the early photograph quickly developed into what Cathy Davidson calls a "commodified redaction of immortality" (670), it thus seemed to others to enact a murder of its own. In

144 this sense, early writings on photography may be seen as constituting a dialectic between two very different notions of the relic, a conflict between the "medieval" desire to invest the material remains of the photograph with supernatural powers and the "modern" perception of the relic as "residue," "dead shell," "lifeless debris" (Pearce 197). "The daguerreotype. It saddens me," wrote Jules Michelet in 1851, "not to see myself thus with respect to form, but to see myself a corpse, without my inner fire or my spirit: life, more or less!" (quoted in Welling 59). Michelet's words eerily anticipate Barthes: "With the Photograph, we enter into *flat Death*" (*Camera Lucida* 92). Within the space of the photograph, death comes unrelieved and unqualified, prosaic and monotonous, slow-witted and inactive. Entering the photograph, we enter into a broad and shallow death, unlike the death signified by the narrow, deep space of the coffin.

This tension between belief in photography's supernatural powers and the antiphonal response of cynicism so powerfully articulated by Michelet echoes cultural responses to the relic during the Middle Ages.[9] One of the problems that haunted the circulation and reception of medieval relics was, of course, how to distinguish saints' relics from the remains of sinners. The value attached to the special corpses that would be venerated as relics required the communal acceptance of three interrelated beliefs: first, that a person had been, during life and especially after death, a special friend of God, that is, a saint; second, that the remains of a saint were to be prized and treated in a special way, for they partook of the saint's holiness; and third, that the particular corpse or portion thereof was indeed the remains of that particular saint.

To substantiate such conclusions, however, one had literally to scavenge through the remains of the dead, picking one's way through the polluted in order to select the miraculous. Relics of saints, whether physical remains, particles of clothing, or objects associated with them during their lives, had no obvious value apart from a very specific set of shared beliefs. The relics most eagerly sought—bodies or portions of bodies—were superficially similar to thousands of other corpses universally available. Not only were they omnipresent and without intrinsic economic value, they were normally undesirable: an ordinary body was a source of contamination, and opening graves or handling remains of the dead was considered abhorrent (Geary 201).

Like bodies, photographs are universal, banal, and inherently val-

ueless; they also experience the same brief mortality as human beings:
"The only way I can transform the Photograph," Barthes writes, "is
into refuse: either the drawer or the wastebasket. Not only does it
commonly have the fate of paper (perishable), but even if it is attached
to more lasting supports, it is still mortal: like a living organism, it is
born on the level of the sprouting silver grains, it flourishes a moment,
then ages. . . . Attacked by light, by humidity, it fades, weakens, van-
ishes; there is nothing left to do but throw it away" (*Camera Lucida* 93). The dilemma facing Victorians was thus the inevitably futile
project of somehow sustaining a spiritual aura about what was obviously so quotidian and perishable a product of a materialist era. This
paradox informs much early writing on photography; for every response that celebrated the photograph as something spiritually tran-
scendent, another articulates anxiety about death and its finality,
about the inherent irony of investing so much spiritual potency in a
mere piece of paper.

Part of the reason for such a response lay in the rarity and frailty
of photographs. Before the advent of Kodak, portrait photographs
were generally seen as unique, formalized objects whose singularity
represented a distinctive moment in the individual's life. The average
middle-class American family in the 1860s may have owned four or five
photographs, as opposed to the hundreds, even thousands, that most
middle-class families possess today. The photograph thus functioned
as fetish in a way it cannot do today, given the sheer ubiquity of photographs as well as the unprecedented capacity through digital photography not only to reproduce images but to alter them. As a relatively rare object, the portrait photograph before Kodak frequently
evoked thoughts of mortality precisely because its uniqueness and
frailty signified all too clearly that of its subject.

One account by a Victorian photographer illustrates this situation
with heartbreaking clarity. Describing a mother's trip to his studio to
see if she can purchase a portrait taken some years ago of her now
dead child, the author explains that "search was made among old and
rejected plates in hopes that the picture might still be in existence . . .
but after looking for a day or two, the mother coming frequently during the time, the search was abandoned as hopeless. The shadow, fixed
in a wonderful and mysterious manner by a ray of light, had faded
also, and the only image of the child that remained for the mother was
on the tablet of her memory" (quoted in Welling 101). Given both the

146 relative scarcity and the mortality of early photographs, it seems plau-
◇ sible that the photograph and its referent were tied together in a
much more palpable way than they are now—that Barthes's notion
that all photographs function as traces of their referents holds more
relevance to the Victorians than to most contemporary viewers of photographs. Such singularity is most vividly dramatized by the postmortem photograph, a person's death being of course an event that can
never be repeated.

Moreover, because there was no corporate institution authorizing
and determining the meanings of photography to the extent that Kodak soon would do, early responses to photographs—particularly
portrait photographs used for domestic purposes—were notoriously
diaphanous, punctuated by ambivalence, awe, and uncertainty. "In
regard to photography," claims Trachtenberg, "the process of acclima-
tization was neither as spontaneous nor as unequivocal as is often assumed" (61). What is remarkable about early responses to the photograph—even as late as the 1880s—is the surprise viewers expressed
when they discovered details they had not looked for or expected.

What John Berger calls the "accidental" nature of photography
thus mirrored in a sense the accidental nature of memory. Photography's ability to present unsought details can be seen as akin to memory's tendency to overwhelm us occasionally with its "unauthorized"
images. Moreover, as Barthes provocatively suggests, it is those details
that reside outside the photographer's intention or the viewer's expectation that hold the most potential to wound. Existing beyond an academic or conventional framework, beyond the "codes" that determine
the photograph's general reading, these details point to the very heart
of photography—the project of freezing in time what will ultimately
be destroyed. In his famous distinction between what he calls the
"studium" and "punctum" of the photograph, Barthes describes the
punctum as "that item which pricks me (but also bruises me, is
poignant to me). . . . It suggests meanings other than the literal one"
(*Camera Lucida* 27). As such, the punctum constitutes the center of
photography's subversiveness for Barthes, for photography is most subversive "not when it frightens, repels, or even stigmatizes, but when it
is pensive, when it thinks" (38).

With no corporate institution like Kodak to direct their responses,
early and mid-nineteenth-century viewers arguably had more freedom
to discover those details that could evoke a range of responses outside

intentionality, as Oliver Wendell Holmes's description of a stereo-
scopic image of a church and its graveyard makes clear:

> Here is Alloway Kirk, in the churchyard of which you may read
> a real story by the side of the ruin that tells of more roman-
> tic fiction. There stands the stone "Erected by James Russell,
> seedsman, Ayr, in memory of his children," three little boys,
> all snatched away from him in the space of three successive
> summer-days, and lying under the matted grass in the shadow of
> the old witch-haunted walls. It was Burns's Alloway Kirk we paid
> for, and we find that we have bought a share in the griefs of James
> Russell, seedsman, for is it not the stone that tells this blinding
> sorrow of real life and not the roofless pile which reminds us of
> an idle legend? (745)

Striking about this passage is the tension between Holmes's own reading of the image and the apparently more generalized one authorized
by its status as picturesque commodity. Such readings, catalyzed by
the unexpected details of a photograph, were quite common in the
mid–nineteenth century, testifying to a cultural moment in which, despite the fact that photographs were already clearly being marketed
as commodities, the meanings of photography were still actively in
contest.[10]

The confusion of image and afterlife, in the punctum of Barthes
as well as in the literal afterlife of the unintended image Holmes describes, has always haunted photography, however covertly. This legacy
arguably stems from the fact that, in essence, every photograph functions potentially as relic, since the material photograph is always con-
tingent upon its living, or once living, subject. To the laity and clergy
of the Middle Ages, relics *were* saints, continuing to live among hu-
mankind. They functioned as available sources of supernatural power
for good or ill, and close contact with them or possession of them was
a means of participating in that power. Their gross materiality didn't
matter; it was their intimate connection to the saint that endowed
them with value. Like the relic, the photograph itself is invisible. What
matters to most viewers in most cases is the image's immediate relation to its subject, and that relation, as Barthes suggests, shares the
relic's peculiarly erotic and metonymic attachment to the dead or always dying body it represents.

148
◇ Such a perception was especially acute during the first few de-cades after photography's invention, when an amazingly rich animistic discourse surrounded the photographic image. Early metaphors por-trayed the photograph as an intelligible presence with magical prop-erties, evidenced by such phrases as "mirror with a memory," "the pencil of nature," and "secure the shadow ere the substance fade." In fact, as Alan Trachtenberg observes, an entire vocabulary developed around the medium that was at once familiarizing and alienating: a bizarre language of animated portraits, shadows, haunted spaces, un-conscious desires, and talismanic properties (64). In this discourse, the portrait photograph—seemingly domesticated but actually con-nected to a larger, supernatural world—reveals the inner motives and even soul of a person.

Every relic needs a home. Relics were generally housed in "reli-quaries," decorated wooden or stone structures designed to keep safe the remains of saints. Note how much attention was given to *enshrin-ing* the early photograph, especially the daguerreotype. Like physical remains, the daguerreotype typified vulnerability. It was fragile, deli-cate, one of a kind, and extremely sensitive to light. Daguerreotypes were thus frequently encased in small, jewel-like boxes of Moroccan leather with embossed designs ranging from conventional medallions to vases of flowers to musical instruments, the inside of the cases padded with red or blue velvet and ornamented in gold. Like reliquar-ies, these leather cases were designed to offer much more than physi-cal protection. They dramatized the experience of viewing the da-guerreotype, like the solemn ritual that surrounded the opening of a saint's grave or reliquary. The opening and closing of the case al-lowed the viewer a brief experience of witnessing the miraculous, fol-lowed by the reverent gesture of returning the image to its undisturbed space.

Given the persistence of the confused and contradictory rhetoric surrounding nineteenth-century photography, the tendency to see the photograph as both supernatural object and material residue, it comes as no surprise that the invention came to be so closely linked with the increasingly popular movement of spiritualism through the practice of "spirit photography." The term refers to the practice of taking pho-tographs in an effort to produce visual evidence of ghosts, spirits, and other supernatural elements. Spirit photography, in essence, afforded an opportunity to reawaken medieval notions about the potency of

relics, to distinguish the miraculous image from the banal. With the 149
flourishing of spiritualism during the 1860s in England and the United ◇
States, photography became the method by which those who believed
in an afterlife could actually offer "proof" of the truth of their convic-
tions. Over the next several decades, mediums, photographers, and
even scientists experimented in the "resurrecting art," and hundreds
of articles on the subject appeared in journals ranging from *Harper's*
and the *Strand* to the *British Journal of Photography*.

The first recorded spirit photograph appeared in Boston in 1861,
produced by an amateur photographer named William Howard Mumler, who subsequently created and sold at high prices hundreds of
such images (including one of the dead President Lincoln and his
widow). As an 1869 cover story on Mumler titled "Spiritual Photography" in *Harper's Weekly* shows, the striking characteristic of virtually
all Mumler photographs is their illusion of normality (figure 31). Most
of them portray a nebulous and static figure posed behind the sitter,
with his hands on her shoulder and his gaze affectionate and serene.
The obvious effect is the suggestion of intimacy between the spirit and
the bereaved. The bourgeois family is reunited; clients actually framed
these photographs or placed them in family albums. Mumler's photographs thus offered domesticated ghosts who performed the same
roles or gestures popular in paintings of the time, as in the photographs depicting a dutiful (though dead) wife consoling her afflicted
husband. The dead could thus appear as they would have done in an
ordinary domestic photograph.

The aura of the medieval relic derived in part from the widespread
practice of passing off ordinary remains as those of saints. Similarly,
as spirit photography gained notoriety, a concomitant anxiety intensified about fraud. In 1868 Mumler left Boston to set up a new practice in New York City. Within a year, however, his practice had incited
so much controversy that the mayor of New York ordered him brought
up on criminal charges of "swindling the public." The trial lasted ten
days and aroused a great deal of public attention. And as dozens of
entries in the American photographic and popular press attest, spirit
photography aroused suspicions (figure 32).

By the late nineteenth century, anxieties about fraud seemed
verified by the images themselves as they became increasingly stylized
and sensational. Spirit photographs had developed into elaborate
theater—in some cases even into miniature horror shows—as they

HARPER'S WEEKLY.
A JOURNAL OF CIVILIZATION

VOL. XIII.—No. 645.]   NEW YORK, SATURDAY, MAY 8, 1869.   [SINGLE COPIES, TEN CENTS. $4.00 PER YEAR IN ADVANCE.

SPIRITUAL PHOTOGRAPHY.

The case of the people against William H. Mumler, of 630 Broadway, is one so remarkable and without precedent in the annals of criminal jurisprudence that we devote this page to illustrations bearing upon it. The charge against Mr. Mumler is that, by means of what he terms spiritual photographs, he has swindled many credulous persons, leading them to believe it is possible to photograph the immaterial forms of their departed friends.

The case has excited the profoundest interest, and, strange as it may seem, there are thousands of people who believe that its development will justify the claims made by the spiritual photographer. We shall not attempt to give an expression to our own opinions, but simply to follow the developments of the case through the testimony offered during the first few days of the trial.

It is through the instrumentality of Marshal Joseph H. Tooker that the case has been brought before the courts. He deposes that he was ordered by Mayor Hall to investigate the case, which he did by assuming a false name, and by getting his photograph taken by Mr. Mumler. After the taking of the picture the negative was shown him, with a dim, indistinct outline of a ghostly face staring out of one corner; and he was told that the picture represented the spirit of his father-in-law. He, however, failed to recognize the worthy old gentleman, and emphatically declared that the picture neither represented his father-in-law, nor any of his relations, nor yet any person whom he had ever seen or known. With this evidence the prosecution rested.

The counsel for the defense have brought forward a number of witnesses who testify to the genuineness of spiritual photographs taken for them by Mr. Mumler. William P. Snelu, a photographer, of Poughkeepsie, testifies that Mumler succeeded in producing spiritual photographs at his gallery in Poughkeepsie, and he was unable to discover how it was done. Judge Edmonds, one of the most distinguished advocates of Spiritualism, deposed that he had two photographs taken by Mumler; the spirit form in one of them he thought he could recognize, but not the one in the other. He said: "I believe that the camera can take a photograph of a spirit, and I believe also that spirits have materiality

—but that gross materiality that mortals possess, but still they are material enough to be visible to the human eye, for I have seen them; only a few days since I was in a court in Brooklyn when a suit against a life assurance company for the amount claimed to be due on a certain policy was being heard. Looking toward that part of the court-room occupied by the jury, I saw the spirit of the man whose death was the basis of the suit. The spirit told me the circumstances connected with his death; said that his suit was groundless, that the claimant was not entitled to recover from the company, and said that he (the poor whose spirit was speaking) had committed suicide under certain circumstances; drew a diagram of the place at which his death occurred, and on closing it in the counsel, was told that it was exact in every particular."

A large number of witnesses deposed that they recognized the forms of departed friends (in some cases of those long dead) in the photographs taken for them by Mumler. The most striking case was that of a gentleman of Wall Street, whose deceased wife's features both he and his friends distinctly recognized in a photograph taken for him in this way.

If there is a trick in Mr. Mumler's process it has certainly not been detected as yet. To all appearance spiritual photography rests just where the rappings and table-turnings have rested for some years. Those who believe in it at all will expect no rapping organisms, and disbelievers will reject every tenable hypothesis of explanation. Mr. Mumler has certainly been very fortunate. He has believed in, in the first place, by a large number of people. He has obtained, again, a good price for his photographs; for who could expect spirits to be called "from the vasty deep" for less than ten dollars per head? And, finally, he has been prosecuted, and thus extensively advertised. Beyond this, the trial, like all legal prosecutions of this nature, will amount to nothing.

In addition to our illustrations of specimens of Mr. Mumler's spirit photographs, we give also representations of similar photographs taken by Mr. Rockwood, of this city. The latter were taken by natural means, but not so as to escape detection as to the trick resorted to to secure the result. Mr. Mumler has certainly the advantage of a longer experience in the business.

W. H. MUMLER.   MRS. W. H. MUMLER.—BY MUMLER.   SPIRIT PHOTOGRAPH BY MUMLER.

SPIRIT PHOTOGRAPH BY MUMLER.   SPIRIT PHOTOGRAPH BY MUMLER.   SPIRIT PHOTOGRAPH BY MUMLER.

SPIRIT PHOTOGRAPH BY MUMLER.   P. V. HICKEY.—BY ROCKWOOD.   C. S. BULL.—BY ROCKWOOD.

SPIRITUAL PHOTOGRAPHY.—[Specimens Furnished by Mumler and Rockwood.]

Figure 31. Cover of *Harper's Weekly*, 8 May 1869

1. "Mr. Dobbs, at the request of his Affianced, sits for his photograph.
   Unconsciously happens in at Mumler's.
2. Result-Portrait of Dobbs, with his five Deceased Wives in Spirituo!!!"

Harper's Weekly, 1869

Figure 32. Cartoon of Howard Mumler, *Harper's Weekly*, 1869

depicted entranced mediums flailing about, collapsing, spitting out
ectoplasm, exhausting themselves into, ironically, a tranquil and seemingly joyful spirit. Along with the usually serene-looking spirit, photographs in the 1880s and 1890s frequently depicted a tormented
medium (and her impassioned sitters) in a setting complete with
photographic equipment and props. They brought to the surface
and made an elaborate production of the desires and fears of the
participants.

The relationship between sitter and spirit in these portraits had
thus changed dramatically, so that the ghost functioned not as simply
a static image independent of the sitter's will but as a specter produced
from her overwrought mind. "Through human agents [medieval relics]

152   moved about at will," Patrick Geary explains, "even changing their res-
◇   idence from one church to another as they wished. They made their
pleasure or displeasure known in no uncertain terms and, like the
Eucharist, tolerated no disrespect" (153). Spirit photos thus came to
reflect the fact that those who participated in the practice desired a
more dynamic engagement with the supernatural, similar, perhaps, to
that realized by their medieval counterparts. Ironically, though, it
seems that the only way to prove the active presence of a ghost in the
late nineteenth century was through the wildly gesticulating and tor-
tured body of a medium.

A far cry from Mumler's flat and static images, these photographs
also reveal a cinematic turn in spirit photography. By the mid-1890s,
film had emerged as the newest technological marvel. And as spirit
photography was transformed into "cinema," cinema itself exploited
supernatural images and events. Among the first films witnessed by
the public, for example, were those of the director George Melies,
whose eerie images were often the result of double exposures, one of
the techniques by which a spirit photograph could be produced. The
content of these films explored the same themes and images that are
found in nineteenth-century writings on photography: the age-old
fears about the magic potential of duplicating the human form, the secret shudders of necrophilia, inversions of the Pygmalion motif in
which a creation outstrips its creator. These films thus cast as their
subject the dark underpinnings of technological image making. Surprisingly self-reflexive, early cinema appears to have meditated on its
spectral nature and origin. And the individual images of spirit photography during this time echoed their cinematic counterparts: some of
them exhibit a dramatic use of light and shadow, an attention to gesture as sign of character, and an expressionist or surrealist portrayal of
objects.

One wonders, then, how so many people could have continued to
accept photographic images that had become stylized enough to draw
attention to their cinematic counterparts. A possible answer resides in
the historical explanations offered for the rise of German Expressionism in film, arguably the most haunted of all artistic movements and
the culmination of cinema's early spectral phase. Spirit photography,
whose popularity in the United States effectively died out by the 1880s,
met with a brief resurgence of interest at the peak of World War I—
the same event that propelled German Expressionism. As Lotte Eisner

has suggested, "mysticism and magic had flourished in the face of death on the battlefields. A new stimulus was thus given to the eternal attractions towards all that is obscure and undetermined" (5).

The statement might well be applied to the resurgence of spirit photography in England and the United States during the war. A practice that barely held any vestiges of respect outside of spiritualist circles suddenly became reinvented as grieving spouses, children, and parents sought proof that their loved ones were not gone forever. More important, however, these images transposed the surreal elements of war into fantastic image making. Arguably, the images' individual content became less important than the mental act of the transference—which perhaps explains why Arthur Conan Doyle (who had lost his son during the war) could believe in images so obviously artificial as those he claimed were genuine. In its final stages, spirit photography's importance may have resided less in offering its believers "proof" of an afterlife than in casting their frightful memories into a magical technology.

In any case, once the war ended, so did spirit photography, and with it the rhetoric of the supernatural that had surrounded the early photograph. Kodak had already destroyed what the war only briefly revived. Spirit photography marked the climactic attempt to invest the medium with preternatural potency; once it deteriorated into grotesque performance, there was no chance of another development. The darkroom was closed to ghosts, saints, President Lincoln, ectoplasm, and every other trace of the otherworldly. All that remained was "flat death."

The Photograph as Antique

By the time Eastman patented his roll film and Kodak No. 1 camera in 1888, Americans' responses to death had shifted substantially since the 1840s, when the postmortem daguerreotype had been produced. Improved preventive medicine and increased public health measures caused life expectancy to rise to the late forties for the average American, and child mortality rates had begun to decline. By 1915, the average age an American could be expected to live had reached fifty-four years (Fulton 86). Dramatic shifts in religious belief near the turn of the century made the afterlife of Christian doctrine increasingly harder to accept. Postmortem photography had already become a

154 much less common practice by the late 1880s, no longer discussed in
◇ photographic journals or promoted in advertisements with the frequency it had enjoyed only twenty years earlier.

By 1900, as Geoffrey Gorer, Elisabeth Kübler-Ross, Philippe Ariès, and David Stannard have all famously explained, death had become a forbidden subject among the American middle class. "The natural process of corruption and decay had become disgusting," claimed Gorer, "as disgusting as the natural processes of copulation and birth were a century ago; preoccupation with such processes was morbid and unhealthy, to be discouraged in all and punished in the young" (79). These and other factors—not least Kodak's refocusing of the objects of photography—gradually erased death and other representations of sorrow and loss from domestic photographs in American culture; viewers' memories were reconstructed to focus on the supposed timelessness of family moments that celebrated youth and vitality. Photos of dead loved ones were increasingly put away, too painful now for Americans to display. In their place came highly nostalgic depictions of family life.

As Rita Felski, David Lowenthal, and Maurice Halbwachs have argued, nostalgia is a relatively modern phenomenon.[11] While nostalgic evocations date back to Virgil, who sought to immortalize the heroic and pastoral past in his poetry, they did not begin to pervade Western culture until the late eighteenth century, intensifying most notably near the turn of the twentieth century. Diagnosed originally in 1688 by Johannes Hofer, nostalgia was at first perceived and discussed as a physical complaint: once away from their native land, sailors languished, wasted away, and even perished. Clear symptoms of nostalgia could even be identified in the diagnosed patient, such as the rejection of food and drink; the impossibility of getting out of bed; emaciation, marasmus, and eventually death.

By the late nineteenth century, as David Lowenthal has noted, nostalgia had been transformed from a physical complaint into a modern malaise: "Today rarely associated with homesickness, nostalgia has become strictly a state of mind" (11). It reflects a culture characterized by a growing rebellion against the present and an increasing longing for the past. As Rita Felski also argues, "If the experience of modernity brought with it an overwhelming sense of innovation, ephemerality, and chaotic change, it simultaneously engendered multiple expressions of desire for stability and continuity. Nostalgia, understood as a mourning for an idealized past, thus emerges as a formative theme of the modern" (40). What we see, then, is a fascinating dialectic taking place during Kodak's formative years, one that reflects a culture bombarded by change and yearning for a mythical and stable past. Such a past could give consumers the illusion that their individual lives had meaning that transcended the graphic death so vividly represented in the postmortem daguerreotype.

"Nostalgia is now even planned for," claims Lowenthal (12). Like Kierkegaard's character in *Either/Or* who imagines herself as a grandmother recalling the infancy of her yet unborn daughters, we look back in the midst of enjoyment to recapture it for memory. No single force has so well conditioned this mentality as snapshot photography. Posing for a photograph in the midst of an experience, we already imagine that experience as an idealized memory before the camera's button has even been pressed. In looking at photographs of themselves, Victorians often saw their death inscribed in their present. Today we look at snapshots and see a realm seemingly untouched by death. No wonder that Americans are so eager to transform their experiences into snapshots, for it is in the space of the snapshot that we can still enjoy the illusion of youth and happiness and the continuity of experience embodied in the family album, that nearly indispensable fixture which promises the wholeness of narrative rather than the violence of disruption. Nostalgia always imagines the wholeness of ideal experience, satisfying our craving for what Lowenthal calls "evidence that the past endures in completely recoverable form" (121).

In this sense, Kodak's transformation of photography played its part in the commodification of nostalgia, a commodification most strikingly marked in the late nineteenth century by the advent of the antique industry. Antiques vividly illustrate the way yesterday's novelties become commodified as artifacts of an impossibly distant past. How can something as instant and disposable as a snapshot be regarded as an antique? Matsuda's description of the function of memory in modern culture provides an apt response. Commenting on Walter Benjamin's analysis of the Paris arcades, Matsuda notes that Benjamin saw in late nineteenth-century Paris an emerging society in which structures were constantly raised and leveled. Amidst such rapid change and movement, a search for the ever new transformed "shop windows from displays into museums, housing yesterday's objects as fossils of an antedated fashion and technology" (12). The new

156 was almost instantly transformed into the old in such a culture: "What
◇   was new, active, part of history, was immediately nothing more than
the prehistory of an eternally changing present. The ever-new instantly
became an ever-same of objects and events relentlessly created and
destroyed by an accelerated, sequential scheme of time. The persistence of memory was the record of things strangely familiar for being
so quickly gone, only half-forgotten" (12).

Nothing more than paper and yet everything more than paper,
photographs are instant antiques, objects that condense to nothingness the increasingly smaller amount of time required to make something past into something cherished. "Formerly contained in time and
place, nostalgia today engulfs the whole past," claims Lowenthal (6),
so that nearly everything that can be distanced as "past," from an Art
Deco alarm clock to a kitchen set from the 1950s to a pair of platform
shoes, has become an object of tender regard or curiosity.

Kodak advertisements that employ a frame motif vividly illustrate
this phenomenon of accelerated nostalgia. Take the 1901 advertisement for the St. Louis world's fair shown in plate 1. Consciously promoted—and experienced—as midways to a new era, world's fairs reduce the world to a simulacrum of accelerated, intensified modernity.
Promoting this event, Kodak thus advertises itself as a central participant in a new, modern era. Yet what is so remarkable about this image
is the way it converts the promise/threat of a technological future into
a thing of the past. The ornate leaf border already frames the advertisement as a keepsake, as if the exposition becomes memory even before it has occurred. Embodying this transposition is the woman in the
advertisement, who with her parasol and organza gown looks like a
picture of old-fashioned femininity; contained within another frame,
that of the snapshot, she becomes a souvenir herself. At once, then,
she represents modernity and slows it down.

This nostalgia for the antique, like all forms of nostalgia, masks a
disturbing possibility—that in seeking to create a warm and continuous narrative that neatly enfolds the past into the present, we have
turned utterly aesthetic; that indeed, no other choice is possible. "In
order to entertain an antiquarian sensibility," Stewart claims, "a rup-
ture in historical consciousness must have occurred, creating a sense
that one can make one's own culture other—distant and discontinu-
ous. Time must be seen as concomitant with a loss of understanding,
a loss which can be relieved through the reawakening of objects and,

thereby, a reawakening of narrative" (142). The enfolding of the past 157
into the present manifested by antique collecting suggests, in other ◇
words, that past and present are really, irreparably sundered. Richard
Terdiman makes a similar argument when he suggests that the latter
half of the nineteenth century was infected by a "memory crisis."

A central claim of Terdiman's *Present Past* is that, as modernity
came to be experienced as a way of life that presented the individual
with too much of everything, including experience, a vague sense developed that human memory couldn't possibly accommodate itself to
such bombardment. And with this sense came an uneasy feeling that
both the historical past and the personal past were slipping away, indeed had already gone.

One easy attempt to integrate the two would now be an *aesthetic*
one, readily available for consumption. When we look at a range of ads
near the turn of the century, it becomes clear that one of Kodak's primary strategies was to market the photograph as antique. In so doing,
Kodak promoted the present moment as always already part of the
past, thus engendering the notion that one could single out from the
dense flux of modern reality timeless, tasteful, consumable, and col-
lectable moments. "Kodak moments."

Terdiman was speaking of European thought, but such anxieties
about the relation of the past to the present was especially pronounced in the United States, the heartland of an attitude that makes
cultural value into commodities precisely because of its own self-
production of culture. One symptom of this "memory crisis" was the
burgeoning interest in antiques in the late nineteenth century. When
the Kodak No. 1 camera and roll film appeared in 1888, antique collecting had become almost a full-fledged industry, generating a host of
handbooks, manuals, catalogs, and essays in publications as varied as
Godey's Lady's Book and *The Art Journal*. And with the expansion of
collecting American antiques after the turn of the century, more and
more printed material appeared on the subject, most of it aimed at
the novice. Among these general, sometimes vaguely organized books
were *The Furniture of Our Forefathers* (1901), *Chats on Old Furniture* (1916), *The Lure of the Antique* (1916), and *The Charm of the
Antique* (1916).

As Elizabeth Stillinger frames it, we can locate the origins of antique collecting in the United States sometime in the 1850s, in isolated
efforts by individuals who seem to have been motivated mainly by

patriotic sentiments; the common interest at that time was in colonial furniture. By the 1880s, according to Stillinger, "a general interest in history and its famous participants had expanded to encompass one's own family, town, or region. People began to have what might be described as a genealogical orientation toward old things" (xiii). Perhaps. Yet what much of the literature during this time reveals is a much more careless and uninformed attraction to antiques in which an "authentic" family history matters much less than the appearance of one. In 1878, for example, the editors of *Godey's Lady's Book* described what they called the "latest mania among fashionable people" for collecting old furniture. "A curious feature of this fashion," they observed, "is the aid it affords people desiring to lay claim to a respectable ancestry" (quoted in Davidson et al. 196).

The sarcasm would certainly not have been missed by their readers, for even by the late 1870s, a wealth of literature was already ridiculing the cultural desire for instant history reflected in the lure of the antique. Clarence Cooke pointed out that in Boston "a polite internecine warfare" ensued between rival collectors of "old pieces." "The back country" was being "scoured by young couples in chaises on the trail of old sideboards and brass andirons" (ibid.).

By the 1890s, then, American antiques had become commodifed status symbols. If acquired by inheritance, they represented social background, for a family in which they descended had been in America since colonial or early federal times. If they weren't acquired by inheritance, however, one could take comfort in the fact that they reflected what by this time had almost become a mantra in discourses on home furnishing: "good taste." Another alternative then, as now, was simply to purchase new furniture imitating the forms and ornaments of earlier days. As the editors of *The American Heritage History of Antiques* explain, "Most early manufacturers went to great pains and expense to turn out machine-made goods that resembled in design and ornament traditional handmade products. Looking backward rather than forward for inspiration, they appropriated the styles of the more or less distant past—often indiscriminately and with little care or understanding—to lend prestige to their mechanically contrived articles" (Davidson et al. 6). Indeed, by the 1890s, a kind of wholesale revivalism had infected much of the eastern part of the country. Cooke also commented on this phenomenon with characteristic sar-

donicism: "The things we see for sale in the shops are all either good 159
or bad or indifferent copies of old-fashioned things, . . . hardly any- ◇
thing with the stamp of our own time and country is to be had"
(quoted ibid. 14).

The distinctively American lack of a national style of home furnishings was noted by other nineteenth-century critics as well. Touring the mansions of Newport, Rhode Island, in the early 1890s, the
French poet and novelist Charles Joseph Paul Bourget was horrified
not only by the extravagant wealth he witnessed there but by the
"twenty, thirty, forty different styles of construction" he saw in the antique furniture and architecture. "In this country, where everything is
of yesterday, they hunger and thirst for the long ago" (quoted in Davidson et al. 195). Like the Disneyland of which Jean Baudrillard writes,
Newport emerges here as a concentrated and exaggerated center of a
uniquely American inauthenticity, more like than unlike the rest of
the country in its pathetic absence of any "real" history.

Unquestionably, one of the motivations for antique collecting at
this time was a general dissatisfaction with the newness, distraction,
and excessive stimulation of modern life. If modernity can be defined
in part as a condition of ideological shelterlessness, one way of com-
bating that condition was to invest unprecedented energy in the
home—to infuse one's modern house with the serenity and stability of
an idealized past. Miss Elsie de Wolfe, the first prominent female interior decorator, touted as "the Chintz Lady," observed, "We have not
succeeded in creating a style adapted to our modern life. It is just as
well! Our life, with its haste, its nervousness, and its preoccupations
does not inspire the furniture makers" (quoted in Davidson et al. 201).
She thus recommends that antiques be purchased as a means of
avoiding the "uninviting" look of new houses. "It is frequently remarked that new houses have a stiff, uncomfortable look, and that
people moving into them are continually conscious of their newness
and want of home-like feeling. The practice, however, of reviving old
fashions does away with much of this" (ibid. 136).

The advent and development of the antique industry thus clearly
coincided with a new cultural attention to transforming the home
into a space of nostalgia. Imagined as a place that embodies the illusion of intimate history, the home is deliberately constructed in these
writings as an antithesis to the modern—to the flux, movement, and

160   assumed decadence of the present. The selling of the importance of
◇   the home marks Kodak's participation (particularly after roughly 1910)
in the complex of ideas that were associated with the commodification
of antiques: nostalgia as a refuge from change, from uncertainty, from
the "memory crisis."

Beginning around 1913, the year Kodak film improved enough to
allow the amateur photographer to take high-quality photographs indoors, provided the subject was near a window, advertisements began
to feature home interiors and to stress the value of home portraiture.
"At Home with a Kodak" headlines one 1920 advertisement, which explains that "after all, Kodak means most in the home—because home
pictures mean the most." In fact, "At Home with the Kodak" became
one of Kodak's most frequently used slogans. "Little home incidents
that may not mean so much at the time are the little things that
count—in pictures. An album full is a prized possession in any home";
"The personal pictures in and about the home—pictures of the children and grown folks, pictures of the familiar surroundings and of the
family pets—these as well as the travel and vacation pictures make
Kodakery worth while," claims a 1912 advertisement. Beginning in
1915, Kodak periodically published a booklet titled *At Home with the
Kodak,* with articles informing readers how to make the best "pictorial
record of the home—the little intimate pictures that can be secured
in no other way" (4).

Participating as well in the new emphasis on cultivating the look
of the old in home furnishing, Kodak frequently marketed its products
as evocative of a bygone era. In plate 15, for example, a group of customers stand outside a Kodak store. Although the ad was published in
1902, the figures are costumed in fashions of the mid–nineteenth century. Quite aside from the period costumes, there's a curiously old-
fashioned feel to this image. As we move our eye toward the top right-
hand corner, our suspicion is confirmed. A banner reads "Ye Kodak
Camera Loads in ye Light of Day." The obviously archaic "ye" (a word
that effectively went out of use by the sixteenth century) draws our attention to Kodak's self-conscious exploitation of Americans' fascination with the antique. Our attention is directed, moreover, to "Kodak
Simplicity." By 1902, simplicity in interior decoration had become almost synonymous with the charm of a preindustrial era, the artless-
ness of the handmade meant to stand in opposition to the rushed complexity of the factory-made.

Beginning shortly after the turn of the century, Kodak advertisements frequently describe the photograph as an object whose value, like that of the antique, grows as it ages. Listen to this 1906 caption: "The Story of the Kodak Album. It's the intimate, personal story of the home—a picture story that interests every member of the family. And the older it grows, the more it expands, the stronger its grip becomes; the greater its fascination." The text of a 1907 advertisement proclaims that "the Kodak Story of Summer days grows in charm as the months go by." Many of these ads picture elderly men and women looking serenely on with their children and grandchildren at photo albums (figure 33). The photo album thus becomes something that's shared from one generation to the next, implying that past and present are united through the act of both taking and looking at photographs. Perhaps more surprising are ads that picture relatively young men and women, occasionally even children, looking longingly at photographs in solitude. In a 1907 advertisement, a young woman sits alone, gazing at Kodak photographs of her summer vacation (figure 34). The original ad was reproduced in muted purples and golds, colors clearly meant to evoke sunsets and thus endings. The tone of the advertisement is remarkably melancholy, exploiting the bittersweet enterprise of nostalgia, which always authenticates the past while discrediting the present. Thus, as summer fades into autumn, the young woman must return to memory for the experience of pleasure; and that reenactment effectively removes her from the world of the present, enclosing her within her own atemporal, lace-curtained world of reverie.

As the photograph underwent its transmutation from relic to antique, a rhetoric of theft gradually gave way to a rhetoric of collection.[12] Relics get stolen; antiques get collected. Early writing on photography often linked it metaphorically with stealing. In literature ranging from Nathaniel Hawthorne's *House of the Seven Gables* (1850) to Thomas Hardy's *A Laodicean* (1881), the photographer is literally cast as a thief, bent on securing property that doesn't belong to him. He watches, schemes, and cases a house for the right opportunity to invade it. This literary trope participated in a larger cultural discourse that projected the act of photography itself as theft. "Secure the shadow ere the substance fade," one of the earliest advertising slogans aimed at photographers, connotes the importance of seizing, of acquiring now. And Honoré de Balzac, infamous for his superstitious distrust of the invention, postulated a bizarre notion called "the Theory

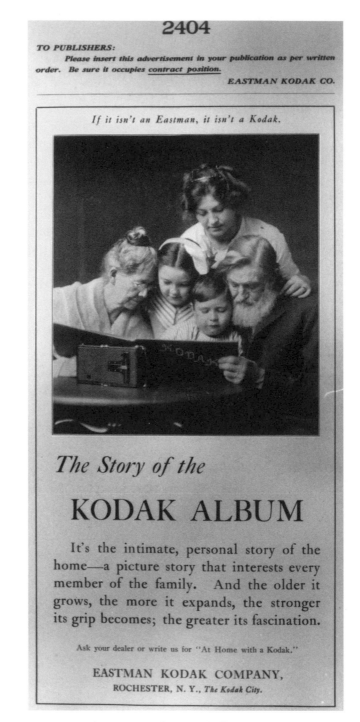

Figure 33. Advertisement for Kodak albums, 1910s. (Reprinted courtesy of Eastman Kodak Company)

Figure 34. Advertisement for Kodak cameras on summer vacations, early 1900s. (Reprinted courtesy of Eastman Kodak Company)

164 of Specters," in which he asserted that each time a photograph was
◇ taken, an actual layer of skin was destroyed. Before Kodak, we stole;
since Kodak, we collect.

Whereas theft generally stresses the singularity of items (the most
notorious cases of theft have been those that focused on stealing one
coveted priceless object, as in the 1912 theft of the *Mona Lisa*), collecting emphasizes the value of things in relation to one another. Russell Belk and his colleagues "take collecting to be the selective, active,
and longitudinal acquisition, possession and disposition of an interrelated set of differentiated objects (material things, ideas, beings,
or experiences) that contribute to and derive extraordinary meaning
from the entity (the collection) that this set is perceived to constitute" (quoted in Pearce 49). The statement raises another important point: one spends one's life collecting; collecting creates—or at
least ratifies—continuity. Stealing, on the other hand, implies impatience—immediate gratification as opposed to the quasi-masochistic
attraction of waiting, of prolonging anticipation. Collecting emphasizes the (idealized) past; stealing emphasizes the (actual) present.

In this light, consider the photograph album. The collection of
pictures in an album also involves waiting—waiting for the next
"Kodak moment" worthy of a space among the rest; waiting, in other
words, for the next episode in an alternate version of the life that slips
by as one collects. Collecting photographs, moreover, combines a
preindustrial aesthetic of the handmade with the postindustrial mode
of ready-made production. Photo albums are thus profoundly "antique" in the way they transform the singular, potentially transitory,
and ready-made photograph into a timeless, handmade, and personal
piece of a collection.

Collecting is intensely ahistorical; it erases difference in the attempt to offer an integral set or insular world. "The collection seeks a
form of self-enclosure which is possible because of its ahistoricism,"
says Stewart. "The collection replaces history with classification, with
order beyond the realm of temporality. In the collection, time is not
something to be restored to an origin; rather, all time is made simul-
taneous or synchronous within the collection's world" (151). The collection's function is not the restoration of origin but rather the creation of a new context, a context standing in a metaphorical relation
to the world of everyday life. And that context effectively allows the
collector the illusion of controlling and organizing not only the chaos

of the past but the present and future as well. In the collection the
potential terrors of infinity are always contained by the illusion of in-   ◇
finity's wholeness.

This, perhaps, is the ultimate consolation of the antique: the illusion that we can delimit a world we perceive as terrifyingly limitless.
Kodak's most significant impact in this transformation from relic to
antique was that it confined photography's vision—a vision that in
the nineteenth century extended even to the ectoplasmic. Seeing too
much, perhaps the nineteenth-century viewer wanted less: wholeness
without remainder, time without its losses, a remembered life marked
by the materiality of skin, not its withering in death. In the 1880s
Nietzsche described wisdom in terms of its "skin coveredness"; Kodak
at the same time trafficked in images without skin—in Marxian terms,
without the materiality of use-value. That is, Kodak transformed the
material relic into the immaterial commodity. And so what Kodak offered *was* less; in every advertisement, every caption, every image, it
expunged all traces of sorrow, all traces of death. It managed to do so,
as we will see, even in the face of war.

6

"Let Kodak Keep the Story"

Narrative, Memory, and the Selling of the
Autographic Camera during World War I

Among the many slogans devised by L. B. Jones's department to extol photography's narrative capabilities, "Let Kodak Keep the Story" did the job so well that it became famous. Begun in 1907 and extending into the 1930s, this campaign enjoyed one of the longest lives of all Kodak campaigns, and it numbered among the most popular, too. Within only months of its creation, "Let Kodak Keep the Story" had become almost as resonant a slogan as "You Press the Button, We Do the Rest."

To link photographs with stories is, of course, to assert that photography functions as its own language, with its own codes, rhetoric, agency, and reading practices separate from those of written language.[1] And while some of the ads produced for the Story Campaign draw attention to this idea, my interest resides in an aspect of the ads that assumed much more prominence: the relentless message to consumers that their memories could not be trusted to preserve their life stories.

"Let Kodak Keep the Story," states one 1916 ad. "Memory has a most aggravating way of storing up details for which we don't care a crooked sixpence—and of dropping out of sight forever things that we really want to know—especially dates." This caption comes from an advertisement for the Autographic Kodak, a type of camera invented in 1913 that allowed the amateur photographer to record information about the photograph right on the negative of the film.[2] Kodak used the Story Campaign to advertise the Autographic Kodak especially. Through its promotion of this camera, from 1914 to the mid-1920s,

Kodak stressed the frailty of human memory and photography's potential to compensate for that frailty by "keeping stories" that were
doubly legitimated by the accuracy of the photographic image and the
factual information that could now be inscribed on it.

In actuality, the Autographic Kodak allowed for the inscription of
only minimal text—enough space to title and date the photograph and
to provide a brief description (such as "Our first Christmas together,
Dec. 1915"). Consequently, most owners used the autographic feature
to record factual information only, hardly the stuff of "stories." Yet in
these ads, the facticity of informational text, like the facticity of the
photo it accompanies, gets sold through fiction—fiction not as *making up* but as *making good.* This strategy depended on Kodak's subtle
conflation of the concept of story with the separate but related concept of memory, a conflation that underscores Kodak's reconfiguring
of memory as nostalgia. Nostalgia, according to Susan Stewart, "is always ideological: the past it seeks has never existed except as narrative" (23). That is, Kodak's confluence of memory and story constitutes
nostalgia itself.

Kodak also collapses the distinctions between documentation and
authenticity in ads for the Autographic Kodak, with statements that
assure viewers that the inclusion of written information on the photograph makes the image "doubly valuable" by providing "authentic history." The Autographic camera's documentary function of recording
details thus translates into the narrative power of authenticity. Unlike the more neutral concept of documentation, authenticity falls
squarely within the province of narrative, and thus of nostalgia, because it fetishizes origin. As a "structure of feeling" (to use Raymond
Williams's term) that privileges origin in its yearning for the past, nostalgia relies heavily on the notion of authenticity, as any trip to an antique dealer will remind us.

Both the Autographic Kodak and the Story Campaign reached the
height of their popularity during World War I.[3] As Fred Davis notes,
nostalgia thrives particularly in wartime, when people wish to escape
a present that seems overwhelmingly bleak and disruptive.[4] As we
shall see, Kodak responded to the disruptions of the Great War by suggesting to consumers that the horrors of war could be balanced and
neutralized, even forgotten, through reassuring narratives implicit in
photographs of home and family.

The Autographic Kodak

During the summer of 1914, Kodak announced the invention of the autographic feature in popular magazines worldwide, touting it as "the greatest photographic invention of the last twenty years." Cameras equipped with the feature seem to have been simple to operate. After shooting a picture, the photographer opened the back door of the camera and wrote her information with a metal stylus or pencil on either the bottom or left margin of the negative. The film cartridge was designed so that a strip of tissue lay between the paper and film, the tissue both lightproofing the cartridge and permitting the recording, by light, of the writing on the film. After jotting down her information, the photographer held the camera up to the light for 2 to 10 seconds so that sunlight could act on the film to fix the handwriting. At the end of the last exposure, the photographer turned the winding key until the letter *A* appeared in the center of the window on the back of the camera; then she raised the spring door and wrote her name on the last exposure, thus ensuring proper identification for the developer.

Judging from articles in the *Kodak Trade Circular* as well as in-house correspondence, it is clear that the company expected this feature to be one of its most momentous and lucrative inventions. Kodak immediately redesigned nearly all its cameras, even the Brownie, to come equipped with the feature and manufactured them in the tens of thousands, to be sold at prices ranging from $6 to $75. Public response was tepid at first, but within a year the demand was overwhelming. A 1915 advertisement explains: "The Autographic Feature has scored a hit, and a big one. At first, perhaps, the interest was mild. . . . Then the real advantages of the simple method to, for all time, accurately record the 'who, when and where' struck home, so that now, in considerably less than a year, it is pretty hard to sell a camera without the Autographic Feature."

In 1915 Kodak made all its folding Kodak cameras autographic. Indeed, the two most popular Autographic cameras were the Autographic Kodak Juniors and the Vest Pocket Autographic Kodaks, both of them folding cameras. By 1922, sales had risen so high that an advertisement for the No. 1 Autographic Kodak Special boasted that "since the introduction of the Kodak thirty-four years ago there has been no greater single achievement in hand camera construction."

The earliest advertisements for the Autographic Kodaks are characterized by a notable appeal to a presumably masculine practicality. Matter-of-fact in design and text, these ads were directed toward professionals who needed to keep accurate information regarding inventory, dates, and other such matters. "Write it on the film—at the time. Record the 'Who, When, Where' on every negative," begins one of the first Autographic advertisements. The ad continues with the same matter-of-fact appeal to the value of information: "Architects, engineers, and contractors who make photographic records of progressive work, can add greatly to their value by adding notes and dates permanently on the negatives by means of the Autographic Kodak. The amateur photographer who wants to improve the quality of his work can make notations on his negatives, of the light conditions, stop and exposure."

Within several months, however, the look, content, and tone of these ads changed considerably, no doubt prompted by the public's initially lukewarm response to the invention. Kodak apparently recognized that it needed a series of advertisements more glamorous and sentimental, ads that would appeal to women as well as to men. One of the first new strategies it employed was to capitalize on the name "Autographic" and its various connotations. "Autograph," a signature, especially the signature of someone famous, evokes the aura of celebrity status, suggesting that every subject that appeared within the viewfinder of the Autographic camera would be recognized as important. Indeed, one of the later tips for using the camera was to have the subject inscribe his or her signature on the exposure.

In the 1920s advertisement shown in plate 16, for example, a man is pictured writing something on the camera while two women look on. Judging by the expressions and body language of the women—one looks adoringly at his face; the other gleefully leans over to get a glimpse of the signature—the advertisement suggests that this "ordinary" man has attained the status of movie star, and that his image, like a celebrity photo, will be treasured even more by these women because he has autographed it. The advertisement's springtime setting, reproduced in romantic shades of pink and green, accentuates the amatory dynamics of the pictured scenario, the overhanging cherry blossoms functioning as a traditional symbol of romance. The fact that two women are pictured here, rather than one, diffuses the charged implications of the scenario, however, suggesting that this man is somehow unattainable. What *is* attainable, the ad makes clear, is his

170 photograph and accompanying autograph, a feature that makes "every
◇ negative doubly valuable."

The captions accompanying the images in ads for Autographic Kodaks often ran for several paragraphs. Kodak captions are notoriously
short, usually no more than a sentence or two, in keeping with the
company's philosophy of simplicity and with modern advertising's tendency to avoid extensive text. When the text does exceed two or three
lines, it is generally to provide technical or retail information about
the product. But in many of the ads for the Autographic Kodak we find
up to three or four paragraphs of copy. Rather than including practical information, moreover, these captions offer extensive meditations
on such subjects as the fallibility of human memory, the bittersweet-
ness of parenthood, and the transitoriness of childhood.

Functioning as a type of narrative, captions call to mind Walter
Benjamin's observation that "the camera will become smaller and
smaller; more and more prepared to grasp fleeting, secret images whose
shock will bring the mechanism of association in the viewer to a complete halt. At this point captions must begin to function, captions
which understand the photography which turns all the relations of life
into literature, and without which all photographic construction must
remain bound in coincidences" ("Short History" 215). According to
Benjamin, captions perform a crucial narrative function because they
give structure and meaning to the otherwise fugitive nature of photographs. They anchor the image.

Hence, when verbose captions are employed for a campaign
that promotes the narrative qualities of photography, consumers are
doubly encouraged to view captions as meaning-making devices.[5] Eric
Margolis argues that captions "force meanings on the picture that are
neither explicitly nor implicitly part of the image. The words over-
determine and legislate meaning, further limiting critical evalua-
tion" (42). While I disagree with the absolutism of Margolis's claim,
believing that most photos allow for much more play between image
and caption, I do recognize its relevance in the case of these ads. As
advertising photos that aspire to the obvious rather than the ambiguous, Kodak's images are already overdetermined; accompanied by extensive meditations on their supposed meaning, they leave the viewer
little room to see much other than what Kodak intends her to see.

In a 1919 ad for the Autographic Kodak titled "His First Dress
Suit," family members admire the eldest boy's tuxedo as he goes to his

first dance. Any casual viewer would agree that here, as in most cases
of Kodak advertising, she requires no text to interpret the image. The
photograph contains signs formed to ensure that the viewer reads its
predetermined meaning correctly: a "first dress suit" marks an important occasion in a young boy's life, evidenced by the boy's proud air and
the admiration of his parents and siblings. Nevertheless, Kodak fur-
nishes an extensive description, part of which reads: "Bill, Jr. is conscious of a newly acquired dignity; little Jim is envious; Mother sits in
rapt admiration; Betty has an attack of the giggles, and Dad, in spite
of his sense of humor, realizes that this is a great day in the history of
his son and heir."

Kodak violates modern advertising's tenet about letting the image
"speak" for itself because it assumes that viewers, charmed by the
emotions conveyed through facial expressions and gestures in the photograph, will want to hear more about this fictionalized event in order
to imagine (or reflect upon) a similar one in their own lives. More important, the five-paragraph description suggests that the kind of
snapshots endorsed by Kodak (particularly those produced by the
Autographic Kodak) inspire imaginative readings that produce what
Barthes calls "second signifieds"—that is, meanings that are "retroac-
tively projected into the image" (*Image* 27). That is, snapshots inspire
imagination, feeding written text and thereby also calling attention to
the text's weaker status, an observation that reinforces Barthes's claim
that, with the advent of the newspaper photograph, illustration shifts
from a secondary role in the relation between text and image to a
dominant one.

Within less than a year of the camera's debut, Kodak had shifted
from accentuating the Autographic Kodak's practical value to stressing its sentimental value. In this effort, text was not all that assumed
a larger role; so did memory. In an article in *Kodakery* titled "On the
Negative," the writer advises the reader to "pick up a handful of your
old prints—look them over and try to tell from memory when the
negatives were made—and you will in future never fail to date the
negative" (25). After explaining the steps required to take an Autographic photograph, another advertisement ends with the guarantee
that "you have now titled your picture against a truant memory." "Truant" is a provocative choice, suggesting as it does that memory is delin-
quent, the camera a policing agent that will correct it, and the Kodak
system infallible. If Kodak's emphasis on simplicity emphasized that

172   consumers could depend on the company for the technical aspects of
◇   photography, it now intimated something far more extreme: that we
could now rely on the company, not on our own memories, for an accurate preservation of our personal histories.

Unquestionably, the strongest selling point for the Autographic camera was its role in alleviating the traumatic memories of World War I, as we shall see; but a close second was its supposed indispensability in the chronicling of children's activities and development. In one 1914 advertisement, the caption advises the consumer to "make your Kodak story of the children doubly valuable by dating every negative, by making brief notes that will help, in after years, to recall happily to memory the incident that led to the taking of the picture." What this ad implies, as so many of them do, is that parents whose children have grown up will yearn to relive a time when their children were younger, and that photographs will help alleviate the pain of watching their children mature. A 1926 advertisement promises, "Children are always little, and the scenes just as they used to be—in your Kodak album"; another one, also from the mid-1920s, reads: "With children in your home, there certainly should be Kodak pictures in your album. And the time will come when you'll never forgive yourself if the chance slips by." Manipulating consumers into feeling guilty if they fail to take pictures of their children, the ad also hints at a future sense of loss. It encourages *anticipation* of nostalgia, or, as Margaret Drabble so aptly phrases it, the state of being "sad in advance" (93).

In a remarkable advertisement from the 1920s, a young boy is pictured as he carves a toy boat (figure 35). So immersed is he in his hobby that he doesn't notice his father recording the scene with an Autographic camera. "For the Days to Come," the caption informs us, this foresighted "Dad, with his Kodak, has caught the boyish story" and "is writing the autographic record—the date and title on the film; the record that will give double value to the picture when time has played sad tricks with memory."

The most striking aspect of this advertisement is the fact that the man, with his thinning hair and his wrinkled face and hands, looks much older than we would expect the father of a young boy to be. Old age is already approaching, the ad suggests, and with it the "sad tricks" played by time on memory. Soon, too soon, the father will begin to forget this experience, but his Autographic Kodak will preserve the memory for him.

For the Days to Come.

Building his boat of pine and dreaming, as he works, of the days when he will sail a real ship on a real ocean—a regular boy, that.

And Dad, with his Kodak, has caught the boyish story. Now he is writing the autographic record—the date and title on the film; the record that will give double value to the picture when time has played sad tricks with memory.

Make the family chronicle complete. Let every picture of the children bear at least a date. It's all very simple, as simple as taking the picture itself —with an

Autographic Kodak

EASTMAN KODAK CO., Rochester, N. Y., *The Kodak City*

Figure 35. Advertisement for the Autographic Kodak camera with boy and his father, 1910s. (Reprinted courtesy of Eastman Kodak Company)

Storytelling

"Nothing seems more natural and universal to human beings," J. Hillis Miller writes, "than telling stories" (66). Miller proceeds to argue that narrative provides modes of ordering experience, two "closely related forms of 'order-giving' and 'order finding'" (68). It both creates its "orders" out of the stereotyping of experience and, at its best, allows those stereotypes to be transformed into insight and comprehension. A story, he maintains, "makes something happen in the real world: for example, it can propose modes of selfhood or ways of behaving that are then imitated in the real world. It has been said, along these lines, that we would not know we were in love if we had not read novels." Still, "if novels coach us to believe that there is such a thing as 'being in love,' they also at the same time subject that idea to effective demystification, while perhaps at the end showing the triumph of love beyond or in spite of its demystification" (69).

Nostalgia, as I have suggested, participates in the first task of narrative Miller describes: it orders the world by simplifying social and family life through narratives of self-evident community and conflict-free relationships. What makes narratives "simple" is their structure of a beginning, middle, and end, where the end is understood as a comprehension of the whole: the end of a story is implicit in its beginning and harmonizes the apparent difficulties and contradictions presented in the middle. If narrative can "demystify" experience, as Miller argues, it does so by not short-changing the difficulties of the middle of the story—the place where we all, as tellers and listeners to stories, find ourselves. A story's cheerfulness is its promise that the difficulties and confusions of its middle will eventually make sense. But when that "sense" does not grapple with the personal and social difficulties, contradictions, and cross-purposes that shape our experience, but instead reduces them to simple, stereotypical formulas, narrative impoverishes rather than enriches experience.

The task of narrative can clearly be discerned in the uses of nostalgia. Thus, as any antique dealer would acknowledge, one of the most successful strategies for selling an antique is to provide a story with a complicated middle and a simplifying end that makes the time period it represents seem more intimate to the potential buyer. Without such narratives, antiques threaten to become what in fact they are: timeworn, often useless objects of a remote and irrecoverable era.

Likewise, without some kind of accompanying story, photographs can
denote historical bankruptcy, their silence, fragility, and sheer profusion stubbornly resisting any attempt to assign them an intimate
meaning. Susan Stewart has argued that the starting point of nostalgia is narrative; a more accurate statement would be that nostalgia
dramatizes what is implicit in every memory act—the imposition of a
story on retrieved information.

Daniel Schacter reminds us that memories are not, like photographs, "passive or literal recordings of reality." They "are records
of how we have experienced events, not replicas of the events themselves" (46). They constitute highly subjective realities. Their subjec-
tivity, however, involves the actual transformation of retrieved information (which forms the basis of memory) into a meaningful scenario:
"In order to be experienced as a memory, the retrieved information
must be recollected in the context of a particular time and place and
with some reference to oneself as a central participant in the episode" (17). Memory, in other words, depends on a personalized narrative; nostalgia transforms that narrative (including the possible stresses
and uncertainties of events in progress) into fullness, innocence, and
simplicity.

If narrative lends usability to memories, however, it arguably de-
limits them as well—at least according to Gary Saul Morson:

> Narrative structure . . . falsifies in several distinct but closely re-
> lated ways. It violates the continuity of experience by imposing a
> beginning and an ending; it reduces the plurality of wills and pur-
> poses to a single pattern; it makes everything fit, whereas in life
> there are always loose ends; and it closes down time by confer-
> ring a spurious sense of inevitability on the sequence actually re-
> alized. The very possibility of possibility is ultimately eliminated.
> Whenever structure is present, there is no truly eventful process,
> only the execution of a pregiven plan. (38–39)

In other words, narrative's gift of bestowing value on experience (or
memory) necessarily involves the transmutation of multiple possibilities into one possibility. While such an observation could indeed be
countered by any number of exceptional cases of narrative making, it
is difficult to dispute Morson's claim in regard to Kodak's Story Campaign. For undoubtedly the business of advertising is to convince us of

176
◇

one particular way of seeing a product or concept—even when the subject is as elusive as photography. And especially when "story" gets relentlessly equated, as it does in these ads, with a "pregiven" emphasis on family and social harmony.

Photographs and the Stories They Tell

As objective and fragmentary records, photographs resemble retrieved information, their facticity similar to the details we remember before we have located them within a personal framework such as the details of household furniture we remember as part of our childhood home. Roland Barthes writes of such facticity when he says that "the Photograph does not necessarily say what is no longer, but only and for certain what has been. . . . In front of a photograph, our consciousness does not necessarily take the nostalgic path of memory . . . , but for every photograph existing in the world, the path of certainty: the Photograph's essence is to ratify what it represents" (*Camera Lucida* 85). It should be clear by now that in the Story Campaign Kodak sought to recreate photography's essence, to ensure that snapshots followed the path of nostalgia.

Although none of the ads produced under this campaign explicitly denigrate written language, they frequently imply that snapshots can now supersede words as the primary medium for recording personal events and relationships. Indeed, Kodak published dozens of articles on the superiority of photography to written language, the overall aim being, as one historian put it, to "convince the world that photography could become the principal instrument for education and the recording of history" (Brummett 45).

"Which will give you the most concise and most accurate information regarding an incident or a scene for your travel diary—a written description or a photograph?" rhetorically asks the author of "A Pictorial Diary" (21). Note his assumption that his readers will value concision and accuracy over elaboration and interpretation as desirable traits for their diaries. Such an assumption is especially ironic when one considers the historical role of the diary as a genre meant to valorize personal impression and encourage extended reflection. Rather than providing a limited and inevitably distorted account of a scene, as written descriptions do, photographs provide what he calls "comprehensive accuracy"—an interesting phrase, given the dual meaning of "comprehensive" as both inclusive and having a wide mental grasp.

The writer concludes with a statement submitted to *Kodakery* by one of its subscribers: "I am traveling over nearly all the States and in lieu of a diary I keep my Vest Pocket Kodak constantly loaded with me—each day taking one exposure as a record of that day—as near as possible the subject chosen being the representative one for that day" (21). In this understanding, experience itself is transformed from activity to passive reception. Moreover, the fact that this subscriber sees one photograph as representative of an entire day's events is remarkable, as if lived experience could somehow be encapsulated—and described in a diary—by one moment of time.

Kodak thus systematically promoted photography as a much more accurate and encompassing means of description than written language, which fails as historical record because it is too bound to the author's limited interpretation. At the same time, however, Kodak knew that its customers would want more than accuracy for their family and personal records; hence the company's deliberate use of the word "story" (as opposed to a more objectivity-laden word such as "history," "record," "account," or "chronicle"). More than most literary genres, as Miller suggests when he describes narrative as conveying "modes of selfhood or ways of behaving" (66), "story" connotes the celebration of individual experience.

In the worlds depicted by ads that associate snapshot photography with storytelling, "ordinary" scenes such as children seated at the breakfast table are framed as events worthy of capturing on film and remembering (figure 36). Indeed, the images and captions employed for the Story Campaign focus almost exclusively on home scenes, rather than, say, vacation settings or other kinds of excursions. To a twenty-first-century amateur photographer, setting up a tripod and manipulating the camera in order to compensate for indoor light, as the mother does in this advertisement, seems like an inordinate amount of effort to capture children eating a meal, but such scenes are precisely the kinds of images the viewer finds in later Kodak ads, particularly those produced for the Story Campaign. According to these advertisements, snapshots provide the basis of stories not only because they record such personal and ordinary events but because they present the photographer's point of view and thus, putatively, her unique way of framing the world. "The Kodak Story of summer days

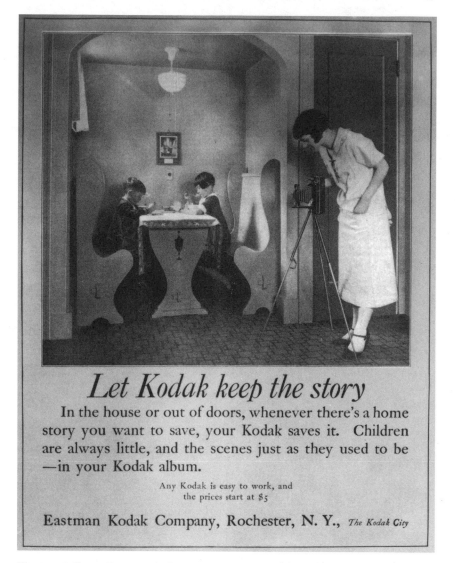

Figure 36. Story Campaign advertisement, *Pictorial Review*, October 1926.
(Reprinted courtesy of Eastman Kodak Company)

grows in charm as the months go by—it's always interesting—it's personal—it tells of the places, the people, and the incidents from your
point of view—just as you saw them."

In their redaction of the photographer's viewpoint, snapshots supposedly embody the selection, discrimination, and specificity so necessary to good storytelling, what Ruth Tooze calls the storyteller's
"sixth sense" of knowing what material will constitute a compelling
narrative. The insistent and characteristic emphasis on "you" in this
caption alerts us once again to Kodak's encouragement of the largely
illusory notion that the amateur photographer's independent interests,
perceptions, and judgment are at work in each production of a snapshot. Such an illusion builds upon narrative's ability to simplify experience by making its beginning (interests), middle (perceptions), and
end (judgment) a seeming whole.

Seen nostalgically, stories are the literary province of children—
the genre most associated with their education, their entertainment,
and their participation. In this sense, Kodak's association of photography with storytelling extends its portrayal of children as embodiments
of Kodak simplicity and innocence. Just as children are popularly regarded as the ideal audience for stories, they are also represented in
Kodak advertising as the consummate viewers and practitioners of
snapshot photography. Such a message is vividly conveyed in a 1922
advertisement that pictures a young mother or older sister about to
photograph a grandmother reading to four children (figure 37). The
costume, hairstyle, and pose of the older woman are notably out of
date for the time period, rendering her the stereotypical grandmother
and thus transforming the contemporary scene into a picture laden
with the nostalgia of storybook sentiment. Framed at the front porch
of the house, the notably staged snapshot suggests that such domestic scenes are the kind of spontaneous, domestic "stories" Kodak cameras can record; indeed, the accompanying caption explains that Kodak stories depend on candid and natural moments that take place
within the home or family unit: "Today it's a picture of Grandmother
reading to the children. Tomorrow it may be Bobbie playing the traffic
policeman or Aunt Edna at the wheel of her new car or Brother Bill
back from college for the week-end or—There's always another story
waiting for your Kodak."

The caption's emphasis on spontaneity belies the staged quality
of the snapshot, compensating for its artifice and at the same time

Figure 37. Advertisement for Autographic Kodak with grandmother reading to children, 1922. (Reprinted courtesy of Eastman Kodak Company)

transforming the image into narrative. More significant, this ad suggests that when the photograph the young woman is about to take has assumed its place in the photograph album, these four children will "read" it at some later point in time, just as Grandmother now reads a story in a book. The compositional symmetry of the photograph, in fact, reinforces the similarity between the acts of reading and picture taking, a symmetry sharpened by the fact that two women are represented as the storytellers. One of the less noticeable but equally compelling aspects to this advertisement is that while the younger children stand in rapt attention to their grandmother's story, the eldest girl, on the far right, looks directly at the photographer, perhaps implying that she is too old to appreciate the stories in the book but mature enough to sense the importance of the domestic stories created by the camera. An observer outside both activities, she seems to be reflecting on the storytelling capacity of the camera as she distances herself from her grandmother's narrative. Photography thus becomes subtly aligned here with an initiation into womanly maturity at the same time that it is contextualized within the narrative of childhood and growth.

This insistence on describing photographs as simple, spontaneous, accessible to children, and comprehensive enough to be classified as stories that unite a beginning, middle, and end is especially remarkable when we consider that photographs have historically been described as possessing an unsettling combination of silence and fragmentation, on the one hand, and a tendency to include frustratingly extraneous information, on the other. John Berger calls this triangulation of characteristics photography's "accidental" nature; Barthes defines it as photography's "stupidity." As transcripts of reality, photographs—especially snapshots—stare us blankly in the face with their apparent lack of an interpreting and organizing eye, their annoying—or what Barthes even calls their "violent"—tendency to encompass details that seem to exceed or violate the intention of the photographer or the overall narrative they might otherwise convey. These extraneous elements (to which Barthes famously referred as the photograph's "punctum") are precisely what make snapshots potentially subversive, for they jeopardize the intended reading of the photograph, threatening to displace it with the more imaginative and expressive reading of the no longer guided viewer. By promising consumers that photographs could indeed tell "their" stories, Kodak advertising thus not only sought to reinforce a personal dimension to

182 snapshot photography; it effectively purged the medium of its more
◇ subversive meanings, the snapshot's potentially fugitive characteristics
now wholly ballasted by the promise and domestication of story.

If narrative has the potential, as Miller says, of "effective de-mystification" (69), the snapshot narratives of the Story Campaign rely solely on the mystifications of stereotype. Hence the oft-noted fact that so many family snapshots look remarkably similar, that they tend to generate a much more limited range of readings and meanings than other sorts of photographs. Conditioned to believe that photographs can tell stories of family unity and harmony, most amateur photographers have fallen into the habit of taking stock images—children at play, family members grouped on front porches, automobiles, Christmas trees—that are striking only in their resemblance to the images in Kodak ads. What is left out of the storytelling snapshot as Kodak depicts it—with its stereotypical grandmother, its repeatable families, its easy ironies—is precisely what Benjamin calls the "catastrophe" of the image, the catastrophic fact of the mortality of the older woman inscribed in every retrospective viewing of the snapshot, which the narrative of family harmony (which has room enough for the elder daughter's sympathetic irony) cannot accommodate.

Narrative, Community, and the Privatization of Experience

Of all literary genres, stories arguably come closest to the ideal behind all written language, the desire to impart to listeners the cohesion and value of one's own intentions, perceptions, and interpretations—the beginning, middle, and end of experience. Viewed in traditional terms, stories celebrate community and continuity, a fact reinforced by their associations with oral tradition and live performance. Unlike most other literary genres, they are frequently meant to be heard and performed. Like dance, they are popularly regarded as a "living art," with words becoming a "living substance for all who listen" (Sawyer 30). But photography has no such quality. Indeed, as Barthes and Sontag so famously argued, photography is a murderous art, the camera enacting its own version of death in the transmutation of living subject into frozen image.

Less extremely, we might note that photographs serve to solidify identity whereas stories (at least oral stories) encourage the temporary

suspension of identity through the vicarious act of listening to another's experience. By contextualizing the photograph within the discourses and practices of storytelling, Kodak advertising thus sought to
endow snapshot photography with an illusory animation, suggesting
that photographs can be animated upon each viewing, just as stories
are animated upon performance, and that, just like stories, they can
unite their audience through coherent experience that is also shared.

Indeed, according to histories of storytelling roughly contemporaneous with the Autographic Kodak, storytelling has its roots in the desire for vicarious pleasure and experience. "In his goings and comings,
and all that he told of life outside his group's experience, [the ancient
storyteller] widened their horizons, lengthened their point of view, and
even deepened their understanding. And if he had great skill, something of the story entered into their very souls, their essential beings,
and became a part of them. If a story becomes part of the experience
of many people, this quality of universality makes it live" (Tooze 6). As
readers during the 1910s and 1920s would generally have viewed it, the
storyteller's idealized role was thus to convey a deeper and more ex-
pansive view of the world, while at the same time reformulating alien
experience into the familiar and recognizable. Photographs also pur-
port to offer such vicarious pleasure; indeed, one of the earliest and
most common uses of photography after the invention of the wet collodion process in 1851 was to market foreign scenes as substitutes for
actual travel, as miniature simulacra of the real locales.

One of the major transformations in photography effected by
Kodak, however, has been the increasing tendency to limit our expectations and practices of snapshot photography. Kodak ads effectively
instilled in consumers a sense of snapshot photography as a highly private activity, as private as the immediate family. In so doing, it ensured
that the nuclear family and the events that help maintain its survival—births, marriages, vacations, holidays—would form the dead
center of photographic culture and, indeed, of culture as a whole. It
is as if the enormous dislocations of the early twentieth century—
the "rearrangement" of the relationships between men and women,
masters and servants, employers and workers that Virginia Woolf
had in mind when she wrote that "on or about October 1910, human
nature changed" (194)—called for the stereotyping simplicity of com-
prehending experience only on the level of domestic life. The strongest

184 historical moment of such early twentieth-century dislocations is
◇ World War I, which, as Paul Fussell argues, gave rise to the "one domi-
nating form of modern understanding: that it is essentially ironic; and
that it originates largely in the application of mind and memory to the
events of the Great War" (35). As we shall see, irony threatened to
transform myths, legends, and folk heroes into the fragmentary memories arising out of World War I.

Thus Kodak's Story Campaign promised to erase the opposition
between private family harmony and public disruption simply by domesticating and forgetting the world of public turmoil. Kodak went so
far in reducing all experience to private stereotype that it became increasingly difficult to respond to photographs with the kind of imagination necessary for stories. Amateur photographers go on vacations
and return with photographs to show friends and family members, but
the truth is that no one but the people in the photographs can enjoy
viewing them. It is as if all the pleasure in taking photographs resides
in the possibility of recreating the experience rather than sharing it.
Any attempt to share photographs with others who did not participate
in the event almost immediately turns flat; hence the cliché about the
ordeal of sitting through someone else's home movies and vacation
slides.

Interestingly, Kodak published several articles in the *Kodakery*
on this very problem. In "Telling the Story with Your Kodak," Harry
Phibbs asks: "Have you ever shown your pictures to friends and found
that they looked at them with a bored air of indifference? If so, the
reason is that the prints, which may be good as photographic records,
and may also be very interesting to you and to the people who posed
in them, meant nothing to others, because they were merely a collection of photographs of one or more people smiling vacantly into
the lens" (9).

The salient aspect here is the attempt to encourage a view of photographs as more than private records despite all the company's notable efforts to effect this very perception. The writer then proceeds to
offer a series of examples illustrating how photographs can be transformed into stories, one of which I'll quote in its entirety:

> Just to show what I mean let's join two young people as they walk
> through the woods. They wish to be photographed, of course. A

common procedure is to pose the pair, then say something that   185
will make them smile, and snap the picture at a moment when   ◇
they are smiling a sheepish grin into the lens. Let's avoid this
method and make the picture tell a story.

They are sweethearts taking a stroll through Lovers' Lane. An
old fence and the shade of a tree form the setting. We ask the girl
to lean against the fence and request her companion to place his
hand on the fence post and lean forward while he engages her in
conversation . . . and the result is "Lovers' Lane." (10)

Anyone who has fallen into the trap of taking frontal shots and awkward poses would appreciate this suggestion, encouraging as it does a
more imaginative response to the act of photographing. But in dis-
suading readers from taking stock pictures, the writer creates a pictorial story out of a narrative cliché, as if exhausted literary elements can
be viewed as creative precisely because they are taken by the amateur
photographer and his instrument of nostalgia.

One of the aims behind Kodak's association of snapshots with stories was to endow the realism of the photograph with a fictional quality, thus engendering in consumers a sense that their photographs
could indeed provide a narrative that would enrich or romanticize relationships as well as events, just as stories enrich actual events for its
listeners and, I might add, for its tellers as well. Kodak thus appropri-
ates the fabulist nature of the storyteller in order to compensate for
the reportorial nature of the camera. But whereas stories often celebrate the magical and extraordinary, photography has always operated
under the burden of accurate depiction. Our desire, then, to embel-
lish or recreate our actual experiences in the manner of storytellers
can always be curtailed by the photographs we take, which offer insistent proof of what actually occurred.

A salient question arises out of these observations: How has photography's emphasis on honesty, accuracy, direct and unadulterated
reporting limited our imaginative capacities? The worst kind of stories,
claims Ruth Sawyer, are those that seek only to impart information.
And yet the "stories" produced by Kodak are more often than not limited to this function. "Imagination, perception, insight, enthusiasm,
spontaneity, concentration—these are the qualities of a creative artist.
Add to these the desire to share experience with listeners, sensitivity

186

◇   to the needs and moods of those listeners, sincere joy in the sharing
process, and you have the makings of a good storyteller," promises
Sawyer (17).

The camera, of course, lacks all of these characteristics. It merely
records information, a fact dramatized by the marketing and extreme
popularity of the Autographic camera. And it is precisely because we
fear the loss of these qualities ourselves that we turn to photography
as a means of recording, indeed of certifying, our experiences and relationships. This is Benjamin's argument in "The Storyteller," but he
adds that we have lost them precisely because of the individualism of
storytelling as it is practiced by the novelist, whose aim is to impart information and an "end," whereas a story's aim is to be continued and
retold by others, so that storytelling remains, essentially, a social activity. It is for this reason that he defines the opposite of experience
as "information" (87), just as he argues that "the epic side of truth,
wisdom," is dying out in the face of the informational grab bag of
the newspaper, which we might call "snapshots" of information in
the news.

"Every morning," Benjamin writes, "brings us the news of the
globe, and yet we are poor in noteworthy stories. This is because no
event any longer comes to us without already being shot through with
explanation. In other words, by now almost nothing that happens
benefits storytelling; almost everything benefits information" (89).
The "explanation" Benjamin describes is the stereotyping of narrative
I have been touching upon, modes of comprehension that are pre-
conceived, orderly, and shot through with the nostalgia of private
meaning.

No wonder, then, that no one else shares our interest in our own
photographs. Experience can never simply be passed on to another
without some effort to recreate that experience through a narrative
that transcends factual information, solely personal experience, and
charged stereotype. Individual experience, in other words, must be re-
formulated into larger patterns of human experience or no one listens.
If Kodak is "keeping the story," who are the listeners? Only those, presumably, who have already been through the experience, or who are
intimately tied to the subjects the snapshots depict. And even that
small group soon loses interest. After breathlessly waiting for their
photographs to be developed, most amateur photographers soon put

them away in boxes, up on shelves, and in albums, often letting years 187
go by before they look at them again, bored by the reduction of their ◇
experiences to information, a reduction Tooze claims marks the death
of all stories.

Kodak and World War I

What is the wisdom World War I imparts? This is the great question
that troubles all the chroniclers of that overwhelming disruptive moment in modern cultural history, when all the forces of Enlightenment
"progress"—wealth, the enormous growth in Western populations,
the fantastic knowledge and information gained through the triumphs
of Newtonian science, the emerging social sciences, and the great
technical achievements of the late nineteenth century—conspired to
create one of the greatest catastrophes of shared history. In "The
Storyteller" Benjamin tries to answer the problem of the "wisdom"
that we might take from the war:

> Every glance at a newspaper demonstrates that [experience] has
> reached a new low, that our picture, not only of the external
> world but of the moral world as well, overnight has undergone
> changes which were never thought possible. With the [First]
> World War a process began to become apparent which has not
> halted since then. Was it not noticeable at the end of the war that
> men returned from the battlefield grown silent—not richer, but
> poorer in communicable experience? . . . For never has experi-
> ence been contradicted more thoroughly than strategic experi-
> ence by tactical warfare, economic experience by inflation, bod-
> ily experience by mechanical warfare, moral experience by those
> in power. A generation that had gone to school on a horse-drawn
> streetcar now stood under the open sky in a countryside in which
> nothing remained unchanged but the clouds, and beneath these
> clouds, in a field of force of destructive torrents and explosion,
> was the tiny, fragile human body. (84)

Here Benjamin attempts to articulate the loss of communication conditioned by the Great War, the ways it destroyed institutions of
community—including the institutions of storytelling—that allowed

188 people to comprehend "public" modes of understanding. Like the history of snapshot photography, World War I ended in private experiences, even though many people retained a prewar sense that the war was a kind of play—what Modris Eksteins calls "a game, deadly earnest, to be sure, but a game nevertheless" (123)—something that Ekstein argues the Great War made impossible to imagine afterward.

We can find evidence of the incommunicability Benjamin speaks of in the official and press photos produced during the war, remarkable mainly for what they *don't* tell about combat, suffering, disillusionment, and death. Caught been government censorship on the one hand and its own technical limitations on the other, photography failed to communicate to the American public World War I's actual atrocities and tragedies. Susan Moeller develops this observation:

> What seems so disappointing about the World War I photographs is the near-total absence of either a sense of the horror or the thrill of the danger. The photographs are remarkably static— more so than the camera technology insisted. They portray neither a sense of emotion nor one of movement. No photographs were published during the war of individual faces showing the glazed eyes of the shell-shocked or the naive look of the recruits. With the exception of studio portraits, few pictures of individuals were published at all. There were many dull, pedestrian images of groups, interesting now for their quaint sepia-toned evocation of times gone by. But periodicals did not publish pictures of U.S. troops vaulting desperately over trenches of American bodies lying soddenly in heaps. The scenes existed, but they either were not photographed or, if they were, the negatives were not printed. (126)

To a large extent, the blandness of Word War I's pictorial record may be blamed on censorship and propaganda. Along with the suppression of numbers of dead soldiers during the war, the censorship of written commentary that criticized the United States' involvement, the attempts to hide reports of human errors and technological failings, and the fictionalized accounts of German atrocities, photographs participated in a systematic effort to glorify the United States' role in the war. The American Expeditionary Force, which employed more than fifty print correspondents and photographers, issued such severe

restrictions on what could be represented that some photographers resorted to taking photos clandestinely to illustrate their articles despite
the risk of dismissal and even imprisonment (Moeller 111). No photos
that could affect the morale of the American soldier, the public at
home, or the United States' relations with the Allied governments
were allowed to be taken. Consequently, soldiers in compromising
situations or poses were not to be photographed, nor were mangled
airplanes, wrecked war vessels, trenches of American dead, operating
rooms in hospitals—anything, in short, that would "cause unnecessary and unwarranted anxiety to the families of men at the front"
(quoted in Moeller 114).

What the photographs did show were anonymous battlefields,
titled generically with captions such as "Our Heroes at the Front."
Neither individual photographers nor picture agencies were credited.
At home, the closest Americans came to seeing death in the *New
York Times* was the studio portraits of men killed in the war and
photographs of battleside graveyards. In the studio portraits, the soldiers all seemed to convey small-town American upbringing: very few
blacks were featured, nor were men from cities such as New York
and San Francisco. Photos of dead enemy soldiers did occasionally appear, however, reinforcing the impression that the enemy was indeed
defeatable.

The result was not only public ignorance about the war but a response to photography that remained within the confines of Barthes's
studium. Official photographs of the war, whether released by the
press or by a government agency, encouraged a sense of being disaf-
fected and outside—a tendency to explore the subjects pictured in
war photographs as a theme or question rather than as a "wound"
(*Camera Lucida* 27). The response, in other words, was carefully conditioned to lack the private urgency of death—an urgency that, for
Barthes, lies at the heart of photography.

Like the official photos of the war, the Autographic Kodak contributed to the loss of communication Benjamin describes by its refusal to feature tragedy or atrocity. It differed from the official photos,
however, in its insistence on the seeming self-contradiction of the essential privacy of experience, on the one hand, and the universality of
the forms and structures of that experience within the nuclear family,
on the other.

Paul Fussell describes a recruitment poster for the war effort that

190   comports in interesting ways with both the official photos of the war
◇   and Kodak's advertising campaigns.

> The Great War was perhaps the last to be conceived as taking
> place within a seamless, purposeful "history" involving a coher-
> ent stream of time running from past through present to future.
> The shrewd recruiting poster depicting a worried father of the fu-
> ture being asked by his children, "Daddy, what did *you* do in the
> Great War?" assumes a future whose moral and social pressures
> are identical with those of the past. Today, when each day's expe-
> rience seems notably *ad hoc,* no such appeal would shame the
> most stupid to the recruiting office. But the Great War took place
> in what was, compared with ours, a static world, where the val-
> ues appeared stable and where the meanings of abstractions
> seemed permanent and reliable. Everyone knew what Glory was,
> and what Honor meant. It was not until eleven years after the war
> that Hemingway could declare in *A Farewell to Arms* that "ab-
> stract words such as glory, honor, courage, or hallow were ob-
> scene beside the concrete names of villages, the numbers of
> roads, the names of rivers, the numbers of regiments and the
> dates." In the summer of 1914 no one would have understood
> what on earth he was talking about. (21)

What Fussell is talking about is a particular kind of "story campaign"
for the Great War, which to twenty-first-century eyes and ears seems
to traffic in cliché and stereotype—to reduce, as Benjamin says, experience to "bottomlessness" ("Storyteller" 84).

According to Fussell, such a recruitment campaign could never be
produced again after the war was over, for no surviving soldier could
see a poster like the one Fussell describes without some temptation to
read it ironically. The difference between the years before the war and
those after it, Fussell argues, is the striking, apocalyptic nature of the
war, which, like death itself, violently linked together the play of a particular moment and a past comprehended as irretrievably lost. Thus,
on the day after Britain joined the war, Henry James wrote that "the
plunge of civilization into this abyss of blood and darkness . . . is a
thing that so gives away the whole long age during which we have supposed the world to be . . . gradually bettering, that to have to take it all

now for what the treacherous years were all the while really making for and *meaning* is too tragic for words" (quoted in Fussell 8). The "moment" of the Great War falsified the past, rewrote it so that its pleasures and its stories all seemed, as they did to Hemingway, somehow obscene. Out of it arose what Fussell describes as the great irony of the war—the pervasion of memory by irony—so that after the war serious memory could function only with the aid of what he terms the mechanisms of "irony-assisted recall." "By applying to the past a paradigm of ironic action, a rememberer is enabled to locate, draw forth, and finally shape into significance an event or a moment which otherwise would merge without meaning into the general undifferentiated stream" (30).

Needless to say, what Fussell describes here isn't the only mechanism of memory. Another one, promulgated by Kodak, uses paradigms of harmonious story and stereotype, the very import of the glory, honor, and courage that the war erased for Hemingway. Stories attached to such terms functioned at home even while, as Fussell demonstrates, they were rendered impossible for the men who lived for months on end at the front. They functioned in the very recruitment advertising Fussell describes, and they were the heart of Kodak's response to the Great War.

In one advertisement, a young mother and child prepare to send photographs of their presumably ordinary daily lives to the father overseas (figure 38). The caption reads: "The morning letter of cheer and hope has been written and with it pictures are going, simple Kodak pictures that will bring a cheery smile to his face, a leap of joy to his heart, that will keep the bright fire of courage in his soul as with the home image fresh in mind he battles for the safety of that home and for the honor of his flag." Through the intimacy of a letter, these photos will be situated in the extraordinary and catastrophic world of war, where they will then become the memories that sustain the soldier. The stereotyped image of a state rather than of action transforms the soldier into the idealized father, and the family at home can "remember" him as such rather than as subject to the war's catastrophes. The star prominently displayed in the window, as the caption says, tells the story—their soldier is over there. Like snapshots, the star traffics in cliché, reducing the pain and violence of absence with a reassuring symbol of pride and patriotism. A certain kind of memory—seemingly

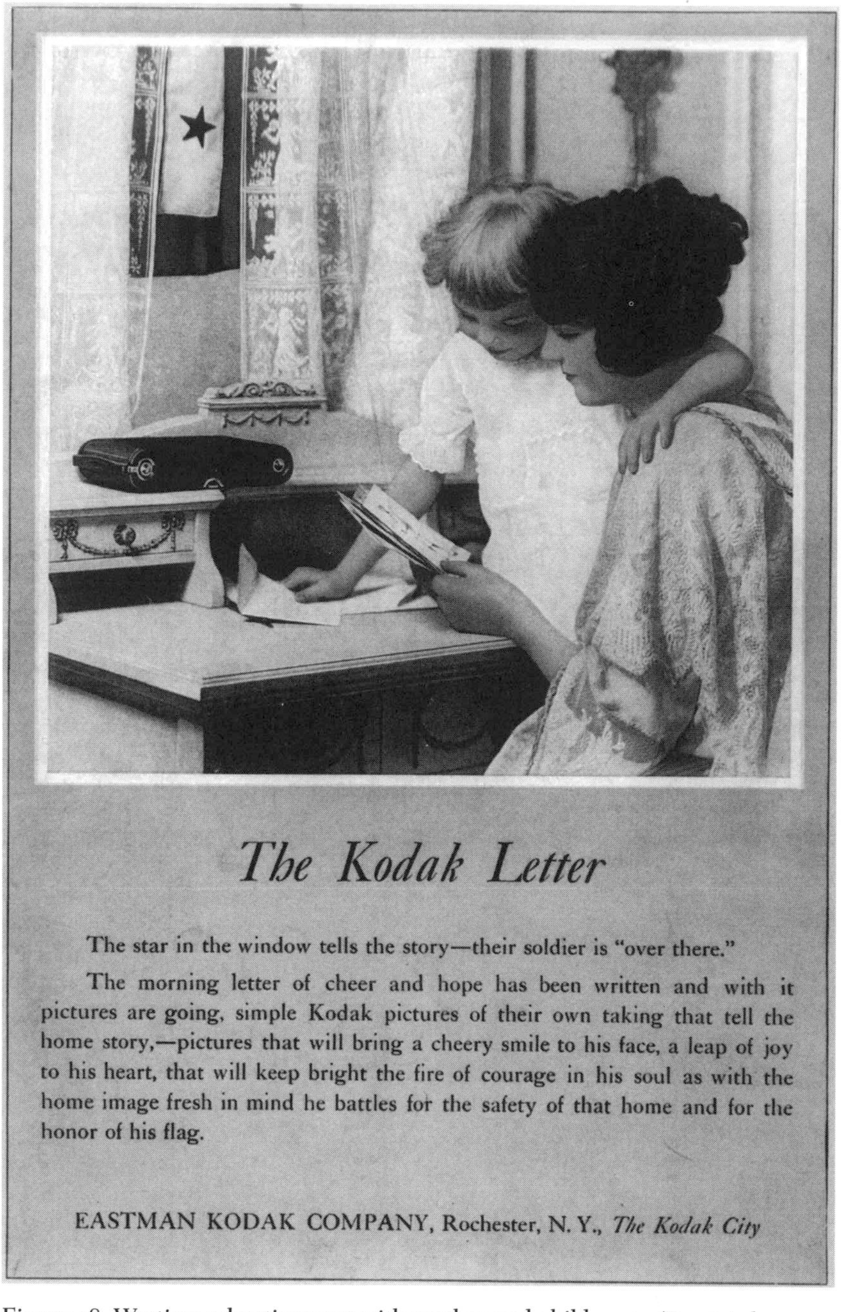

The Kodak Letter

The star in the window tells the story—their soldier is "over there."

The morning letter of cheer and hope has been written and with it pictures are going, simple Kodak pictures of their own taking that tell the home story,—pictures that will bring a cheery smile to his face, a leap of joy to his heart, that will keep bright the fire of courage in his soul as with the home image fresh in mind he battles for the safety of that home and for the honor of his flag.

EASTMAN KODAK COMPANY, Rochester, N. Y., *The Kodak City*

Figure 38. Wartime advertisement with mother and child, 1917. (Reprinted courtesy of Eastman Kodak Company)

storied, but hardly touching the pathos of Benjamin's "horse-drawn
streetcar"—is provoked at the home front rather than at the battle
front so that the war itself can be forgotten.

Many ads picture a father holding his child as his wife takes a photograph of them, with a caption underneath headed "Before He Goes"
(figure 39). The captions explain that as he fights overseas, he will
treasure such photos as reminders of what he fights for and will return
to. But in this advertisement the sheer physical distance between wife
and husband undercuts such sentiment, visually reminding us of the
impending separation. Indeed, the tension in this photograph resides
precisely in its sentiment of family affection and unity, despite the fact
of war, and in its visual attention to the overwhelmingly empty space
between husband and wife. Just as important, the possibility also exists that this photo will become an object of solace, not for the father
and husband overseas but for the widow and orphaned daughter he
has left at home.

What I am doing, of course, is reading the photograph with the
kind of irony that Fussell finds inhabiting all narrative just on the
other side of the timeless narratives of stereotype. I am able to do so
because this image provides one of the very few possibilities in the history of Kodak advertising to read an image ironically, despite the
"overdetermined" nature, to return to Eric Margolis, of the caption.
The fact that such an opportunity occurs in an ad centered on separation caused by war, moreover, testifies to the overwhelming ironies
of World War I, traced here even in the midst of packaged nostalgia.

Most of the time, however, the ads of the Story Campaign resist
such irony. The majority of advertisements during the war picture
wives and children at home; those that do feature men overseas never
locate them in an identifiable landscape, just as the official photographs of the war rarely were accompanied by captions that specified location or battle. The men are in camp, either alone or in groups,
looking at photos of home and family (figure 40). The pictures suggest
above all a domestic story in which the privacy and intimacy of the
snapshot allow the soldier to create his own interior world within the
landscape of war. Such ads privatize the war just as the Story Campaign privatizes experience, with such captions as "An Intimate Story
of the War" and "The Pictures from Home." One caption even enjoins
its reader to "Let Your Kodak Album Keep the Home Story of the War.
Today that story means history, and more than ever it is important that

194
◇

Figure 39. Wartime advertisement with mother taking photo of father and child, 1917. (Reprinted courtesy of Eastman Kodak Company)

it be authentic history—that every negative bear a date. Let Kodak keep the date." Here war gets collected as a subject for the family album, an episode in the narrative of domestic life, presumably along with the wedding, the baby's first steps, the graduation, and family vacations. Kodak thus allows war to be domesticated, in every sense of

The Picture From Home

Figure 40. Wartime advertisement with American soldier, 1917. (Reprinted courtesy of Eastman Kodak Company)

196
◇ the word, and its meaning resides in its relation to the subjects of the other photographs in the album. That is, war becomes part of a family history, rather than, as Benjamin has it, a historical "catastrophe."

In a remarkable article in the *Kodak Salesman* that attempts to transform war to personal experience and success in war to maintaining a proper personal psychology, the writer boldly announces that

> pictures are going to help us win this war; not only those made by intrepid observers in the air and other war photographers but those made by the folks at home. The elements which compose human courage are complex; it takes more than a sound body and mind and a belief in the cause for which he is fighting; it requires in addition the sustaining of morale to make the fighting man content with his job. Nostalgia—homesickness—will take a man's nerve far quicker than anything else, but give him a cheery letter from home, and some snapshots of the loved ones, and of the familiar home scenes, and the hun had best have a care. ("Snapshots from Home" 12)

Note the reference to nostalgia, which gets described by its most archaic definition, as "homesickness." Kodak ads rarely, if ever, refer to nostalgia, no doubt because of its associations with delusion and excessive sentimentality. In this case, nostalgia emerges as a by-product of the war, not of photography; indeed, photography functions as the antidote to it. The article begins by advancing the importance of snapshots as equal to that of documentary or strategic photos of the war, an interesting statement given Kodak's development of special film and equipment that would aid the U.S. Army in its tactical maneuvers, as well as in Kodak's six-week training program for selected recruits to take aerial photos of the war. It was in the area of aerial photography, argues Susan Moeller, that the war produced its most exceptional photographic accomplishments. Thanks largely to Kodak, soldiers could take photos, develop them in the daylight developing tank, fix them, and rinse them all while on board an airplane. The negatives were then parachuted to the ground, where a waiting messenger rushed them to a darkroom. The photos were processed and, within fifteen minutes, in the hands of a commanding officer planning his next attack (117).

Still, this particular essay clearly privileges the private snapshot over the public or army document. While everyone else may view official photographs, it suggests, only the soldier at war will view those made for him by his family. At the same time it also implies that no "official" activity can replace the soldier's private and personal morale; that war is, at bottom, a private affair—but a private affair quite different from the kind Eksteins describes as a common postwar anxiety: "If the war as a whole had no objective meaning, then invariably all human history was telescoped into each man's experience; every person was the sum total of history. Rather than being a social experience, a matter of documentable reality, history was individual nightmare, or even, as the Dadaists insisted, madness" (293).

Kodak rarely hints at the possibility of such individual nightmares. One exception is a surprising article titled "The Ways of Peace" in *Kodakery*, which begins by describing how the Kodak camera, like the soldier, has borne witness to sights it must now learn to forget: "The peacefulest, kindliest person you know could not suggest a less turbulent companion than a Kodak. Yet, of a sudden, by the accident of war, the camera came under pressure. Like the kindliest person it had to be shut out here and there. Its very truthfulness became a hazard, for war must have its secrets, and its secrets must be kept" (3–4). The cryptic language in this passage skirts around the violence of war, the ironies of its apprehensions, the losses suffered on the front and at home. It admits, through its very evasiveness, that Kodak refuses confrontation with death and the black-humor ironies that Fussell sees permeating memory transformed by the Great War. "Now that the war has ended," this article proceeds, "the camera can turn its face away from scenes of excitement and devastation to scenes of beauty and tranquility. And where it has lived at home—the picture-hungry soldier was glad of its work at home—it is better able than it had been for a long time to express simple and comfortable things that help the world to forget its troubles" (4). Like the nostalgic image of a soldier returning home, photography can once again see the innocence and beauty of the world. If, as Fussell argues, the Great War transformed and contaminated memory itself with irony and cynicism, photography is here portrayed as the antidote to such memory, the forgetfulness of stereotyped nostalgia.

An article in *Kodakery* describing a book produced by the company called *Kodak War Portraits* explains how Kodak photographers have managed to find shots of heroism and comradeship in the scenes

198

◇

of war. "It is impossible not to feel freshly grateful to the camera, to the wonderfully compact and weapon-like Kodak, every time one sees a graphic series like this. Such pictures keep us close to the human heart that is beating 'over there.' They tell us vividly about the figures in the biggest drama that ever was acted. They carry to us the cheery smile of the man who is staking all on a simple duty that has behind it the most eloquent of all possible meanings" ("Picturing the World War," 4). Here a soldier's participation in war gets described much like a snapshot—"simple" but immensely meaningful in that simplicity. The writer concludes by saying that "we are not least grateful for every fragment of proof that the war is not all cheerless or inhuman, that not every moment is filled with horrors and that even the fringe of tragedy may have elements of beauty" (4).

To call the war a "fringe of tragedy"—to assert that the Great War barely approximates tragedy—and at the same time to clothe it in, of all things, the discourse of fashion is to encapsulate the import of all of Kodak's uses of the war in its advertisements and publications. This writer wishes to aestheticize the war for his readers, to transform apocalyptic event into domestic comedy. This is a far cry from the "modern memory" Fussell describes as ironic, growing out of "a world where myth is of no avail and where traditional significance has long ago been given up for lost" (58). Moreover, the aestheticization of experience that this article and the Story Campaign in general call for is tied up with the stereotyping and anti-irony of all stories with harmonies of beginnings, middles, ends. Irony is the aesthetic of cacophony, not harmony. That is why it is the ironies and anxieties of non-narrative poetry that most fully capture the ethos of modern memory that Fussell describes. Thus Fussell quotes H. M. Tomlinson's observation that "the parapet, the wire, and the mud" are now "permanent features of human existence." This is to say, Fussell concludes, "that anxiety without end, without purpose, without reward, and without meaning is woven into the fabric of contemporary life" (320). Such anxiety is the opposite of story and narrative; and it is precisely what Kodak aimed to eliminate from memory.

The Great War thus drew the line between the play of the camera and its possibilities of recovering nostalgic history. It did so by presenting to experience cataclysmic events that threatened to transform memory into irony and experience into anxiety. Kodak's Story Campaign did exactly the opposite: it transformed memory into stereotype

and experience into paradigm. Just as the leisure and play of the earlier Kodak advertisements responded to a world of new disposable ◇
wealth and disposable time, so the work of memoried Kodak responded
to a world where memory itself was threatening to disappear in the
face of unheard-of and "inexpressible" experience. Fussell claims that
the Great War created "a world where myth is of no avail and where
traditional significance has long ago been given up for lost" (58).
Needless to say, he is wrong in this, or at least not altogether right. Because the Great War also created a world in which cliché could replace catastrophe and a lost tradition of significance could be replaced
by kitsch. While such forms impoverish experience, helping to produce historical amnesia, they also help offset brutal memories of violence and tragedy.

On a more positive note, then, we might see Kodak's Story Campaign as having provided a valuable compensation to those who lived
through the war: the promise to make meaning out of chaos, separation, and death. Drawing on narrative's associations with unity, structure, and closure, Kodak encouraged viewers to see the war years as a
necessary part of their lives' stories. War could be remembered safely
if one took the right kind of photos—the soldier going off to war, the
family waiting at home, the fortunate soldier returning home. As Leo
Spitzer demonstrates in his reflections on the seeming incongruence
between the cheerfulness of the snapshots produced by his family during their escape from Nazi-occupied Austria and the bleak reality of
their situation, such images do not have to be written off as mere tools
of forgetting. They can also function as a means of survival, even if the
price of that survival is "stories" that omit much more than they tell.

Coda

Kodak's Death Campaign

D
URING THE summer of 1932, the J. Walter Thompson agency de-
signed a series of advertisements for Kodak called the "Death
Campaign." In all the reading I had done on Kodak, published
and unpublished, I had never come across any reference to these ads.
In all my extensive talks with curators, librarians, photo technicians,
and historians during my numerous trips to the Kodak Company, the
George Eastman House, and the Hartman Center for Sales, Advertising, and Marketing History, no one had ever mentioned them to me.
As with most real finds in research, I learned about the Death Campaign completely by accident. Having just finished my final research
trip to the Hartman Center, which had produced nothing surprising
or new, I was preparing to leave when an assistant mentioned the ads
to me. "Weird stuff," she commented with a shudder. That description
was all I needed: I took off my coat, requested the material, and went
back to work.

All that remains now of the Death Campaign is housed at the
Hartman Center in a big white box: a collection of unfinished designs
for advertisements, the text in someone's handwriting, and some of the
photographs existing only as negatives. None of these ads was ever
published. None was even completed. At some point in 1932, the
campaign was aborted. But no one can tell me why. Indeed, no one
seems to know anything about the ads. Like Eastman's suicide that
same year, the campaign feels like Kodak's family secret, hushed up
and forgotten.

"There is hardly a thought more offensive than that of death," claims the philosopher Zygmunt Bauman (12). Not surprisingly, then, the advertising historian finds it nearly impossible to come up with campaigns that have addressed the subject of death in some way. Advertisements for funeral homes and life insurance do so, but these ads rarely appear on national television or in magazines. Many of their campaigns (including a recent one that featured a burial service from the bottom of a grave with a priest and mourners looking inward) have in fact been rejected by the Advertising Standards Authority as "distressing," "in bad taste," and "too emotive" (Summers 12).

The most notorious example of advertising's deployment of death is undoubtedly the Benetton campaign that began in 1989 in an effort to promote the clothing company's image as politically engaged, humanitarian, and scornful of marketing conventions. One ad pictured the blood-soaked uniform of a Croatian soldier; another featured a man's arm tattooed with "HIV positive"; a third focused on a war cemetery. These ads generated a storm of controversy, prompting boycotts and dozens of lawsuits by store owners whose sales had declined dramatically when the ads appeared. The complaints voiced by Benetton's opponents focus mainly on what they see as the double victimization of the subjects depicted in the ads. Codifying positions of the pathetic and the privileged, they argue, the ads exploit human tragedy and suffering to sell clothes.

But these arguments skirt the more powerful reasons for our objection to death in advertisements. Reminders of death are precisely what we do not want from advertising, whose narrow, instrumental purpose of selling goods belies advertising's pivotal role in shielding us from death. "The first activity of culture," argues Zygmunt Bauman, "relates to survival—pushing back the moment of death, extending the life-span, increasing life expectation and thus life's content-absorbing capacity" (31). In other words, culture provides us with a means of forgetting death, or allowing us to feel we can transcend it, however briefly. As one of our most trenchant cultural formations, advertising pushes death back by filling our lives with desires so consuming that we forget about the absurdity of life in the face of death.

Someone might counter such an argument with the observation that representations of death pervade culture. But these representations usually occur in socially sanctioned, specified places for a confrontation with death: the pages of literature, the theater, the museum, the art gallery. Unlike novels, film, or painting, for example, advertising

202

◇

is so ubiquitous that it cannot embrace death, for as Paul Ricoeur argues, "The desire for death does not speak, as does the desire for life. Death works in silence" (294). This silent work involves an admission that death is the one area where we must admit uncertainty or ignorance, that there is no intrinsic grounds for authority in the discourses and practices surrounding it—an admission that, arguably, advertising cannot make. As the limit of cultural representation—"the blind spot the representational system seeks to refuse even as it constantly addresses it" (Bronfen and Goodwin 14)—death refutes and mocks the rhetoric of promises, guarantees, and certainties on which advertising so heavily depends.

Given these observations, as well as Kodak's relentless efforts to promote memory as untouched by death, the existence of Kodak's Death Campaign is stunningly incomprehensible. Indeed, the campaign itself is now a relic, a piece of Kodak history that cannot be fitted into a narrative of wholeness. As I have argued throughout this book, Kodak's most important contribution to popular perceptions of photography was its systematic attempt to expunge all traces of sorrow from photographs. The Death Campaign violated the very foundation on which Kodak advertising had been based—indeed, on which all advertising is based. In this campaign, Kodak acknowledged for one brief moment that we take photos to ward off death and sorrow—and that when death does strike, photos can have a meaningfulness that outweighs and cuts through the usual nostalgia when such documents are taken for granted. Such thoughts are too overwhelming for advertising, especially for advertisements that have trafficked in cliché and stereotype as much as Kodak's have done.

"That was the last time Dad was with us" describes a snapshot of an older man helping his young grandson move a wheelbarrow, the activity obviously meant to underscore the symbolism of planting and reaping. "Thanksgiving 1930—the last time we were ever to be together," reads another caption above a photograph of an extended family—a young father with his three children and two grandparents who have just arrived for a visit. Although the subtext seems to be that one or perhaps both of the grandparents died shortly thereafter, the vagueness of the language leaves open the possibility that one of the other family members, including a little girl in patent-leather shoes and white dress, could have been the one to die. We look at the ad and cannot help but wonder which one of these joyful subjects fell victim

to the random violence of death. That response foregrounds what
Barthes argues is implicit in every viewing of a photograph: the awareness that the living subject will die. "By giving me the absolute pose of
the past . . . the photograph tells me death in the future" (*Camera
Lucida* 96).

Edgar Allan Poe once remarked that "the death of a beautiful young woman is the most poetical topic in the world." As Elisabeth Bronfen has argued, Poe's observation speaks to the ubiquitous
aestheticizing of dying or dead women in nineteenth- and twentieth-
century media, from Millais's *Ophélia* to Hollywood's *Camille*. Certainly these ads participate in such representation, inciting our sympathy precisely because the women featured in them are so young and
attractive. One ad depicts a woman in her early thirties, wearing a
tennis outfit and looking vibrant, healthy, and in love. The caption beneath the photograph reads, "Your Mother was the loveliest woman
that ever lived, my son." The contemporary look of her clothing suggests that the photograph could not have been taken very long ago, so
that her death was also recent. The poignancy of the advertisement is
also reinforced by the scenario the viewer imagines as she reads the
caption: father and son looking at the photograph, both yearning for
the woman whose death has left them alone, the photograph creating the scene of mourning shared by those who are left to look at the
picture.

"She died the year after Sally was born, you know—" says the caption accompanying a photograph of another young woman in a summer dress holding a straw hat. Drawing on the Victorian preoccupation with death and childbirth, the ad leaves open the possibility
that the woman's death may have been a result of her child's birth,
its poignancy thus framed by notions of maternal sacrifice and aban-
donment. Another young woman, this one only in her early twenties,
also poses in summer costume; the accompanying text reads, "Sylvia—
the day we were engaged." We are left to assume here that the marriage never occurred, that this woman never got to experience all the
typical events that circumscribe marriage according to Kodak: an elaborate wedding, the pleasure of watching her children at play, the celebration of family holidays and vacations. Unlike the other Death Campaign advertisements, however, this one does not confirm that the
woman died. Such indeterminacy underscores the relation between
these ads and all photographs, a relation hinging on the possibility

that the experience depicted in the individual snapshot may be the last of its kind.

One of the striking aspects of these ads is the employment of facial close-ups. Close-ups rarely appear in early Kodak advertising, probably because they lend too much attention to the individual subject and therefore complicate Kodak's effort to promote its images as representations of archetypal people and experiences. Here the focus on the subject's face makes her vulnerability to death even more poignant. One might recall in this context Benjamin's observations about the face in photographic portraiture. Writing in 1936 with an obvious trace of regret, he posed the possibility that the reproduction of the human face served as the last retrenchment of photography's cult value: "It is no accident that the portrait was the focal point of early photography. The cult of remembrance of loved ones, absent or dead, offers a last refuge for the cult value of the picture. For the last time the aura emanates from the early photographs in the fleeting expression of a human face. This is what constitutes their melancholy, incomparable beauty" ("Work of Art" 226).

Most of these advertisements feature very young children. A little girl walking by the ocean is framed by the words "It was the last picture we got of her—" and a young boy plays with his dog at the beach above the words "Here's our boy with his first dog—I'll never forget how happy he was." The death of a child, as Carol Mavor and James Kincaid have established, has enjoyed powerful iconic significance ever since the early nineteenth century, when child mortality rates were extremely high. "The good child is patient, quiet, submissive; the best child is eternally so," claims Kincaid (234). Mavor explains that "both the photograph and childhood accept their shape and their poignancy from death. If there were no death, why would childhood hold its appeal? If there were no death, why would our desire to photograph and to preserve lost moments be so urgent?" (5–6). Such rhetorical questions get at the very heart of this campaign, which focuses almost entirely on children not only because their supposed purity and goodness make their death especially poignant but because their connection to life also seems especially tenuous.

As we have seen, part of what makes Kodak advertising after 1901 so powerful is its incorporation of snapshots that seem completely "authentic." As we look at them we forget that most were taken by professional rather than amateur photographers, with models rather than housewives, and with equipment often much more sophisticated than the Kodak cameras and film actually being advertised. We see these simulated snapshots as proof of the "real." And that response to them is largely like the response we have to all photographs: "The Photograph does not necessarily say what is no longer, but only and for certain what has been. This distinction is decisive. In front of a photograph, our consciousness does not necessarily take the nostalgic path of memory (how many photographs are outside of individual time), but for every photograph existing in the world, the path of certainty: the Photograph's essence is to ratify what it represents," writes Barthes (*Camera Lucida* 85). The most important aspect of the photograph, in other words, is its supposedly evidential force. Hence it is easy to forget the constructedness of these images, the fact that we are invited to mourn for what actually never occurred.

Such power is reinforced by the captions, almost all of which use dashes ("It was the last picture we got of her—"; "She died the year after Sally was born, you know—"). On the one hand, dashes mark the moment when language fails, when the speaker is so overcome that she cannot find the words to express her feelings, when subjects are too painful to describe. On the other hand, dashes can suggest the continuation of language—the words that were voiced or the stories that were told beyond the frame of the advertisement. Looked at this way, the captions provide us with the rhetoric of mourning—the attempt to recover a voice in the face of overwhelming experience. In this sense, these captions draw more attention to their rhetorical importance than perhaps any other caption found in Kodak advertising, for, as Ronald Schleifer argues, "mourning is the scene of rhetoric, the place where the 'rhetoricity' of rhetoric cannot be erased, where there is nothing else between ordinary lives and the nothingness or pure non-sense of death than the gestures of rhetoric" (*Rhetoric* 228).

Schleifer here follows the thinking of Benjamin, who suggested that a crucial relation exists between death and storytelling:

Not only a man's knowledge or wisdom, but above all his real life—and this is the stuff that stories are made of—first assumes transmissible form at the moment of his death. Just as a sequence of images is set in motion inside a man as his life comes to an end—unfolding the views of himself under which he has encountered himself without being aware of it—suddenly in his expressions and looks the unforgettable emerges and imparts to everything that concerned him that authority which even the poorest wretch in dying possesses for the living around him. This authority is at the very source of the story. ("Storyteller" 94)

Ended before they barely begin, the captions of the Death Campaign suggest that stories wait to be told about the dead subjects depicted in the ads. These stories, if they had been told by people to whom such events had actually happened—and we can imagine such a possibility much more easily than we can other possible parallels between our daily lives and those represented in the advertisements—would assume a much more poignant, singular, and meaningful form than any of the "stories" promoted during Kodak's Story Campaign. Those stories were represented by unusually long captions, as we saw in chapter 6, because they are easily told and warmly received. The stories inspired by death are not the kinds of stories Kodak can sanction; even though the truncated captions of the Death Campaign only hint at these stories' existence, the few words that make up the captions are enough to remind us of death. And so it is no wonder that they never made the printed page.

Although no one can tell me how or why the Death Campaign was ever started, it's intriguing to speculate. One possible reason lies in the year; 1932 marked the depths of the Depression, a period when advertising needed to justify its existence with weightier, more urgent, and more thoughtful reasons than it had in the past. By 1932, thousands of advertising clients had cut back or canceled orders, sending a rash of firings through the ranks of copywriters and account executives. "Advertisements themselves became shrill, sometimes even hysterical," states Jackson Lears, "as they clamored for scarce consumer and client dollars" (236). Perhaps the Death Campaign testifies to Kodak's participation in this hysteria.

Or perhaps it represents an attempt on the part of the Kodak Company to acknowledge George Eastman's death in March 1932. Eastman committed suicide knowing that his condition—atherosclerosis of the spinal cord—would leave him an invalid, confined to a chair or bed and being waited on by nurses. "There isn't much to live for. All that people come here for is to have me sign on the dotted line," he remarked to a friend only days before he died (quoted in Brayer 519). Unlike the deaths implied in the Kodak advertisements,

Eastman's was meticulously planned. He put a Lucky Strike in his cigarette holder, took one drag, and then put it out. He folded a wet towel over his chest in order to prevent powder burns, pointed the muzzle of a German automatic at the center of his heart, and pulled the trigger.

Although no one can tell me for certain whether the Death Campaign was initiated in response to Eastman's suicide, the connection seems too close to have been coincidental. Benjamin argued that death achieves its representations only in dispersed and particular instances. As material event, death bears a problematic relation to generalization because it is always unique, always singular. Eastman's suicide—committed upstairs in the privacy of his bedroom, away from family and friends—dramatizes this observation. Perhaps Kodak wished to render the material singularity of his death into generalizable experience, something as shared as leisure, fashion, family albums, even war. This time, however, Kodak confronted a subject that couldn't be advertised. This time, as always, death won out.

Notes

PREFACE

1. *The Home of Kodak,* which was revised and published every several years beginning in the 1920s, provides a vivid example of this tendency. Accompanied by an
aerial photo of "Kodak Park," one passage describes the facilities by accentuating the
frenetic energy that occurs within a tranquil and even domestic atmosphere: "Wide,
well trimmed lawns and ivy covered buildings surround the main entrance, giving a
feeling of repose in marked contrast to the activities within the plant itself" (11).

2. See Swasy's *Changing Focus* for a journalistic account of Kodak's financial
troubles since the late 1980s. Focusing particularly on company layoffs and termina-
tions, Swasy locates extravagance and complacency as the primary reasons for the
company's downfall: "It was a gentle world for Kodak employees because Kodak was
the unrivaled king of world photography. Its virtual monopoly on photographic film
meant managers simply had to make sure the production machines were running
twenty-four hours a day" (4).

3. See Stieglitz, "Hand Camera" 215.

INTRODUCTION

1. My book thus aligns itself with such cultural histories of advertising as the
Ewens' *Channels of Desire* (1992), Leach's *Land of Desire* (1993), and Lears's *Fables of
Abundance* (1994), all of which treat advertising as a lens through which to view American culture as they address such wide-ranging issues as the rise of patent medicines,
women and consumerism, and the shift from earth to factory as the representational
locus of abundance for nineteenth-century Americans. Other cultural histories of
American advertising include Fox's *Mirror Makers,* Marchand's *Advertising the American Dream,* and Norris's *Advertising and the Transformation of American Society.*

2. Sontag, *On Photography* 34–41.

3. This is not to say, of course, that there were no large-scale companies producing and distributing commercial photographs or selling photographic equipment in the
decades before Kodak's invention. As Elizabeth Brayer explains: "While eventually
Eastman would easily outstrip all other American companies in diversification, innovation, advertising, and attention to foreign markets, at the beginning he had to labor
diligently to get a foothold in the domestic photographic industry" (34). Although still
in its infancy, the photographic world already had an establishment; its leading firm
was E. and H. T. Anthony of New York City. In 1842 the Anthonys opened a daguerreotype gallery in Manhattan, and they soon expanded into selling photographic

supplies. Thirteen years later sales had reached $225,000, making the company one of the top two in the trade. The other was Scovill, a branch of Scovill Brass of Waterbury.

4. I am basing this estimate on conversations I have had with other photo historians, particularly with members of the listserv PhotoHistory.

5. For discussions of commodity culture, see Fox and Lears, *Culture of Consumption;* Bronner, *Consuming Visions;* Richards, *Commodity Culture of Victorian England;* Lears, *Fables of Abundance;* Frow, *Time and Commodity Culture;* and Slater, *Consumer Culture and Modernity.*

6. See Schleifer's *Modernism and Time* for a brilliant discussion of this transformation.

7. Even as early as 1855, Cuthbert Bede parodied the oppressive formality of the photographic studio in his book *Photographic Pleasures.* For other accounts that describe the tedium felt by visitors to the photographic studio, see Henisch and Henisch, *Photographic Experience,* and Rudisill, *Mirror Image.*

8. Of course, the antique industry also exploits the rhetoric of authenticity, but its marketing appeal has become increasingly idealized and fantastic. Ever since the turn of the twentieth century, as Lowenthal explains, industries that commodify the past have increasingly attempted to market the past as what he calls a "foreign country." Both tourism and antiques exploit the appeal of authenticity while at the same time commodifying the past as both exotic and imagined.

9. See Mauss, *The Gift,* on gift exchange in ancient and Third World cultures. His famous argument is that gifts must be continually given and returned because they signify the importance of communal relations.

10. For discussions of snapshot photography's aura of naiveté, see several of the essays in Spence and Holland, *Family Snaps,* especially Holland's "Introduction" and Slater's "Consuming Kodak."

11. Kodak actually discontinued the slogan in 1892, the year it first marketed daylight-loading film. With this invention, it was no longer necessary for the customer to send the camera back to the company for reloading, as one had had to do up to this point. Now the amateur photographer was required to do somewhat more than "press the button"; she also had to load and unload her roll film. The old slogan then gave way to others promoting this new development, such as "It's Daylight All the Way with a Kodak." But despite the short time it was in use, the slogan earned a reputation, which it has maintained to this day, as one of the most successful in the history of American advertising.

12. Although Terdiman limits his study to the century's most notable writers on memory—Wordsworth, Baudelaire, and Freud, for example—its thematic scope and rich historical detail suggest that he could easily have included many other writers in his analysis as well.

13. See, for example, Combs, *Reagan Range;* Doane and Hodges, *Nostalgia and Sexual Difference;* and Greene, "Feminist Fiction."

14. Works that specifically address the more positive uses of nostalgia include Tannock, "Nostalgia Critique"; Halbwachs, *On Collective Memory;* Spitzer, *Hotel Bolivia;* and Colley, *Nostalgia and Recollection.*

15. Such rhetoric has also shaped public perceptions of Kodak. In most studies of the company, Kodak emerges as a monolithic institution founded by a genius, run smoothly by innovative employees, and promoted through "advertising giants," such as

L. B. Jones and J. Walter Thompson, who somehow "knew" what Americans wanted out of snapshot photography. Even the title of what is to date the most comprehensive account of Kodak's history, Douglas Collins's *Story of Kodak,* suggests the exclusively descriptive and often celebratory approach that characterizes most accounts of the company's success. One of the striking aspects of many of these studies is how often George Eastman is likened to the resourceful heroes of Horatio Alger's books. Margolin et al., *Promise and the Product,* for example, opens its account of the Kodak company as follows: "George Eastman, in the classic tradition of Horatio Alger, started his career as a floor sweeper, cuspidor cleaner, and messenger boy in Rochester, New York. With genius and determination, he started a dozen industries and helped create several new branches of science and medicine and one basic art form" (59). By emphasizing Eastman's unquestionable "ingenuity" and "resourcefulness," these studies often give the impression that Kodak's early success was largely a result of its founder's entrepreneurial spirit rather than the company's equally important participation in newly emergent cultural formations shaping American life.

16. Spence's work on family photographs, particularly her volume edited with Holland, *Family Snaps,* has extensively addressed the role of snapshot photography in the construction of family life and memories. In *Family Frames,* Marianne Hirsch deploys her theory of "postmemory" as a means of addressing how photographs help create "memories" of family events in people of later generations who in fact never experienced those events. Other such works include Halle's "Displaying the Dream," Musello's "Studying the Home Mode," and Gear's "Baby's Picture."

I. A SHORT HISTORY OF KODAK ADVERTISING

1. Citing such things as the "catchiness" of Kodak's brand name, the simplicity of its slogans, the bright packaging of its products, and the "heartwarming" images reproduced in the ads, most general histories of advertising refer to Kodak as a model of successful marketing. See, for example, Strasser, *Satisfaction Guaranteed,* and Margolin et al., *Promise and the Product.*

2. Kingslake's *Photographic Manufacturing Companies* provides a descriptive catalog of Kodak's competitors in its own city.

3. Bliven, "Teaching the Nation" 112.

4. As Susan Strasser explains, successful businesses such as Singer and McCormick had begun to stamp their products with brand names as early as the 1850s, but it wasn't until the late 1870s, with the passage of the first trademark law, that the brand name began to assume its modern importance and to be seen, in the words of one early twentieth-century advertising theorist, as an "integral part of the commodity itself" (quoted in Strasser 30). People started to make purchases according to their recognition of a brand name rather than relying on the individual retailer's opinions or suggestions. And by marking their products, manufacturers now seemed to be taking more responsibility for them, and therefore presumably for the conditions under which they were produced. Advertising slogans—such as "You press the button, we do the rest" and Morton's Salt's "When it rains, it pours"—emerged as linguistic identifiers for products, their rhetorical simplicity associated with the simplicity of consumption.

5. See Brayer, *George Eastman;* Collins, *Story of Kodak;* and Hungerford, "George Eastman," for further information on Eastman's personal involvement in the advertising details of his company.

6. *British Journal of Photography,* September 14, 1888, 1–2.

7. Written by Edward L. Wheeler, *Kodak Kate* was featured in Beadle's Half Dime Library throughout the year 1891. *Captain Kodak,* written by Alexander Black, apparently enjoyed great popularity among boys in the early 1890s. Interestingly, the foreword to the novel anticipates what would become, upon the invention of the Brownie camera in 1900, one of Kodak's key advertising strategies: to promote photography as an ideal hobby for children because it teaches them to see the familiar in unfamiliar and surprising ways:

> This is the story of the camera hobby; of an amateur photographer and his chums; of a boy's adventures in the company of his camera; of a camera club and the old and young brought together by the influence of a common interest. . . . The pictures are not by any means always intended to show my readers how photographs should be made, but rather to suggest the interest of familiar and accessible things, and that the best thing about a photograph is not always the thing we wished or expected to put into it. (10)

8. This was one of many such ads produced by Kodak in the early 1900s. By the early 1930s, the company had stopped using the name Kodak as anything but a proper adjective in its ads and promotional literature.

9. The production figures were provided to me by Todd Gustavson, Curator of Technology at the George Eastman House.

10. "Lewis B. Jones."

11. See Brummett 13.

12. See Bliven, "Teaching the Nation" 106.

13. Jones made this statement in an interview. See ibid. 4.

14. The memo, in the Eastman Kodak Company archives, Rochester, N.Y., is dated June 10, 1904.

15. See Brummett 46–47 for more information on these contests.

16. *The Kodak Salesman* also featured such regular columns as "Selling to Women," "Between Us," "Overheard at the Counter," and "Ten Minutes with the Boss." George Eastman's insistence on the importance of good salesmanship is legendary, particularly his demands on David Cooper, his original traveling salesman. One letter to David Cooper dated April 2, 1886, reflects this observation: "There is no object whatever in making them or advertising them or demonstrating them, unless it is to result in a sale. There is no reward until the sale; therefore we consider the salesman a very important part of our business" (EKC Letters, February 1885–March 1899, George Eastman House, Rochester, N.Y.).

17. The first two chapters in Fox, *Mirror Makers,* provide a fascinating account of advertising's shift from lack of respectability to professionalism. A much different history of advertising's transition in the United States is offered by Jackson Lears, who argues in *Fables of Abundance* that advertising in the latter half of the nineteenth century was purged of its decadent—and liberating—value once it became the cornerstone of corporate business. "As rhetorical constructions," Lears argues, "[corporate] advertisements did more than stir up desire; they also sought to manage it—to stabilize the sorcery of the marketplace by containing dreams of personal transformation within a broader rhetoric of control" (10).

18. Larson, *Rise of Professionalism,* charts the history of professionalism in the nineteenth century through a focus on medicine, law, and academia.

19. See Scanlon, *Inarticulate Longings* 12.

20. For more information on Eastman's targeting of the "best" magazines, see Strasser, *Satisfaction Guaranteed,* and Brayer, *George Eastman.*

21. See "Advertising Talks" 4.

22. See Scanlon's introduction and chap. 1 in *Inarticulate Longings* for a useful account of circulation rates in the 1890s and early 1900s.

23. For a fascinating discussion of the impact of these new photo technologies and the rising prominence of illustrators on the reputation, prestige, and circulation of magazines, see Bogart, *Artists, Advertising, and the Borders of Art.*

24. For a concise history of the shift in the advertising industry's attitude toward photography, see chap. 2 of Johnston's *Real Fantasies.*

2. "VACATION DAYS ARE KODAK DAYS"

1. For discussions of the popularity of state and national parks near the turn of the twentieth century, consult Kaplan, *Leisure in America,* and Cross, *Social History of Leisure.*

2. See the ad for Oso hammocks in *Ladies' Home Journal,* June 1907, 23.

3. The Kodak Tank Developer was designed as an improvement on the Kodak Developing Machine, invented in 1902, which an article in the *Kodak Trade Circular* describes as "the final triumph. . . . The photographic dark-room is abolished. Cameras will be improved from year to year; photographic processes will be still further simplified and the lens manufacturers will, no doubt, make marvelous strides towards perfection; but nothing which remains to be accomplished in the simplifying of picture making can equal in importance or interest the simple device by means of which the gloom of the darkroom has been dispelled" (August 1902, 1).

Like the developing machine, the Kodak Tank allowed photographers to develop their own photos in daylight, without the need to crank film through a developer. Neither invention performed with stunning success on the market, despite Kodak's apparent ambitions for them. The fact that Eastman would market such a product, which could obviously threaten an entire industry based on the development of amateurs' film, apparently angered many film companies. Eastman remained resolute, however, wagering that the simplification of film development would open up yet another market consisting of amateurs who wished to perform a more advanced form of photography but were not interested in constructing their own darkrooms or engaging in a difficult and time-consuming process. An article titled "For 1905" in the January 1905 issue of the *Kodak Trade Circular* explains the Tank's functioning and Kodak's defense of the commercial value of such a product.

4. Kaplan devotes a chapter of *Leisure in America* to the return to nature as a popular leisure movement in the late nineteenth and early twentieth centuries.

5. For general historical approaches to leisure, see ibid.; Miller and Robinson, *Leisure Age;* Goodale and Godbey, *Evolution of Leisure;* Cross, *Social History of Leisure;* and Grover, *Hard at Play.* Philosophical approaches to leisure include Huizinga, *Homo Ludens;* Anderson, *Work and Leisure;* De Grazia, *Of Time, Work, and Leisure;* Glasser, *Leisure;* and Rybczynski, *Waiting for the Weekend.*

6. After the turn of the century, the increased mechanization and intensification

214

◇

of work in the United States began to ease employers' fears that a reduction in work-time would necessarily reduce profits. Health reformers and unions urged American businessmen to see the value of rewarding their workers with more time off, arguing that intense factory and commercial work required shorter hours in order to restore physiological and mental balance. Refreshed and relaxed workers would produce more than tired ones. Henry Ford was one of the first businessmen to put such a philosophy into action. In 1914 Ford reduced the daily hours in his plants from nine to eight; in 1926 he announced that henceforth his factories would be closed on Saturdays. Ford's five-day week was widely criticized as both uneconomic and irreligious by other businessmen as well as by the National Industry Council and the National Association of Manufacturers. Still, within only a decade many companies would follow Ford's lead. See Cross, *Social History of Leisure,* 185.

7. See Huizinga, *Homo Ludens* 55.

8. Although I limit my discussion here to world's fairs and automobiles, many of these activities and locales could have constituted material for extensive discussion. Kodak's use of beach settings deserves particular attention, since the advent of snapshot photography coincided so closely with the rise to popularity of such resorts as Atlantic City and Coney Island in the 1890s.

9. In chap. 4 of *Theory of the Leisure Class,* Veblen writes: "The basis on which good repute in any highly organized industrial community ultimately rests is pecuniary strength; and the means of showing pecuniary strength, and so of gaining or retaining a good name, are leisure and a conspicuous consumption of goods" (70).

10. Ironically, it was the Great Depression of the 1930s that led to the consolidation of the two-day weekend. Shorter hours came to be seen as a remedy for unemployment: people would work less, but more people would have jobs. From that time forward, the weekend spread quickly, and after the Depression ended it continued to spread until it became a permanent fixture of American life. Businessmen's earlier fears of the pernicious effects of idleness thus gradually gave way to the recognition that recreation was the only arena for restoring the physical and psychological capacity to work.

11. For discussions of Kodak's popularity in the 1890s, see Brayer, *George Eastman,* and Collins, *Story of Kodak.*

12. These figures were provided to me by Todd Gustavson.

13. Among general works on amateurism are Stebbins, *Amateurs* and *Amateurs, Professionals, and Serious Leisure.* For histories of amateur photography, see Chalfen, *Snapshot Versions; Coe, Snapshot Photograph;* Ford, *Story of Popular Photography;* Green, *Snapshot;* King, *Say "Cheese!";* Sciberling, *Amateurs, Photography, and the Mid-Victorian Imagination;* and Moeller, "Ladies of Leisure."

14. Consult Cross's *Social History of Leisure,* Kaplan's *Leisure in America,* and Anderson's *Work and Leisure* for information on reduced work hours in the United States during the nineteenth and early twentieth centuries.

15. In light of this observation, we might consider Roland Barthes's essay "Toys." Here Barthes argues that mass-produced toys encourage the child to respond to them as *owner* rather than creator.

16. The body of publications written for amateurs in the 1870s and 1880s is remarkable for its clear division between works aimed at readers who wished to devote

much time and commitment to a subject of interest and works aimed at readers (assumed to be female) who wished to acquire only a superficial knowledge of the subject. Among the many books written for the amateur during this period we find *Amateur Clubs and Actors*, *Amateur Theatricals*, *The Amateur Spirit*, and *The Amateur Gentleman*.

17. Other titles: "The Amateur Spirit"; "Amateurs: What We Can Learn from Them"; "A Nation of Amateurs"; "What About Amateurs?"

18. Seiberling discusses the marginal role of the serious amateur in her two final chapters, observing that "by the 1880s, it was the amateur who lacked a clear sense of identity in contrast to the well-established commercial photographers active in different fields" (113). Serious amateurs found themselves threatened not only by the proliferation of commercial photography but by the democratization of photography promoted by Kodak; having created so many more amateur photographers, Kodak effectively ensured that the field of amateur photography could no longer boast a sense of shared interests and values, as it had done from the 1840s through the 1860s.

19. For general discussions of the gentleman amateur and the arts, see Adams, *Dandies and Desert Saints*; Freedman, *Professions of Taste*; and Gillett, *Worlds of Art*. Among the works that study the concept of the gentleman amateur in relation to photography are Seiberling, *Amateurs, Photography, and the Mid-Victorian Imagination*, and Green-Lewis, *Framing the Victorians*. For a discussion of the role of the gentleman amateur within the contexts of photography and debates about masculinity, see my essay "Men in the Age of Mechanical Reproduction."

20. Works by American photographers that address the notion of the gentleman amateur include Root, *Camera and the Pencil*.

21. One of the most prominent examples of this phenomenon is Talbot, *Pencil of Nature*. Green-Lewis, *Framing the Victorians*, chap. 3, is a fascinating discussion of how this tendency to ignore the role of the photographer in the production of the photograph was reinforced by popular fiction that literally positioned photographers outside the frame of events while at the same time investing photographs with an almost animistic power.

22. For more information on Eastman's roll holder, see Taft, *Photography and the American Scene*; Collins, *Story of Kodak*; and Brayer, *George Eastman*.

23. Eastman to Tompkins, April 21, 1888, in EKC Letters, February 1885–March 1899, George Eastman House, Rochester, N.Y.

24. Indeed, in Hawthorne's *House of the Seven Gables* (1850), Hepzibah Pyncheon, the novel's representative of a fading upper-class gentility, looks upon the daguerreotypist's stained fingers as signs not only of his working-class background but of his potentially criminal aspirations. Anticipating the stained fingers of the apprehended suspect, whose stained hands after fingerprinting signaled his status as suspected criminal, Hepzibah sees the nitrate stains on Holgrave's fingers as the traces of criminal behavior.

25. Even the catalogs of Kodak products, published every year beginning in 1890, opened with a message of one to three pages addressed to amateur photographers. These statements were generally designed to stress the importance of any new product and, more important, to remind consumers that Kodak was always willing to aid them

216
◇

in their photographic endeavors. The address in the 1915 catalog (headed "Kodak Service"), for example, states that

> the Kodak Company has not been satisfied with merely making mechanical and chemical improvements; it has assumed the responsibility of educating people in picture taking. The very first Kodak, way back in 1888, was accompanied by a so-called "manual" that did more than merely explain the operation of the mechanical features of the camera. It showed how the pictures should be taken, how (and how not) to photograph a tall building, how to photograph a small child—told about the length of exposures in different kinds of light, both in-doors and out. It was really a primary hand-book of photography. From that day on, every piece of Kodak apparatus, every amateur product of the Company has been accompanied by the most concise instructions. (3)

26. Most covers of *Kodakery* between 1913 and 1932 portray women either alone, in the company of other women, or with their children.

27. For more information, see Harding, "Kodak Girl," and West, "Her Finger on the Button."

28. See Lears 221.

29. See Weimann, *Fair Women*; Brown, *Contesting Images*.

30. See Banta, *Imaging American Women,* and Brown, *Setting a Course.* Banta devotes an entire section of her study to the "Outdoors Pal" in early twentieth-century American culture. She sees this image and the two others with which she compares it—the "Beautiful Charmer" and the "New England Woman"—as prominent ideals for young women during this period. The "Outdoors Pal" represented health and fitness; the "Beautiful Charmer" represented poise, social grace, and physical beauty; and the "New England Woman" represented intellect.

31. Representative articles in the *Ladies' Home Journal* between 1903 and 1907 include "If You Are Going Traveling" and "How to Spend Two Weeks on a Vacation in New York on a Working Girl's Budget"; and an advertisement headed "$1000 for What You Do and See This Summer" offers $50 for the "best articles on the best two-week vacation . . . for the self-supporting girl" (July 1903, 45).

32. Among contemporaneous articles on Kodak, risqué behavior, and violations of privacy at the beach is "The Kodak" in the *Cincinnati Herald Presbyterian,* Oct. 17, 1894. The author describes an allegedly recent scenario at Atlantic City:

> The bathing costumes were varied and the waves, rough in their welcome, had put the bathers in very grotesque positions. On the sand of the beach parties had sought comfort rather than elegance. This removal of conventional restraint betrayed into a familiarity that was unusual and gave occasion for serious misunderstandings. All unconscious of these things, the crowd were thoughtlessly enjoying themselves, when the enjoyment was destroyed one morning by finding posted here and there at prominent points on the beach the following notice: "Persons are forbidden to bring or use kodaks on this beach." It was then made known that for several days parties had

been on the beach with kodaks and had been taking snap pictures of different persons in the grotesque positions that they had unconsciously been placed in, and that pictures had also been taken of those who on the sand had acted with unconventional familiarity.

For cartoons that illustrate such scenarios, see in *Puck* "The Peeping Toms of the Camera" (July 15, 1891) and "Turn About Is Fair Play" (Aug. 24, 1892).

33. Informative sources on world's fairs are Augur, *Book of Fairs;* Rydell, *All the World's a Fair* and *World of Fairs;* and Benedict, *Anthropology of World's Fairs.*

34. See Paster, "Advertising Immortality by Kodak."

35. The word "snapshot" as a photographic term was apparently first used by Sir John Herschel in the *Photographic News* (May 13 1860): "The possibility of taking a photograph, as it were by a snap-shot, of securing a picture of a tenth of a second" (quoted in *Oxford English Dictionary* 2889). Hence, even twenty-eight years before the advent of Kodak, the word had already been circulated metaphorically as a means of describing instantaneous exposures.

36. Brown's *Contesting Images* gives a detailed and highly informative account of Eastman's campaign to promote Kodak as a major participant in the Chicago fair. I am indebted to Brown for much of the information presented here.

37. As far as I have been able to discover, Kodak produced a roll of 250 exposures only for this occasion. Although Kodak advertising capitalized on the 1901 and 1904 world's fairs as well, the company apparently did not produce a special roll of film for those events, nor did it rename one of its cameras, as it did for the Chicago fair.

38. See Collins, *Story of Kodak* 156.

39. An article in the *Kodak Trade Circular* headed "Motoring with a Kodak" exemplifies Kodak's efforts to link automobility with photography: "[There] is no disputing the tremendous present popularity of auto touring and there can be no doubt that this year will see a great increase in this fascinating sport—pastime—recreation—fad. Call it what you will. On the other hand, the speed mania is passing. . . . Leisurely touring means pure enjoyment of the country, of the road, of the scenery and of the friends that are along—and all this spells: K-O-D-A-K" (12). In 1910 Kodak also published a booklet titled *Motoring with a Kodak,* which suggested what sort of photographs to take along the road.

40. See Rae, *American Automobile Industry,* and Flink, *Car Culture,* particularly chap. 2.

41. See Rae; Flink; and Ling, *America and the Automobile.*

42. See Ling, chaps. 1 and 2.

43. Rybczynski makes a fascinating distinction between time marked by leisure (the weekend) and time marked by work (the weekday):

Weekday time, like profane time, is linear. It represents an irreversible progressions of days, Monday to Friday, year after year. Past weekday time is lost time. Schooldays are followed by workdays, the first job by the second and the third. . . . Not only is weekday time linear, but, like profane time, it encompasses the unpredictable. During the week, unforeseen things happen. . . . The weekend, on the other hand, . . . is time apart from the world of mundane problems and mundane concerns, from the world of making a living. On weekends, time stands still. . . . Weekend time shares a sense of reenactment with sacred time, and just as sacred time was characterized by ritual, the weekend, despite being an opportunity for personal freedom, is governed by convention. (229–31)

3. "Operated by Any School Boy or Girl"

1. The Brownie camera was first announced to photographic dealers in February 1900; an article in the *Kodak Trade Circular* opened with this comment: "The dollar camera is at last a fact. Of course, there have been pin-hole affairs, with a groove in the back to hold a glass plate, which have sold for almost nothing—and were worth it, but the Brownie is the first really practical instrument at the price" (1). Nor was this mere company rhetoric; the camera's combination of efficiency and low price made it one of Kodak's best-selling instruments until the 1960s, when the Brownie line was finally discontinued. For more information on the camera, see Lothrop, "Brownie Camera."

2. I am indebted to Lothrop for much of this information.

3. See Derks, *Value of a Dollar,* 18–19, for a list of products that could be purchased for $1 in 1900.

4. These sales figures were provided to me by Todd Gustavson.

5. I base this conversion on information provided in "Inflation Calculator," http://www.westegg.com/inflation/ (May 3, 1999).

6. This is a rough estimate based on various statements published in the *Kodak Trade Circular* during this period.

7. See Calvert, *Children in the House,* and Kline, *Out of the Garden,* for informative readings of the rise of a commercialized children's culture in the United States. For other histories on the construction of childhood as both idea and industry in the nineteenth century, see Ariès, *Centuries of Childhood;* Hiner and Hawes, *Growing Up in America;* Pollock, *Forgotten Children;* Cunningham, *Children and Childhood;* Kincaid, *Child-Loving;* Steedman, *Strange Dislocations;* and Jordan, *Victorian Childhood.*

As Ariès has argued, nostalgia for childhood developed with the rise of industrialization in the seventeenth and eighteenth centuries, producing what he and others since have called the "modern invention of childhood." In *Centuries of Childhood,* Ariès traces the emergence of concepts of childhood from the Middle Ages, when in his view there was no such concept at all. Although many historians have taken Ariès to task for his representation of medieval culture as a world where "the idea of childhood did not exist," many of his observations about the representations of childhood in modern culture have been expanded by such historians as Michael Anderson, Hugh Cunningham, and Linda Pollock. As Cunningham claims, "the construction of childhood is of course a continuing process: 'childhood' is never fixed and constant. But between the late seventeenth and mid–twentieth centuries there occurred a major and irreversible change in the representation of childhood, to the point where all children throughout the world were thought to be entitled to certain common elements and rights of childhood" (*Children of the Poor* 7). Since the publication of Ariès's book in 1961, a wealth of criticism has discussed, for example, the nineteenth- and twentieth-century sentimentalization of childhood and the nuclear family as a response to such aspects of modern life as increased urbanization. And most historians now agree that beginning in the eighteenth century, childhood was perceived more and more as a separate stage of life, with its own dynamics and its own culture, and yet possessing—and this was what gave the matter such urgency—the power to mold and determine the life of the adult.

8. Thanks to Colin Harding for sharing this description with me.

9. See Cadava, *Words of Light,* and Rugg, *Picturing Ourselves,* for two provocative and very different discussions of this famous passage in Benjamin's *Berliner Kindheit.*

10. David I. Macleod uses this phrase for the title of his book on childhood in the United States between 1890 and 1920.

11. For discussions of childhood and nostalgia, see Mavor, *Pleasures Taken;* Cunningham, *Children and Childhood;* and most important, Steedman, *Strange Dislocations.*

12. Other such manuals included E. L. Thorndike's *Notes on Child Study* and Ellen Key's *Century of the Child.*

13. Children are featured especially in ads promoting indoor photography and home portraiture.

14. This calculation is based on a survey of all ads produced between 1888 and 1932 that I have collected at Duke University and the Eastman Kodak Company—over 1,400 in all.

15. See Mauss, *The Gift.*

16. Mavor posits this argument in *Pleasures Taken* 4.

17. The films *Fairytale: A True Story* (Paramount, 1997) and *Photographing Fairies* (Starry Night, 1998) are both based on this actual incident.

18. See Green-Lewis, *Framing the Victorians,* for a fascinating history of photography's relation to realism in Victorian culture.

19. Kline's *Out of the Garden* and Cross's *Kids' Stuff* detail the commercialization of children's culture in the United States.

20. I discuss these anxieties at the beginning of chapter 5.

21. Braive, *The Photograph,* contains several illustrations from the 1840s and 1850s depicting the camera as gigantic.

22. See Kuznets, *When Toys Come Alive,* for an extensive discussion of this literature.

23. I am indebted to Kuznets for directing my attention to Joseph Schwarcz.

24. See such varied works as Hawthorne's *House of the Seven Gables,* Hardy's short story "An Imaginative Woman" and his poem "The Photograph," and Kipling's story "At the End of the Passage."

25. With this new transformation of play by a mass economy, it should come as no surprise that toys emerged as a popular literary subject between 1900 and 1920, theorized by advertising agencies, child sociologists, and educators as well as by essayists, poets, and fiction writers. In the mid- to late nineteenth century, playthings were of course often featured in children's literature, often within the kind of animation stories I described earlier. In the early twentieth century, however, a remarkable number of authors who wrote for an adult audience—including H. G. Wells, G. K. Chesterton, and Rainer Maria Rilke—began to devote essays and entire books to the subject. In an enormously popular book on floor games published in 1913, H. G. Wells, an avid

collector of toys himself, writes with remarkable detail about such subjects as toy soldiers and railway sets. What's most interesting about the book is the way Wells speaks both of and for children, treating the subject of toys with as much seriousness and enthusiasm as any other component of modern life. "We don't as a matter of fact think much of toyshops," he writes. "We think we trifle with great possibilities. We consider them expensive and incompetent and flatten our noses against their plate glass perhaps, but only in the most critical spirit" (quoted in Fraser 178). His writing becomes, then, a means of entering the toyshop as both modern consumer and child, someone who brings to the subject both a childlike wonder and adult appreciation of the toy as an important commodity.

26. I am indebted to Cross's *Kids' Stuff* for this information.

27. See Fraser's *History of Toys* and Cross's *Kids' Stuff* for two useful histories of this transformation.

28. Kline's *Out of the Garden* contains an entire chapter on this literature.

29. In *Responsibility of Forms,* Roland Barthes claims that "the single photograph is very rarely (i.e. with great difficulty) comical, contrary to the drawing. The comic requires movement, i.e. repetition (which is readily obtained in the cinema) or typification (which is possible in drawing), these two 'connotations' being denied to the photograph" (quoted in Nodelman 14).

30. Cross's *Kids' Stuff,* chap. 5, provides a fascinating account of how turn-of-the-century child theorists came to uphold play as vital to childhood.

31. After roughly 1910, Kodak ads also shift from depicting young children alone or at home with their Brownie cameras to older children participating in group activities and sports. In Brownie ads published before 1910, children are pictured mainly in solitary play with their toys, illustrating the supposedly insular world of childhood. But as Brian Sutton-Smith has argued in *Toys as Culture,* the solitariness of children's play has a disturbing subtext, arguably reflecting a cultural desire to privatize the lives of infants and children so as to eliminate the need for their parents' attention. Perhaps the recognition of this possibility was part of the new push toward socialization described here. In any case, Brownie ads after 1910 generally picture children with their peers, actively enjoying such activities as hiking, swimming, camping, and baseball.

This pattern seems to reflect a wider transformation in children's culture about this time, with new emphasis on older children's literature and education and on the importance of teamwork and social behavior. As Daniel T. Rodgers explains, the burgeoning public high schools during this time period tried to "offset the self-centeredness of traditional education through an array of athletic and extracurricular activities, mock governments, and civic lessons gathered together under the banner of 'social education'" (130). In addition, the profession of what was called "youth work" began to grow rapidly, spawning Epworth leagues, scouting troops, and youth clubs of all sorts. Stories that had focused on children as lone heroes in the late nineteenth century now gave way to scouting stories, school stories, and sports stories. Children's magazines, in addition, began to actively promote membership in clubs like the Boy Scouts and Girl Scouts.

Among these new clubs was the Brownie Camera Club of America, which encouraged all children under sixteen to join, with "no initiation fees or dues if you own a Brownie." Although it was actually founded by Kodak in 1900, the club was not featured in advertisements until 1909. The club regularly sponsored contests, awarding up to an $85 Kodak camera for the best pictures produced by a Brownie, an impressive prize for a child under sixteen and thus an amazingly strong incentive not only to participate in the contest but to improve one's photographic skills. Kodak actually sent a "constitution" out to all children who wrote in expressing interest in the club, explaining that each child would be issued a certificate of membership, which would entitle him or her to participate in all club contests and to receive an annual art brochure featuring all winning photographs in that year's contest.

32. This column, written by a professional photographer, began in 1914 and was featured every month in *American Boy*. Its subject matter is striking in its technical sophistication and in its commercial emphasis as well; the column frequently contains endorsements for certain products, for example.

33. See Fleming's *Powerplay* for a fascinating discussion of the relation between toys and commodities. Barthes also writes in "Toys" that "all the toys one commonly sees are essentially a microcosm of the adult world; they are all reduced copies of human objects, as if in the eyes of the public the child was, all told, nothing but a smaller man, a homunculus to whom must be supplied objects of his own size" (62).

4. "PROUDLY DISPLAYED BY WEARERS OF CHIC ENSEMBLES"
1. I found this statement in a letter sent by an anonymous member of Kodak's advertising department to Hudnet Cosmetics, Mar. 22, 1927, in a box labeled "Sales and Advertising," Eastman Kodak Company archives, Rochester, N.Y.

2. This column included such articles as "Soft Pedal the Mechanics" and "Forget the Business Talk." In the first of these articles, Leigh advises salesmen to "almost hypnotize [the female customer] into believing there is absolutely nothing mechanical about operating a Kodak" (10).

3. As the Vanity Kodak illustrates, Kodak capitalized on the new importance ascribed to design in general and to industrial design in particular. Lipovetsky says that

> increasingly, a new principle took hold: manufacturers grasped the value of doing aesthetic studies of the shape and presentation of mass-produced articles; they learned to embellish and harmonize their forms so as to seduce the eye, in keeping with R. Loewy's famous dictum: "Ugliness doesn't sell." A revolution in industrial production ensued: design became an integral part of the conception of new products; the industry at large adopted the perspective of elegance and seduction. (138)

4. For cultural histories of fashion, see Wilson, *Adorned in Dreams*; Lipovetsky, *Empire of Fashion*; Benstock and Ferriss, *On Fashion*; Craik, *Face of Fashion*; and Finkelstein, *Fashion*.

5. Although Eastman rarely expressed his particular ideas about using female sales models in writing, much evidence exists that he discussed the matter extensively with his friends, business associates, and employees. See Brayer for more information on this topic.

6. *Random House Webster's College Dictionary* (1991), 254.

7. I am indebted to Kathy Connor at the George Eastman House for alerting me

to an essay written by a Mrs. George Hoyt Whipple, who describes these lunches in affectionate and fascinating detail. Nicknamed the "lobster quartet," four women friends visited Eastman once a week at his home, where they discussed, among other subjects, the Kodak Girl and her wardrobe.

8. For discussions of the cultural importance of the Gibson Girl, see Patterson's essay, Banner's *American Beauty,* Wilson's *Adorned in Dreams,* and Banta's *Imaging American Women.*

9. See Breward's *Culture of Fashion* and Lester and Oerke's *Accessories.*

10. The operetta was written by Arthur A. Penn in 1903. Poems on the Kodak Girl appeared in a variety of newspapers and magazines, including the *Journalist* (July 1902).

11. For cultural histories of commercial illustration, see Bogart, *Artists;* Ewen, *All-Consuming Images;* Meikle, *Twentieth Century Limited;* and Smith, *Making the Modern.* See also Hiller, "Combining Brush and Camera," for a contemporaneous perspective on the use of fine art photography in advertising.

12. Wong, *Oriental Watercolor Techniques,* and Koshkin-Youritzin's "Introduction" to *American Watercolors* are useful studies on the history of the medium.

13. The most representative of Simmel's essays on the subject is "Fashion," written in 1904. For other discussions of Simmel's views on fashion, see Lipovetsky, Finkelstein, and Felski.

5. "Kodak Knows No Dark Days"

1. My reading of this daguerreotype has been influenced by Elisabeth Bronfen's fascinating discussion of visual and literary representations of dead women in *Over Her Dead Body,* particularly her first chapter, where she argues that part of the attraction of viewing paintings such as Millais's *Ophélia* is our recognition that a perfect, immaculate dead body will soon disintegrate into dust and bone.

> Beauty fascinates not only because it is unnatural, but also because it is precarious. Even as the painting articulates stillness, wholeness, perfection, it presages the dissolution of precisely these attributes of beauty. It is not just the translation into the inanimate that defines the relation between beauty and death, but also the fact that this form of beauty, even as it signifies an immaculate, immobile form, potentially contains its own destruction, its division into parts. (5)

2. For an extended and very useful discussion of how frames work in shaping our responses to art, see Gombrich, *Sense of Order,* and Green-Lewis, *Framing the Victorians,* especially 121–23.

3. The subject of nostalgia and its relation to modernity has received wide attention. Lowenthal, in *The Past Is a Foreign Country,* characterizes it as one of the principal forces in the shaping of life in twentieth-century British culture. Stewart, *On Longing,* provides one of the most provocative discussions of the uses of nostalgia in its treatment of how four culturally constructed "modern" forms—the miniature, the gigantic, the collection, and the souvenir—have shaped nineteenth- and twentieth-century reading, viewing, and reflective practices. For other discussions of nostalgia and modern culture, see Davis, *Yearning for Yesterday;* Terdiman, *Present Past;* and Felski, *Gender of Modernity.*

4. Studies of nineteenth- and twentieth-century attitudes toward death are too numerous to list comprehensively. Among the most widely discussed are Kübler-Ross, *On Death and Dying*; Ariès, *Western Attitudes*; and Stannard, *Death in America*. More recent works are Weeler, *Death and the Future Life*; Jalland's wonderfully researched *Death in the Victorian Family*; and Lerner, *Angels and Absences*. For a philosophical study of death in Western culture, see Bauman, *Mortality*.

5. Ruby's *Secure the Shadow* offers the most comprehensive study of postmortem photography in the United States to date, spanning the 1840s to the 1990s. Presenting many photographs taken in a wide range of locales and periods, Ruby convincingly argues that the practice was, in fact, much more common in the nineteenth century than most historians have indicated. Ruby does note, however, that though it is still practiced by many families even today, postmortem photography has not been considered a "respectable" activity for photographers since 1880, if we may judge by its disappearance as a topic in professional photography journals. It is no coincidence, I think, that its disappearance coincides with Kodak's emphasis on happy moments, on the forgetting of sadness and death.

6. Jalland discusses the various examples of memorial likenesses of the dead in *Death in the Victorian Family*, 288–90.

7. For discussions of spirit photography, see Gunning, "Phantom Images"; Davidson, "Sherman, Daguerre"; and my essay "Camera Fiends." Both Gunning and I offer an extended analysis of spirit photography in the mid- to late nineteenth century. Gunning's interest is in how the invention of cinema both appropriated and reinforced the cultural fascination with spectral image making; my interest is in putting spirit photography in historical context by charting photography's earlier connections with the supernatural in a variety of discourses and practices.

8. See Trachtenberg, "Mirror in the Marketplace"; Davidson, "Sherman, Daguerre"; and Green-Lewis, *Framing the Victorians*.

9. I am indebted to the following studies for my appreciation of cultural responses to the relic during the medieval era: Landes, *Relics, Apocalypse, and the Deceits of History*; Geary, *Living with the Dead*; and Bollason, *Saints and Relics*.

10. Marien's *Photography and Its Critics* offers perhaps the most comprehensive account of the competing attempts to define and locate photography's role in nineteenth century art, science, and culture.

11. See Felski, *Gender of Modernity*, chap. 1; Lowenthal, *Past Is a Foreign Country*; and Halbwachs, *On Collective Memory*.

12. For much more detailed discussions of the cultural importance of collecting, see Stewart, *On Longing*; Pearce, *Museums*; and Baudrillard, *Système des objets*.

6. "Let Kodak Keep the Story"

1. For discussions of the relation of photography to language or narrative, see Burgin, *Thinking Photography*; Berger, *Another Way*; Hunter, *Image and Word*; Hirsch, *Family Frames*; and Adams, "Autobiography, Photography, Narrative."

2. For further factual information on the Autographic Kodak, see "Autographic Kodak," "Autographic Kodaks," and "On the Negative."

3. The Autographic Kodak did sell remarkably well for nearly eight years, especially in 1917–18. Sales steadily declined after 1922 until the model was finally discontinued in the late 1920s. Much of the reason for its popularity probably had to do with

224   price: a camera with the autographic feature cost only a few dollars more than an or-
◇   dinary camera.

     4. See Davis, *Yearning for Yesterday,* chap. 1.

     5. For more extensive discussions of the use and nature of captions, see Price, *The Photograph,* Green-Lewis, *Framing the Victorians,* and Margolis, "Mining Photographs."

Bibliography

Adams, James Eli. *Dandies and Desert Saints: Styles of Victorian Masculinity.* Ithaca, N.Y.: Cornell University Press, 1995.

Adams, Timothy Dow, ed. "Autobiography, Photography, Narrative." *Modern Fiction Studies* 40, no. 3 (fall 1994): 459–685.

Adorno, Theodor W. *Negative Dialectics.* 1966. Trans. E. B. Ashton. New York: Seabury, 1973.

"Advertising Talks." *Kodak Trade Circular,* July 1915, 3.

"The Amateur Spirit." *Atlantic Monthly,* August 1901, 270–78.

Anderson, Nels. *Work and Leisure.* London: Routledge & Kegan Paul, 1961.

Ariès, Philippe. *Centuries of Childhood: A Social History of Family Life.* Trans. Robert Baldick. New York: Vintage Books, 1962.

———. *Western Attitudes toward Death: From the Middle Ages to the Present.* Trans. Patricia M. Ranum. Baltimore: Johns Hopkins University Press, 1994.

At Home with the Kodak. Rochester, N.Y.: Eastman Kodak Co., 1922.

Augur, Helen. *The Book of Fairs.* 1939. Detroit: Omnigraphics, 1992.

"The Autographic Kodak." *Kodakery: A Journal for Amateur Photographers,* September 1914, 10–15.

"The Autographic Kodaks." *Kodakery,* November 1914, 1–10.

Badger, Reid. *The Great American Fair: The World's Columbian Exposition and American Culture.* Chicago: N. Hall, 1979.

Banner, Lois W. *American Beauty.* New York: Knopf, 1983.

Banta, Martha. *Imaging American Women: Idea and Ideals in Cultural History.* New York: Columbia University Press, 1987.

Barthes, Roland. *Camera Lucida: Reflections on Photography.* Trans. Richard Howard. New York: Hill & Wang, 1981.

———. *The Fashion System.* 1967. Trans. Matthew Ward and Richard Howard. New York: Hill & Wang, 1983.

———. *Image—Music—Text.* Trans. Stephen Heath. New York: Noonday, 1977.

———. "Toys." In *Mythologies,* trans. Annette Lavers. New York: Hill & Wang, 1972.

Baudrillard, Jean. *Jean Baudrillard: From Marxism to Postmodernism and Beyond.* Ed. Douglas Kellner. Stanford: Stanford University Press, 1989.

———. *Le Système des objets.* Paris: Denoël, 1968.

Bauman, Zygmunt. *Mortality, Immortality, and Other Life Strategies.* Stanford: Stanford University Press, 1992.

"Because This Is the First Number." *Kodakery,* September 1913, 1.

226 ◇ Bede, Cuthbert. *Photographic Pleasures; Popularly Portrayed with Pen and Pencil.* 1855. Garden City, N.Y.: Amphoto, 1973.

Belasco, Warren. *Americans on the Road: From Autocamp to Motel, 1910–1945.* Cambridge: MIT Press, 1979.

Benedict, Burton. *The Anthropology of World's Fairs: San Francisco's Panama Pacific International Exposition of 1915.* Berkeley: Scholar Press, 1983.

Benjamin, Walter. *Berliner Kindheit um Neunzehnhundert.* Frankfurt am Main: Suhrkamp, 1950.

———. "A Short History of Photography." In *Classic Essays on Photography,* ed. Alan Trachtenberg, 199–216. New Haven: Leete's Island Books, 1980.

———. "The Storyteller: Reflections on the Works of Nikolai Leskov." In *Illuminations,* ed. Hannah Arendt, trans. Harry Zohn, 83–110. New York: Schocken, 1968.

———. "The Work of Art in the Age of Mechanical Reproduction." In *Illuminations,* ed. Hannah Arendt, trans. Harry Zohn, 217–51. New York: Schocken, 1968.

Benstock, Shari, and Suzanne Ferriss, eds. *On Fashion.* New Brunswick: Rutgers University Press, 1994.

Berger, John. *Another Way of Telling.* New York: Pantheon, 1982.

Black, Alexander. *Captain Kodak: A Camera Story.* Boston: Lothrop, 1891.

Bliven, Bruce. "Teaching the Nation to Want Kodak." *Printer's Ink: A Journal for Advertisers* 52, no. 6 (Feb. 7, 1918): 3–6, 106–11, 112–17.

Bogart, Michele H. *Artists, Advertising, and the Borders of Art.* Chicago: University of Chicago Press, 1995.

Braive, Michel François. *The Photograph: A Social History.* New York: McGraw-Hill, 1966.

Brayer, Elizabeth. *George Eastman: A Biography.* Baltimore: Johns Hopkins University Press, 1996.

"Brevity in Advertising." *Kodak Trade Circular,* June 1920, 7.

Breward, Christopher. *The Culture of Fashion: A New History of Fashionable Dress.* Manchester: Manchester University Press, 1995.

Bronfen, Elisabeth. *Over Her Dead Body: Death, Femininity, and the Aesthetic.* New York: Routledge, 1992.

Bronfen, Elisabeth, and Sarah Webster Goodwin. *Death and Representation.* Baltimore: Johns Hopkins University Press, 1993.

Bronner, Simon J. *Consuming Visions: Accumulation and Display of Goods in America, 1880–1920.* New York: Norton, 1989.

Brown, Dorothy. *Setting a Course: American Women in the 1920s.* Boston: Twayne, 1987.

Brown, Julie K. *Contesting Images: Photography and the World's Columbian Exposition.* Tucson: University of Arizona Press, 1994.

"The Brownie Acorn." *Kodak Trade Circular,* May 1900, 1.

"The Brownie Camera." *Kodak Trade Circular,* February 1900, 1.

Brummett, John. "A History of Kodak." Manuscript, November 1959. Eastman Kodak Co. archives, Rochester, N.Y.

Burgin, Victor. *Thinking Photography.* London: Macmillan, 1982.

Cadava, Eduardo. *Words of Light: Theses on the Photography of History.* Princeton: Princeton University Press, 1997.

Calvert, Karin Lee Fishbeck. *Children in the House: The Material Culture of Early Childhood, 1600–1900*. Boston: Northeastern University Press, 1992. 227

Chalfen, Richard. *Snapshot Versions of Life*. Bowling Green: Bowling Green University Popular Press, 1987.

Charmasson, Henri. *The Name Is the Game: How to Name a Company or Product*. Homewood, Ill.: Dow Jones–Irwin, 1988.

Cheal, David J. *The Gift Economy*. London: Routledge, 1988.

Coe, Brian. *The Snapshot Photograph: The Rise of Popular Photography, 1888–1939*. London: Ash & Grant, 1977.

Colley, Ann. C. *Nostalgia and Recollection in Victorian Culture*. London: Macmillan, 1998.

Collins, Douglas. *The Story of Kodak*. New York: Harry N. Abrams, 1990.

Combs, James. *The Reagan Range: The Nostalgic Myth in American Politics*. Bowling Green: Bowling Green University Popular Press, 1993.

Comstock, Sarah. "The Girl and the Camera." *Collier's*, December 3, 1910, 16–17.

Cox, Palmer. *The Brownies: Their Book*. 1887. New York: McGraw-Hill, 1967.

Craik, Jennifer. *The Face of Fashion: Cultural Studies in Fashion*. New York: Routledge, 1994.

Cross, Gary. *Kids' Stuff: Toys and the Changing World of American Childhood*. Cambridge: Harvard University Press, 1997.

———. *A Social History of Leisure since 1600*. State College, Pa.: Venture, 1990.

Culler, Jonathan. "Semiotics of Tourism." *American Journal of Semiotics* 1 (1981): 127–40.

Cunningham, Hugh. *Children and Childhood in Western Society since 1500*. New York: Longmans, 1995.

———. *The Children of the Poor: Representations of Childhood since the Seventeenth Century*. Oxford: Blackwell, 1991.

"The Dark-Room Abolished." *Kodak Trade Circular*, August 1902, 1–5.

Davidson, Cathy N. "Sherman, Daguerre, Hawthorne: Photographs of the Dead." *South Atlantic Quarterly* 89, no. 4 (fall 1990): 667–701.

Davidson, Marshall B., et al., eds. *The American Heritage History of Antiques from the Civil War to World War I*. New York: American Heritage, 1969.

Davis, Fred. *Yearning for Yesterday: A Sociology of Nostalgia*. New York: Free Press, 1979.

De Grazia, Sebastian. *Of Time, Work, and Leisure*. New York: Twentieth Century Fund, 1962.

Derks, Scott, ed. *The Value of a Dollar: Prices and Incomes in the United States, 1860–1989*. Detroit: Gale, 1994.

Doane, Janice, and Devon Hodges. *Nostalgia and Sexual Difference*. New York: Methuen, 1987.

Doane, Mary Ann. *The Desire to Desire: The Woman's Film of the 1940s*. Bloomington: Indiana University Press, 1987.

Drabble, Margaret. *Jerusalem the Garden*. New York: Penguin, 1969.

Dumazedier, Joffre. *Toward a Society of Leisure*. Trans. Stewart E. McClure. New York: Free Press, 1967.

Dyer, Walter. *The Lure of the Antique*. New York: Century, 1916.

228

Eisner, Lotte H. *The Haunted Screen: Expressionism in the German Cinema and the Influence of Max Reinhardt.* Trans. Roger Greaves. Berkeley: University of California Press, 1973.

Eksteins, Modris. *Rites of Spring: The Great War and the Birth of the Modern Age.* Boston: Houghton Mifflin, 1989.

Elliot, William Gerald. *Amateur Clubs and Actors.* London: Edward Arnold, 1898.

Ellery, Madge. "Kodak, the Family Historian." *Kodakery,* April 1928, 1–8.

"Every Family Its Own Camera Club." *Kodakery,* November 1916, 1–5.

Ewen, Stuart. *All-Consuming Images: The Politics of Style in Contemporary Culture.* New York: Basic Books, 1988.

Ewen, Stuart, and Elizabeth Ewen. *Channels of Desire: Mass Images and the Shaping of American Consciousness.* 2d ed. Minneapolis: University of Minnesota Press, 1992.

Farnol, Jeffrey. *The Amateur Gentleman.* Boston: Little, Brown, 1913.

Felski, Rita. *The Gender of Modernity.* Cambridge: Harvard University Press, 1995.

Finkelstein, Joanne. *Fashion: An Introduction.* New York: New York University Press, 1998.

Fleming, Dan. *Powerplay: Toys as Popular Culture.* Manchester: Manchester University Press, 1996.

Flink, James J. *The Car Culture.* Cambridge: MIT Press, 1975.

Ford, Colin, ed. *The Story of Popular Photography.* North Pomfret, Vt.: Trafalgar Square, 1989.

"For 1905: Something about the New Goods That Are to Help Business." *Kodak Trade Circular,* April 1905, 1–4.

Fox, Richard Wightman, and T. J. Jackson Lears. *The Culture of Consumption: Critical Essays in American History, 1880–1980.* New York: Pantheon, 1983.

Fox, Stephen R. *The Mirror Makers: A History of American Advertising and Its Creators.* New York: Morrow, 1984.

Fraser, Antonia. *A History of Toys.* New York: Delacorte, 1966.

Freedman, Jonathan. *Professions of Taste: Henry James, British Aestheticism, and Commodity Culture.* Stanford: Stanford University Press, 1990.

Freund, Gisele. *Photography and Society.* Boston: D. R. Godine, 1980.

Frow, John. *Time and Commodity Culture: Essays on Cultural Theory and Postmodernity.* New York: Oxford University Press, 1997.

Fulton, Robert, et al., eds. *Death and Dying: Challenge and Change.* San Francisco: Boyd & Fraser, 1981.

Fussell, Paul. *The Great War and Modern Memory.* New York: Oxford University Press, 1975.

Gear, Josephine. "The Baby's Picture: Woman as Image Maker in Small-Town America." *Feminist Studies* 13, no. 2 (summer 1987): 419–42.

Geary, Patrick J. *Living with the Dead in the Middle Ages.* Ithaca, N.Y.: Cornell University Press, 1994.

Gillett, Paula. *Worlds of Art: Painters in Victorian Society.* New Brunswick: Rutgers University Press, 1990.

Glasser, Ralph. *Leisure: Penalty or Prize?* London: Macmillan, 1970.

Goldberg, Vicki, ed. *Photography in Print: Writings from 1816 to the Present.* New York: 229
Simon & Schuster, 1981.

Gombrich, Ernst Hans. *The Sense of Order: A Study in the Psychology of Decorative Art.*
Ithaca, N.Y.: Cornell University Press, 1979.

Goodale, Thomas L., and Geoffrey C. Godbey. *The Evolution of Leisure: Historical and
Philosophical Perspectives.* State College, Pa.: Venture, 1988.

Gorer, Geoffrey. *Death, Grief, and Mourning in Contemporary Britain.* Garden City,
N.Y.: Doubleday, 1965.

Green, Jonathan, ed. *The Snapshot.* New York, 1974.

Green-Lewis, Jennifer. *Framing the Victorians: Photography and the Culture of Realism.* Ithaca, N.Y.: Cornell University Press, 1996.

Greene, Gayle. "Feminist Fiction and the Uses of Memory." *Signs* 16, no. 2 (winter
1991): 290–321.

Grinnell, Elizabeth. *How John and I Brought Up the Child.* Philadelphia: American
Sunday-School Union, 1894.

Grover, Kathryn, ed. *Hard at Play: Leisure in America, 1840–1940.* Amherst: University
of Massachusetts Press, 1992.

Gunning, Tom. "Phantom Images and Modern Manifestations: Spirit Photography,
Magic Theater, Trick Films, and Photography's Uncanny." In *Fugitive Images:
From Photography to Video,* ed. Patrice Petro, 42–71. Bloomington: Indiana University Press, 1995.

Halbwachs, Maurice. *On Collective Memory.* Trans. Lewis A. Coser. Chicago: University of Chicago Press, 1992.

Halle, David. "Displaying the Dream: The Visual Presentation of Family and Self in
the Modern American Household." *Journal of Comparative Family Studies* 22
(summer 1991): 217–19.

Harding, Colin. "The Kodak Girl." *Photographic World* 78 (September 1996): 8–15.

Hawthorne, Nathaniel. *The House of the Seven Gables.* 1851. Ed. Seymour L. Gross.
New York: Norton, 1967.

Hayden, Arthur. *Chats on Old Furniture: A Practical Guide for Collectors.* London:
T. Fisher Unwin, 1916.

Henisch, Heinz K., and Bridget A. Henisch. *The Photographic Experience, 1838–
1914: Images and Attitudes.* University Park: Pennsylvania State University Press,
1994.

Hiller, Lejarena. "Combining Brush and Camera." *Printer's Ink Monthly* 1, no. 7
(June 1920): 10.

Hiner, N. Ray, and Joseph M. Hawes, eds. *Growing Up in America: Children in Historical Perspective.* Urbana: University of Illinois Press, 1985.

Hirsch, Julia. *Family Photographs: Content, Meaning, and Effect.* Oxford: Oxford University Press, 1981.

Hirsch, Marianne. *Family Frames: Photography, Narrative, and Postmemory.* Cambridge: Harvard University Press, 1997.

Holland, Patricia. "Introduction: History, Memory, and the Family Album." In *Family
Snaps: The Meaning of Domestic Photography,* ed. Jo Spence and Patricia Holland, 1–14. London: Virago, 1991.

230

Hollander, Anne. "Fashion Art." In *The Idealizing Vision: The Art of Fashion Photography*, 33–61. New York: Aperture, 1991.

Holmes, Oliver Wendell. "The Stereoscope and the Stereograph." *Atlantic Monthly*, June 1859, 738–48.

The Home of Kodak. Rochester, N.Y.: Eastman Kodak Co., 1928.

Huizinga, Johan. *Homo Ludens: The Play Element in Culture.* 1938. New York: J. & J. Harper, 1970.

Hungerford, Edward. "George Eastman—Advertiser." *Printer's Ink Monthly* 7, no. 5 (November 1923): 17, 18, 106.

———. "My Kodak Is My Friend." *Kodakery*, May 1916, 1–9.

Hunter, Jefferson. *Image and Word: The Interaction of Twentieth-Century Photographs and Texts.* Cambridge: Harvard University Press, 1987.

Jalland, Patricia. *Death in the Victorian Family.* Oxford: Oxford University Press, 1996.

Johnston, Patricia. *Real Fantasies: Edward Steichen's Advertising Photography.* Berkeley: University of California Press, 1997.

Jones, Lewis B. "Kodak's Fighting Front This Year." *Printer's Ink Monthly* 3 (August 1921): 14–15, 50, 53, 55.

Jordan, Thomas E. *Victorian Childhood: Themes and Variations.* Albany: State University of New York Press, 1987.

Kaplan, Max. *Leisure in America: A Social Inquiry.* New York: Wiley, 1960.

Kermode, Frank. *The Sense of an Ending: Studies in the Theory of Fiction.* New York: Oxford University Press, 1967.

Kern, Stephen. *The Culture of Time and Space, 1880–1918.* Cambridge: Harvard University Press, 1983.

Key, Ellen Karolina Sofia. *Century of the Child.* New York: Putnam, 1909.

Kincaid, James Russell. *Child-Loving: The Erotic Child and Victorian Culture.* New York: Routledge, 1992.

King, Graham. *Say "Cheese!": Looking at Snapshots in a New Way.* New York: Dodd, Mead, 1984.

Kingslake, Rudolf. *The Photographic Manufacturing Companies of Rochester, New York.* Rochester, N.Y.: George Eastman House, 1997.

Kline, Stephen. *Out of the Garden: Toys, TV, and Children's Culture in the Age of Marketing.* London: Verso, 1993.

Kodak and Kodak Supplies. Rochester, N.Y.: Eastman Kodak Co., 1917.

"The Kodak Cure." *Kodakery*, April 1915, 1–8.

"The Kodak Girl." *Kodak Trade Circular*, March 1902, 8.

"Kodak Girls at Home and Abroad." Manuscript. Box "Sales and Advertising," Eastman Kodak Co. archives, Rochester, N.Y..

"Kodak in Advertising." *Printer's Ink Monthly* 9 (August 1905): 6–7.

Kodak Primer. Rochester, N.Y.: Eastman Kodak Co., 1888.

"Kodak's Fighting Front This Year." *Printer's Ink Monthly* 3 (August 1921): 14–15, 50, 53, 55.

Koshkin-Youritzin, Victor. "Introduction." In *American Watercolors from the Metropolitan Museum of Art*, 1–15. New York: Harry N. Abrams, 1991.

Kübler-Ross, Elisabeth. *On Death and Dying.* New York: Macmillan, 1970.

Kuznets, Lois Rostow. *When Toys Come Alive: Narratives of Animation, Metamorphosis, and Development.* New Haven: Yale University Press, 1994.

Landes, Richard. *Relics, Apocalypse, and the Deceits of History.* Cambridge: Harvard University Press, 1995.

Larson, Magali Sarfatti. *The Rise of Professionalism: A Sociological Analysis.* Berkeley: University of California Press, 1977.

Latour, Bruno. *Science in Action: How to Follow Scientists and Engineers Through Society.* Cambridge: Harvard University Press, 1987.

Leach, William. *Land of Desire: Merchants, Power, and the Rise of a New American Culture.* New York: Pantheon, 1993.

Lears, Jackson. *Fables of Abundance: A Cultural History of Advertising in America.* New York: Basic Books, 1994.

Lehmann, Jean-Pierre. *The Image of Japan: From Feudal Isolation to World Power, 1850–1905.* London: George Allen & Inwin, 1978.

Leigh, Ruth. "Forget the Business Talk." *Kodak Salesman,* March 1927, 5–11.

———. "Soft Pedal the Mechanics." *Kodak Salesman,* May 1928, 6–14.

———. "Vanity Kodaks in the Fashion Parade." *Kodak Salesman,* July 1928, 9–10.

Lentricchia, Frank, and Thomas McLaughlin, eds. *Critical Terms for Literary Study.* 2d ed. Chicago: University of Chicago Press, 1995.

Lerner, Laurence. *Angels and Absences: Child Deaths in the Nineteenth Century.* Nashville: Vanderbilt University Press, 1997.

Lester, Katherine Morris, and Bess Viola Oerke. *An Illustrated History of Those Frills and Furbelows of Fashion Which Have Come to Be Known as Accessories of Dress.* Peoria, Ill.: Chas. A. Bennett, 1940.

Lesy, Michael. "Sex and the Automobile: From Rumble Seats to Rockin' Vans." In *The Automobile and American Culture,* ed. David L. Lewis and Laurence Goldstein, 123–33. Ann Arbor: University of Michigan Press, 1983.

———. *Time Frames: The Meaning of Family Pictures.* New York: Pantheon, 1980.

Lewis, David L., and Laurence Goldstein, eds. *The Automobile and American Culture.* Ann Arbor: University of Michigan Press, 1983.

"Lewis B. Jones." Manuscript. Box "Sales and Advertising," Eastman Kodak Co. archives, Rochester, N.Y.

Ling, Peter J. *America and the Automobile: Technology, Reform, and Social Change.* Manchester: Manchester University Press, 1990.

Lipovetsky, Gilles. *The Empire of Fashion: Dressing Modern Democracy.* Trans. Catherine Porter. Princeton: Princeton University Press, 1994.

Lothrop, Eaton S., Jr. "The Brownie Camera." *History of Photography* 2, no. 1 (January 1978): 1–10.

Lowenthal, David. *The Past Is a Foreign Country.* New York: Cambridge University Press, 1985.

Lurie, Alison. *The Language of Clothes.* New York: Random House, 1981.

Macleod, David I. *The Age of the Child.* New York: Twayne, 1998.

Marchand, Roland. *Advertising the American Dream: Making Way for Modernity, 1920–1940.* Berkeley: University of California Press, 1985.

Margolin, Victor, Ira Brichta, and Vivian Brichta. *The Promise and the Product: 200 Years of American Advertising Posters.* New York: Macmillan, 1979.

232   Margolis, Eric. "Mining Photographs: Unearthing the Meanings of Historical Photos."
◇   *Radical History Review* 40 (1988): 33–48.

Marien, Mary Warner. *Photography and Its Critics: A Cultural History, 1839–1900.* New
    York: Cambridge University Press, 1997.

Marx, Karl. *The Process of Capitalist Production.* Vol. 1 of *Capital,* ed. Friedrich Engels.
    Trans. Samuel Moore and Edward Aveling. New York: International Publishers,
    1967.

Matsuda, Matt. *The Memory of the Modern.* New York: Oxford University Press, 1996.

Mauss, Marcel. *The Gift: Forms and Functions of Exchange in Archaic Societies.* Trans.
    Ian Cunnison. London: Coehn & West, 1954.

Mavor, Carol. *Pleasures Taken: Performances of Sexuality and Loss in Victorian Pho-
    tographs.* Durham: Duke University Press, 1995.

McAdams, Dan P. *The Stories We Live By: Personal Myths and the Making of the Self.*
    New York: Guilford, 1997.

Meikle, Jeffrey L. *Twentieth Century Limited: Industrial Design in America, 1925–1939.*
    Philadelphia: Temple University Press, 1979.

Miller, J. Hillis. *Reading Narrative.* Norman: University of Oklahoma Press, 1998.

Miller, Norman P., and Duane M. Robinson. *The Leisure Age: Its Challenge to Recre-
    ation.* Belmont, Calif.: Wadsworth, 1963.

Moeller, Madelyn. "Ladies of Leisure: Domestic Photography in the Nineteenth Cen-
    tury." In *Hard at Play: Leisure in America, 1840–1940,* ed. Kathryn Grover, 139–
    60. Amherst: University of Massachusetts Press, 1992.

Moeller, Susan. *Shooting War: Photography and the American Experience of Combat.*
    New York: Basic Books, 1989.

Morson, Gary Saul. *Narrative and Freedom: The Shadows of Time.* New Haven: Yale
    University Press, 1994.

"Motoring with a Kodak." *Kodak Trade Circular,* April 1910, 12–13.

Musello, Christopher. "Studying the Home Mode: An Exploration of Family Photog-
    raphy and Visual Communications." *Studies in Visual Communications* 6, no. 1
    (spring 1980): 23–42.

Nasaw, David. *Going Out: The Rise and Fall of Public Amusements.* New York: Basic
    Books, 1993.

Nodelman, Perry. *Words about Pictures: The Narrative Art of Children's Picture Books.*
    Athens: University of Georgia Press, 1988.

Norris, James D. *Advertising and the Transformation of American Society, 1865–1920.*
    New York: Greenwood, 1990.

"On the Negative." *Kodakery,* December 1918, 25–26.

"$1000 Dollars for What You Do and See This Summer." *Ladies' Home Journal,*
    July 1903, 45.

Paster, James E. "Advertising Immortality by Kodak." *History of Photography* 10, no. 2
    (summer 1992): 135–39.

Patterson, Martha. "'Survival of the Best Fitted': Selling the American New Woman as
    Gibson Girl, 1895–1910." *American Transcendental Quarterly* 9, no. 2 (June 1995):
    72–85.

Pearce, Susan. *Museums, Objects, and Collections: A Cultural Study.* Washington,
    D.C.: Smithsonian Institution Press, 1993.

"The Peeping Toms of the Camera." *Puck,* August 24, 1892, 7.

Pellowski, Anne. *The World of Storytelling.* New York: Bowker, 1977.

Penn, Arthur A. *The Girl from Kodak Town.* Rochester, N.Y.: Carl S. Hallaver, 1917.

Perry, Bliss. *The Amateur Spirit.* Boston: Houghton Mifflin, 1904.

Phibbs, Harry C. "Telling the Story with Your Kodak." *Kodakery,* June 1915, 1–12.

"A Pictorial Diary." *Kodakery,* May 1918, 21–22.

"Picturing the World War." *Kodakery,* February 1917, 1–7.

"Planted Brownie Acorns." *Kodak Trade Circular,* September 1900, 2.

Pollock, Linda A. *Forgotten Children: Parent-Child Relations from 1500 to 1900.* Cambridge: Cambridge University Press, 1983.

Pollock, Walter Herries. *Amateur Theatricals.* London: Macmillan, 1879.

Price, Mary. *The Photograph: A Strange Confined Space.* Stanford: Stanford University Press, 1994.

Rabinbach, Anson. *The Human Motor: Energy, Fatigue, and the Origins of Modernity.* New York: Basic Books, 1990.

Rae, John B. *The American Automobile Industry.* Boston: Twayne, 1984.

Richards, Thomas. *The Commodity Culture of Victorian England: Advertising and Spectacle, 1851–1914.* Stanford: Stanford University Press, 1990.

Ricoeur, Paul. *Freud and Philosophy.* Trans. Denis Savage. New Haven: Yale University Press, 1970.

Robinson, Julian. *The Golden Age of Style.* New York: Harcourt Brace Jovanovich, 1974.

Rodgers, Daniel T. "Socializing Middle-Class Children: Institutions, Fables, and Work Values in Nineteenth-Century America." In *Growing Up in America: Children in Historical Perspective,* ed. Ray Hiner and Joseph M. Hawes. Urbana: University of Illinois Press, 1985.

Rollason. David W. *Saints and Relics in Anglo-Saxon England.* Cambridge, Mass.: B. Blackwell, 1989.

"The Romance and Mystery of the Kodak Girl." *St. Louis Post-Dispatch,* April 18, 1903, 18–19.

Root, Marcus Aurelius. *The Camera and the Pencil; or, The Heliographic Art.* 1864. Pawlet, Vt.: Helios, 1971.

Ruby, Jay. *Secure the Shadow: Photography and Death in America.* Cambridge: MIT Press, 1995.

Rudisill, Richard. *Mirror Image: The Influence of the Daguerreotype on American Society.* Albuquerque: University of New Mexico Press, 1971.

Rugg, Linda Haverty. *Picturing Ourselves: Photography and Autobiography.* Chicago: University of Chicago Press, 1997.

Rybczynski, Witold. *Waiting for the Weekend.* New York: Viking, 1991.

Rydell, Robert W. *All the World's a Fair: Visions of Empire at American International Expositions, 1876–1916.* Chicago: University of Chicago Press, 1984.

———. *World of Fairs: The Century-of-Progress Expositions.* Chicago: University of Chicago Press, 1993.

Sandweiss, Martha A., ed. *Photography in Nineteenth-Century America.* New York: Harry N. Abrams, 1991.

Sawyer, Ruth. *The Way of the Storyteller.* New York: Viking, 1942.

Scanlon, Jennifer. *Inarticulate Longings: The "Ladies' Home Journal," Gender, and the Promises of Consumer Culture.* New York: Routledge, 1995.

Schacter, Daniel L. *Searching for Memory: The Brain, the Mind, and the Past.* New York: Basic Books, 1996.

Schleifer, Ronald. *Modernism and Time: The Logic of Abundance in Literature, Science, and Culture, 1880–1930.* Cambridge: Cambridge University Press, 2000.

———. *Rhetoric and Death: The Language of Modernism and Postmodern Discourse Theory.* Urbana: University of Illinois Press, 1990.

———. "'What Is This Thing Called Love?': Cole Porter and the Rhythms of Desire." *Criticism* 41, no. 1 (1999): 7–23.

Schwarcs, Joseph H. *Ways of the Illustrator: Visual Communication in Children's Literature.* Chicago: American Library Assn., 1982.

Seiberling, Grace, with Carolyn Bloore. *Amateurs, Photography, and the Mid-Victorian Imagination.* Chicago: University of Chicago Press, 1986.

Seiter, Ellen. *Sold Separately: Children and Parents in Consumer Culture.* New Brunswick: Rutgers University Press, 1993.

Simmel, Georg. "Fashion." In *On Individuality and Social Forms: Selected Writings,* ed. Donald N. Levine, 294–323. Chicago: University of Chicago Press, 1977.

Singleton, Esther. *The Furniture of Our Forefathers, with Critical Descriptions of Plates by Russell Sturgis.* Garden City, N.Y.: Doubleday, Page, 1901.

Slater, Don. *Consumer Culture and Modernity.* Cambridge, Mass.: Blackwell, 1997.

———. "Consuming Kodak." In *Family Snaps: The Meaning of Domestic Photography,* ed. Jo Spence and Patricia Holland, 49–59. London: Virago, 1991.

Smith, Terry E. *Making the Modern: Industry, Art, and Design in America.* Chicago: University of Chicago Press, 1993.

Smithsonian Institution. *The Books of the Fairs: Materials about World's Fairs, 1834–1916.* Chicago: American Library Assn., 1992.

"Snapshots from Home." *Kodak Salesman,* April 12, 1918, 3–8.

Snelling, Henry. "Photography." *Photographic-Art Journal* 1 (January 1851): 1.

Sontag, Susan. *On Photography.* New York: Anchor, 1977.

Spence, Jo, and Patricia Holland, eds. *Family Snaps: The Meaning of Domestic Photography.* London: Virago, 1991.

"Spirit of the Times." *Photography* 2, no. 96 (September 11, 1890): 577.

Spitzer, Leo. *Hotel Bolivia: The Culture of Memory in a Refuge from Nazism.* New York: Hill & Wang, 1998.

Stannard, David E., ed. *Death in America.* Philadelphia: University of Pennsylvania Press, 1974.

Stebbins, Robert A. *Amateurs: On the Margin Between Work and Leisure.* Beverly Hills, Calif.: Sage, 1979.

———. *Amateurs, Professionals, and Serious Leisure.* Montreal: McGill-Queen's University Press, 1992.

Steedman, Carolyn. *Strange Dislocations: Childhood and the Idea of Human Interiority, 1780–1930.* Cambridge: Harvard University Press, 1995.

Stewart, Susan. *On Longing: Narratives of the Miniature, the Gigantic, the Souvenir, the Collection.* Baltimore: Johns Hopkins University Press, 1984.

Stieglitz, Alfred. "The Hand Camera—Its Present Importance." In *Photography in*

Print: Writings from 1816 to the Present, ed. Vicki Goldberg, 214–17. New York: Simon & Schuster, 1981.

Stillinger, Elizabeth. *The Antiquers: The Lives and Careers, the Deals, the Finds, the Collections of Men and Women Who Were Responsible for the Changing Taste in American Antiques, 1860–1930.* New York: Knopf, 1980.

"Story-Telling Pictures." *Kodakery,* September 1915, 7–10.

Strasser, Susan. *Satisfaction Guaranteed: The Making of the American Mass Market.* New York: Pantheon, 1989.

Summers, Diane. "Grave Taboos." *London Financial Times,* June 15, 1995, Marketing and Advertising 12.

Sutton-Smith, Brian. *Toys as Culture.* New York: Gardner, 1986.

Swasy, Alecia. *Changing Focus: Kodak and the Battle to Save a Great American Company.* New York: Random House, 1997.

Taft, Robert. *Photography and the American Scene: A Social History, 1839–1889.* New York: Dover, 1938.

Tagg, John. *Grounds of Dispute: Art History, Cultural Politics, and the Discursive Field.* Minneapolis: University of Minnesota Press, 1992.

Talbot, William Henry Fox. *The Pencil of Nature.* 1844. New York: Da Capo, 1969.

Tannock, Stuart. "Nostalgia Critique." *Cultural Studies* 9, no. 3 (1995): 453–64.

"Telling the Story with Your Kodak." *Kodakery,* November 1915, 9–11.

Terdiman, Richard. *Present Past: Modernity and the Memory Crisis.* Ithaca, N.Y.: Cornell University Press, 1993.

Thorndike, Edward Lee. *Notes on Child Study.* New York: Macmillan, 1901.

Tooze, Ruth. *Storytelling.* Englewood Cliffs, N.J.: Prentice-Hall, 1959.

Trachtenberg, Alan. "Mirror in the Marketplace: American Responses to the Daguerreotype." In *The Daguerreotype: A Sesquicentennial Celebration,* ed. John Wood, 60–74. Iowa City: University of Iowa Press, 1989.

"Turn About Is Fair Play." *Puck,* August 24, 1892, 7.

Updike, John. "Lost Art: What the Author Wanted to Be Before He Decided to Become a Writer." *New Yorker,* Dec. 15, 1997, 75–80.

Urry, John. *The Tourist Gaze: Leisure and Travel in Contemporary Societies.* Newbury Park, Calif.: Sage, 1990.

Veblen, Thorstein. *The Theory of the Leisure Class.* 1899. Boston: Houghton Mifflin, 1973.

Walker, John Brisben. "Beauty in Advertising Illustration." *Cosmopolitan,* December 1902, 491–500.

Walkerdine, Valerie. *Daddy's Girl: Young Girls and Popular Culture.* Cambridge: Harvard University Press, 1997.

Wallace, Albert Crane. "The Charm of the Simple." *Kodakery,* November 1920, 1–9.

———. "The Ways of Peace." *Kodakery,* April 1919, 1–5.

Wallace, Ellerslie. *The Amateur Photographer: A Manual of Photographic Manipulation Intended Especially for Beginners and Amateurs.* 5th ed. Philadelphia: H. T. Coates, 1897.

"Ways of Peace, The." *Kodakery,* October 1919, 1–5.

Weber, Max. *The City.* 1894. Trans. Don Martindale and Gertrud Neuwirth. Glencoe, Ill.: Free Press, 1958.

236

Weeler, Michael. *Death and the Future Life in Victorian Literature and Theology: Heaven, Hell, and the Victorians.* New York: Cambridge University Press, 1994.

Weimann, Jeanne Madeline. *The Fair Women.* Chicago: Academy of Chicago, 1981.

Welling, William. *Photography in America: The Formative Years, 1839–1900.* New York: Crowell, 1978.

West, Nancy M. "Camera Fiends: Early Photography, Death, and the Supernatural." *Centennial Review* 40, no. 1 (winter 1996): 171–206.

———. "Her Finger on the Button: Kodak Girls and the Age of UnRipening." In *Picturing the End of Things: Photography and Apocalypse,* ed. Nancy M. West, 63–92. *Genre* 29, nos. 1–2 (spring/summer 1996).

———. "Men in the Age of Mechanical Reproduction: Photography, Masculinity, and the End of Engraving in the Nineteenth Century." *Victorians Institute Journal,* forthcoming.

Wheeler, Edward L. *Kodak Kate.* Beadle's Half-Dime Library. New York: Beadle & Adams, 1891.

Whipple, Mrs. George Hoyt. "'Key' to the Eastman Scrapbook." *University of Rochester Library Bulletin* 21, no. 1 (fall 1965): 4–18.

Williams, Raymond. *The Country and the City.* New York: Oxford University Press, 1977.

Williams, Val. "Carefully Creating an Idyll: Vanessa Bell and Snapshot Photography, 1907–1946." In *Family Snaps: The Meaning of Domestic Photography,* ed. Jo Spence and Patricia Holland, 186–98. London: Virago, 1991.

Wilson, Elizabeth. *Adorned in Dreams: Fashion and Modernity.* London: Virago, 1985.

Wintour, Anna, ed. *The Idealizing Vision: The Art of Fashion Photography.* New York: Aperture, 1991.

Wong, Frederick. *Oriental Watercolor Techniques.* New York: Watson-Guptill, 1977.

Woolf, Virginia. "Mr. Bennet and Mrs. Brown." In *The Virginia Woolf Reader,* ed. Mitchell A. Leaska, 192–212. New York: Harcourt Brace Jovanovich, 1984.

"You Never Can Tell." *Kodakery,* September 1915, 1–2.

Young, Iris Marion. "Women Recovering Our Clothes." In *On Fashion,* ed. Shari Benstock and Suzanne Ferriss, 197–210. New Brunswick: Rutgers University Press, 1994.

Index

Cultural Frames, Framing Culture

Books in this series examine both the way our culture frames our narratives and the way our narratives produce the culture that frames them. Attempting to bridge the gap between previously disparate disciplines, and combining theoretical issues with practical applications, this series invites a broad audience to read contemporary culture in a fresh and provocative way.

Nancy Martha West
Kodak and the Lens of Nostalgia

Raphael Sassower and Louis Cicotello
The Golden Avant-Garde: Idolatry, Commercialism, and Art